GOOD ENOUGH TO EAT

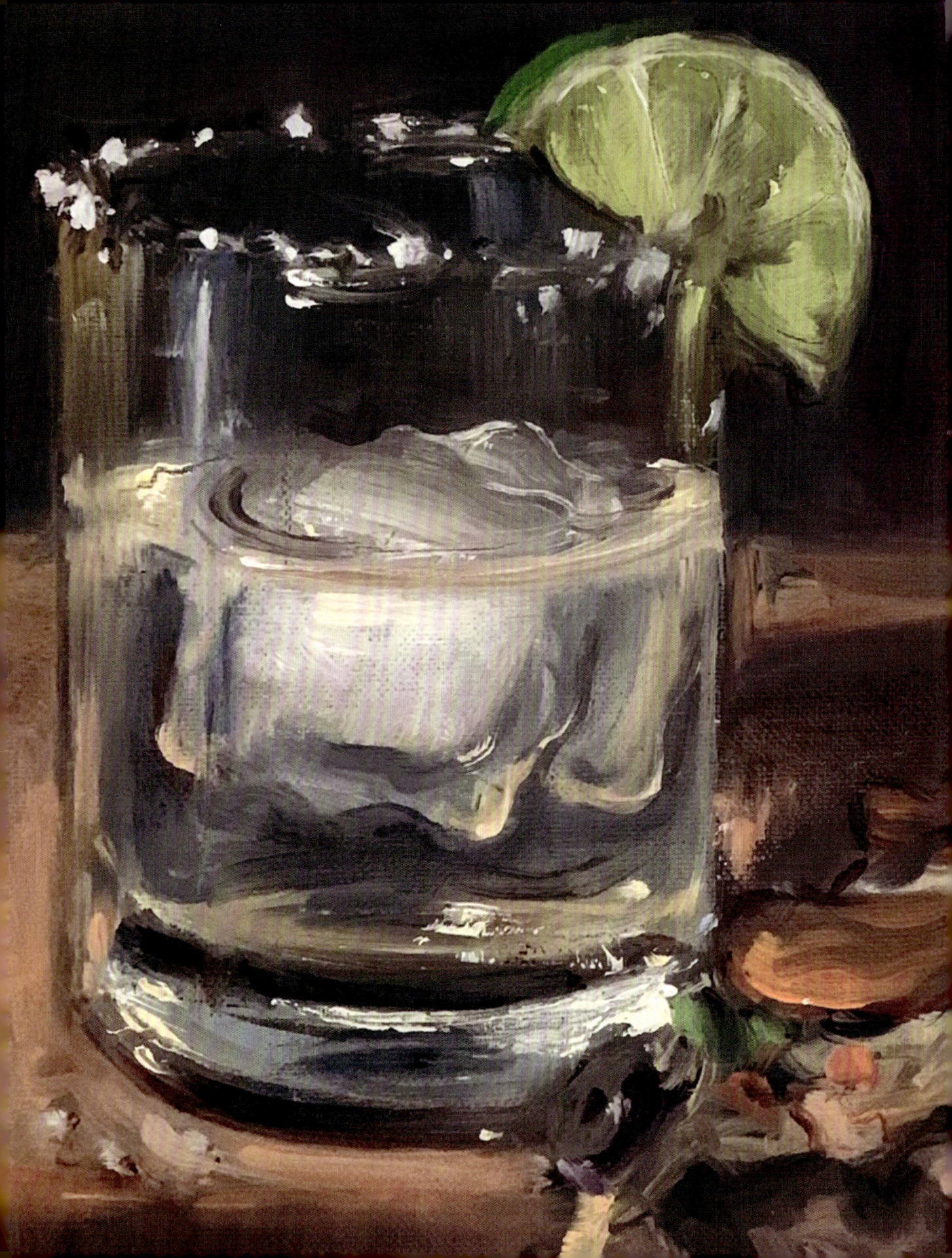

GOOD ENOUGH TO EAT

The Art of Noah Verrier

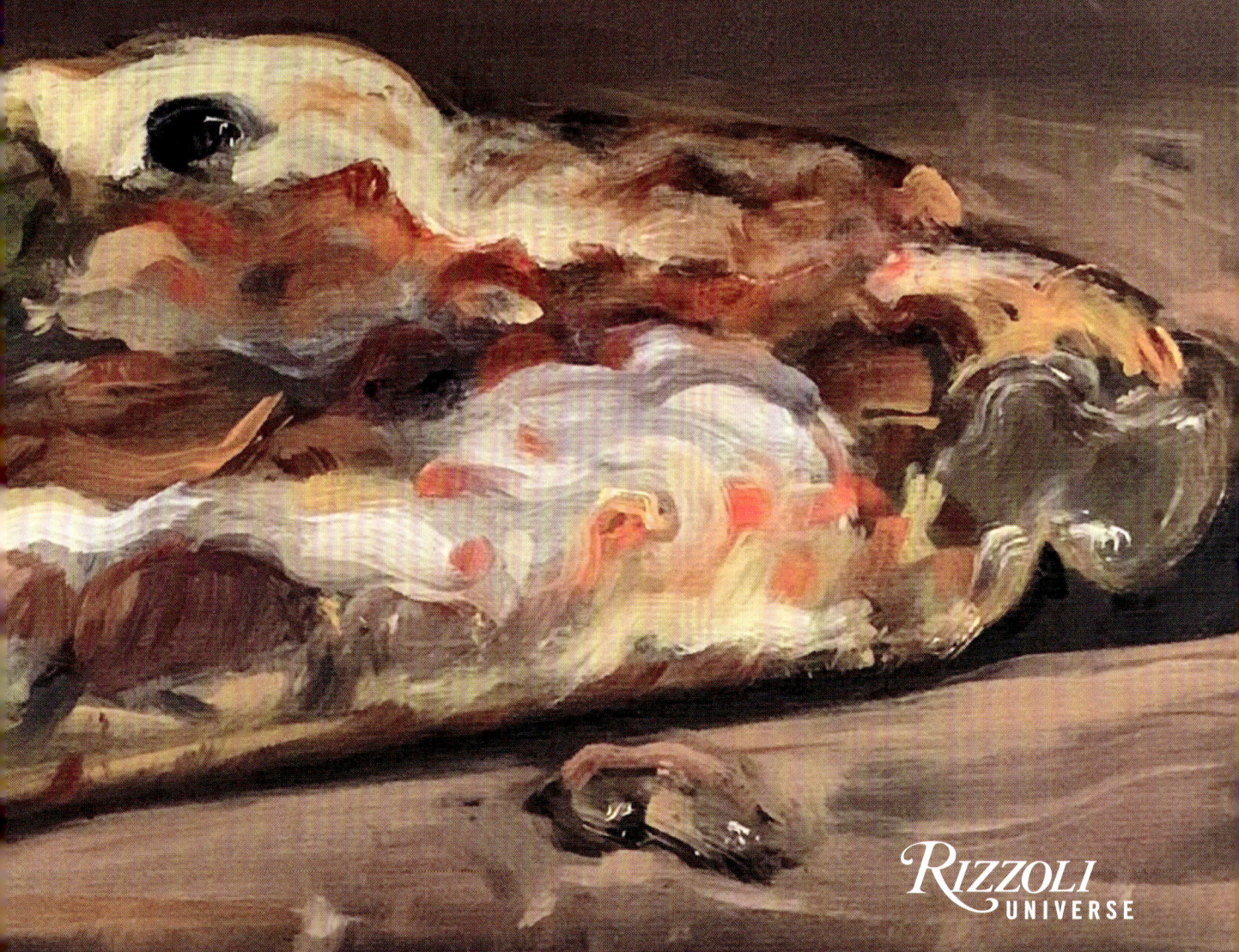

RIZZOLI UNIVERSE

First published in the United States of America in 2026 by
Rizzoli Universe, A Division of
Rizzoli International Publications, Inc.
49 West 27th Street
New York, NY 10001
www.rizzoliusa.com

Publisher: Charles Miers
Associate Publisher: Jessica Fuller
Editor: Sarah M. Sutherland
Production Manager: Colin Hough-Trapp
Design: Makiko Katoh
Design Manager: Tim Biddick

ISBN: 978-0-7893-4621-6

Library of Congress Control Number: 2025940276

Printed in China
2026 2027 2028 2029 / 10 9 8 7 6 5 4 3 2 1

The authorized representative in the EU for product safety and
compliance is
Mondadori Libri S.p.A., via Gian Battista Vico 42, Milan, Italy, 20123,
www.mondadori.it

Visit us online:
Instagram.com/RizzoliBooks
Facebook.com/RizzoliNewYork
Youtube.com/user/RizzoliNY

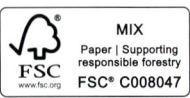

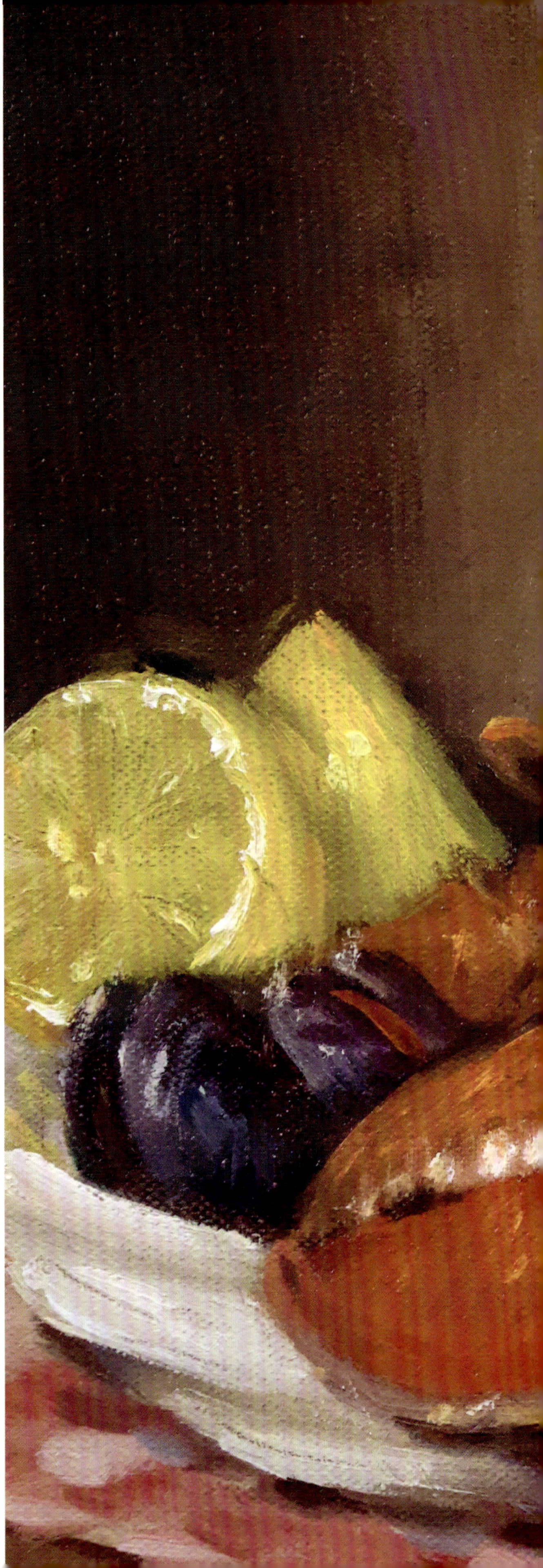

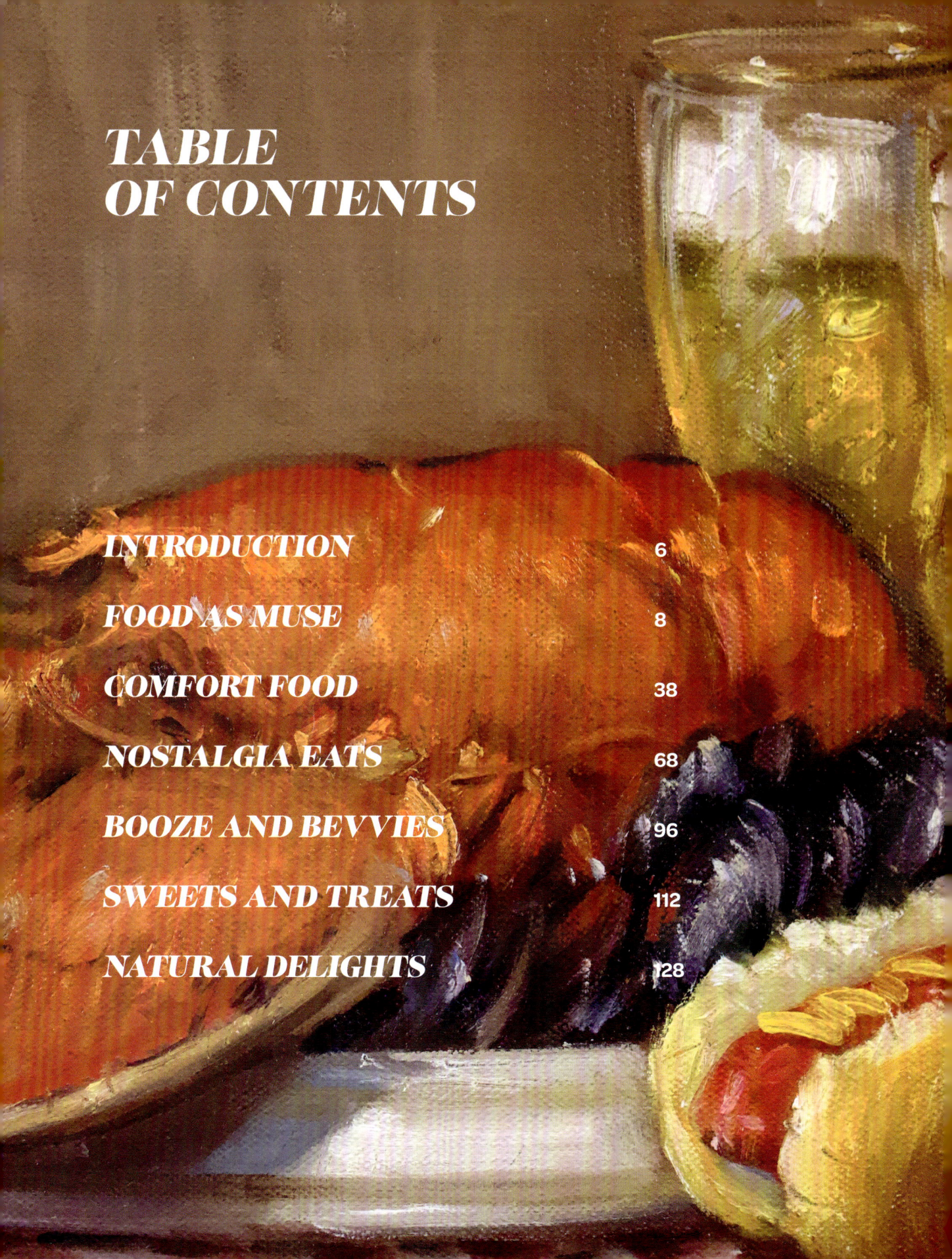

TABLE
OF CONTENTS

INTRODUCTION

There's a long tradition of still-life painting that dates back to ancient art; the earliest still lifes on record were discovered in Egypt around 1,500 BCE. It makes a lot of sense: inanimate objects from daily life, like food or flowers, are undemanding art subjects and were probably readily available.

Art patronage took off in seventeenth-century Europe, where newly prosperous Flemish and Dutch elites sought works of art composed with objects that signified their social status, wealth, and even their patriotism. Still-life subjects usually consisted of food, table settings, and flowers. They could feature exotic foods or opulent tableware, with every item reflecting a world of economic growth and abundance. Some still lifes also included nods to memento mori, where objects like dying flowers or skulls symbolized the passing of time or, more specifically, reminded a spectator of the certainty of death. Memento mori brought a seriousness and extra layer of depth to these already desirable oil paintings.

Still life became its own distinct cultural currency, and its popularity endured over several centuries: from Clara Peeters during the Dutch Renaissance, to French eighteenth-century artist Jean Siméon Chardin, to Henri Fatin-Latour, who painted in France in the nineteenth century.

During art school, I was drawn to oil painting. It wasn't that popular at the time; many artists were making multimedia art. People would wonder why I was pursuing what they felt was an old-fashioned art form. But I saw it differently: my love for and appreciation of still-life painting led me to think about what objects today would make great subject matter. What everyday items could be emblematic of today's world? The art of comfort food was born.

Food like donuts, Taco Bell, or ramen painted in "serious" oil form creates a delicious tension with the nostalgia and light-heartedness of the subjects. The paintings quickly grew in popularity in the most twenty-first–century way—via social media. Now, the patrons of our age include Dunkin', Wendy's, McDonald's, and Netflix, and they commission me to paint the most prestigious commodity of our modern day: objects that feed us and bring us joy.

—Noah Verrier

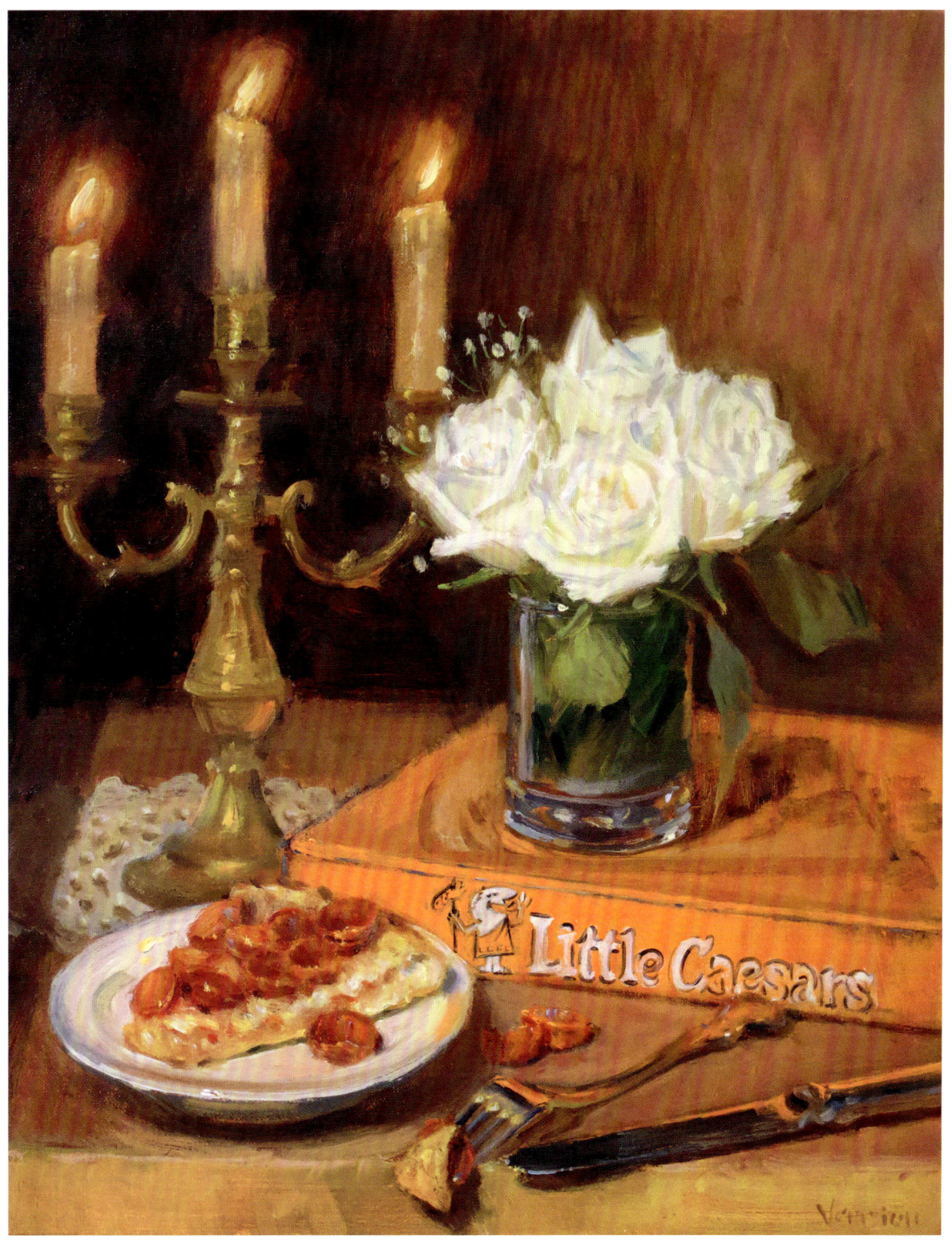

Little Caesars

16 x 20

FOOD AS MUSE

*Carrying on the tradition of still life painting from Chardin and Manet to Andy Warhol and Wayne Thiebaud, my oil paintings use food as a muse. I create scenes that are fun and whimsical, yet serious, aiming to **elevate** everyday delights.*

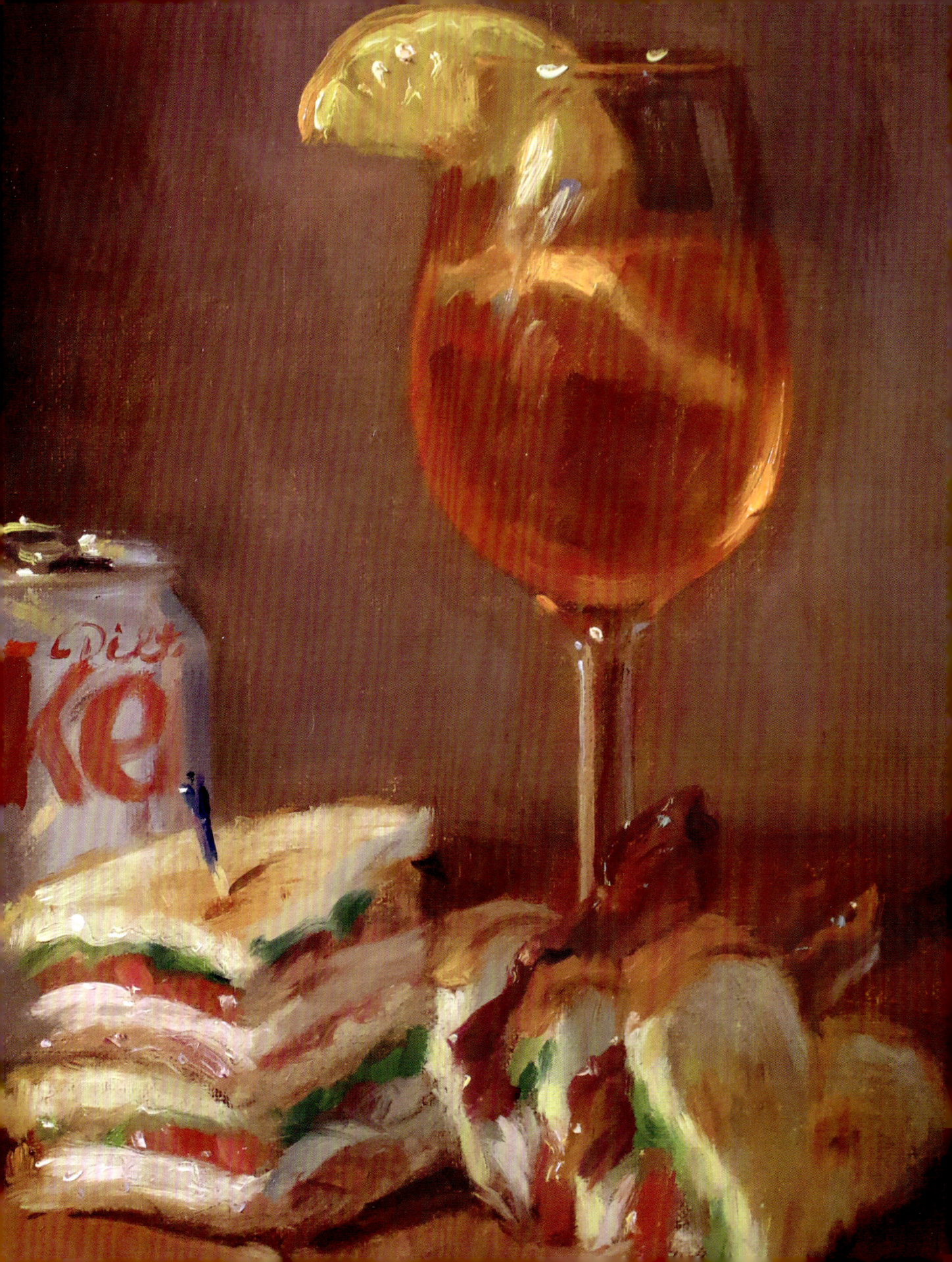

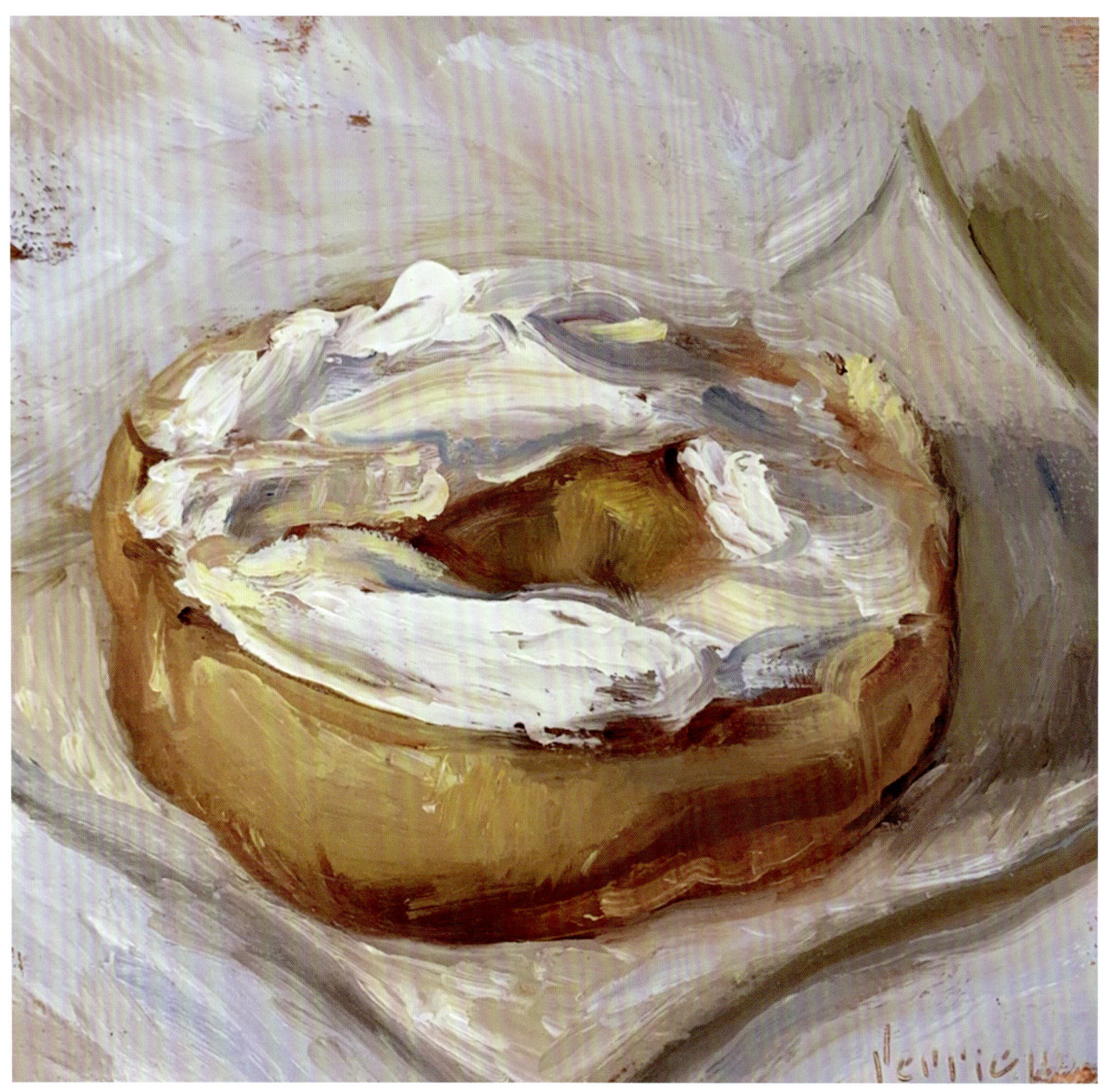

Bagel & Cream Cheese

8 x 8

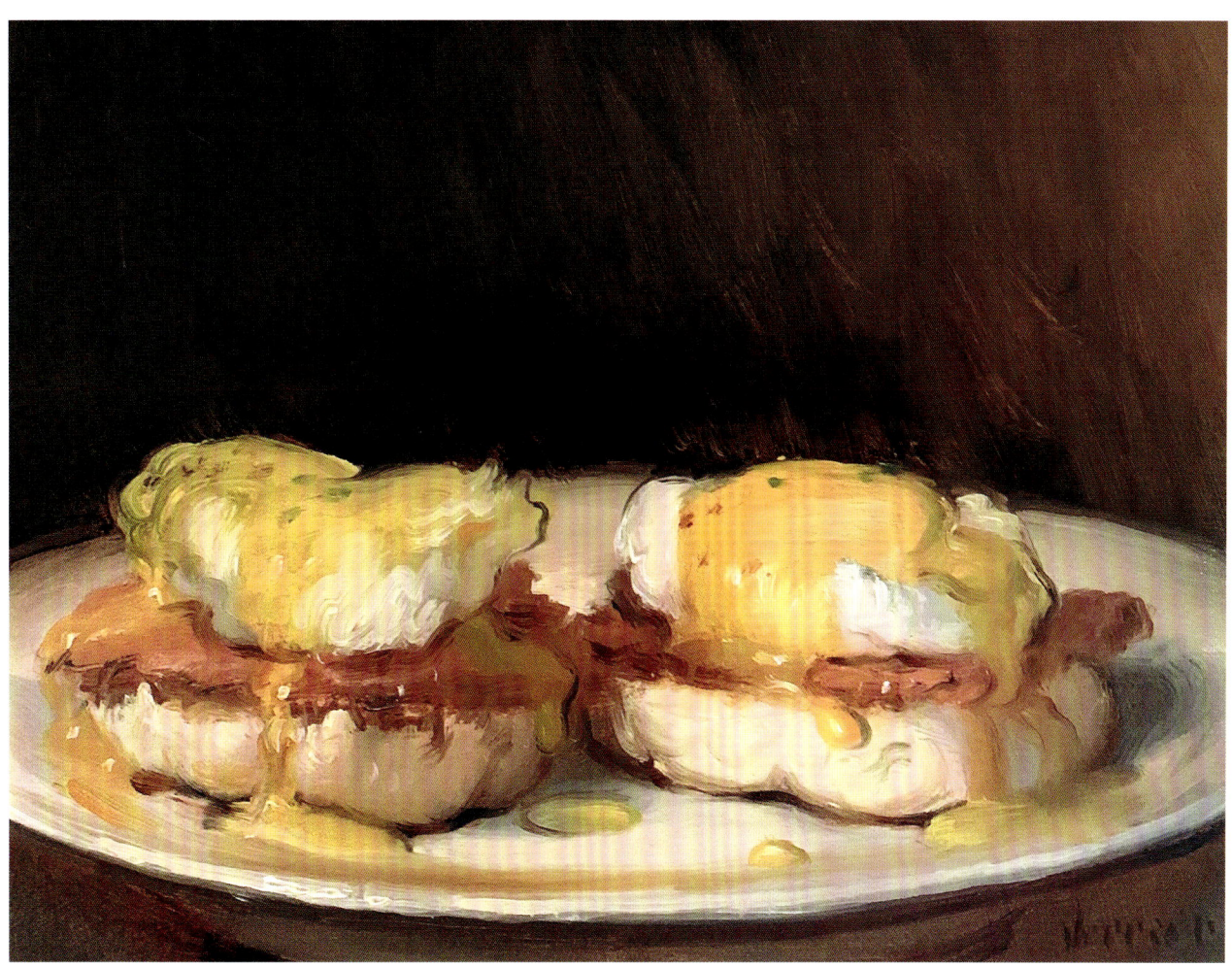

Eggs Benedict

9 x 8

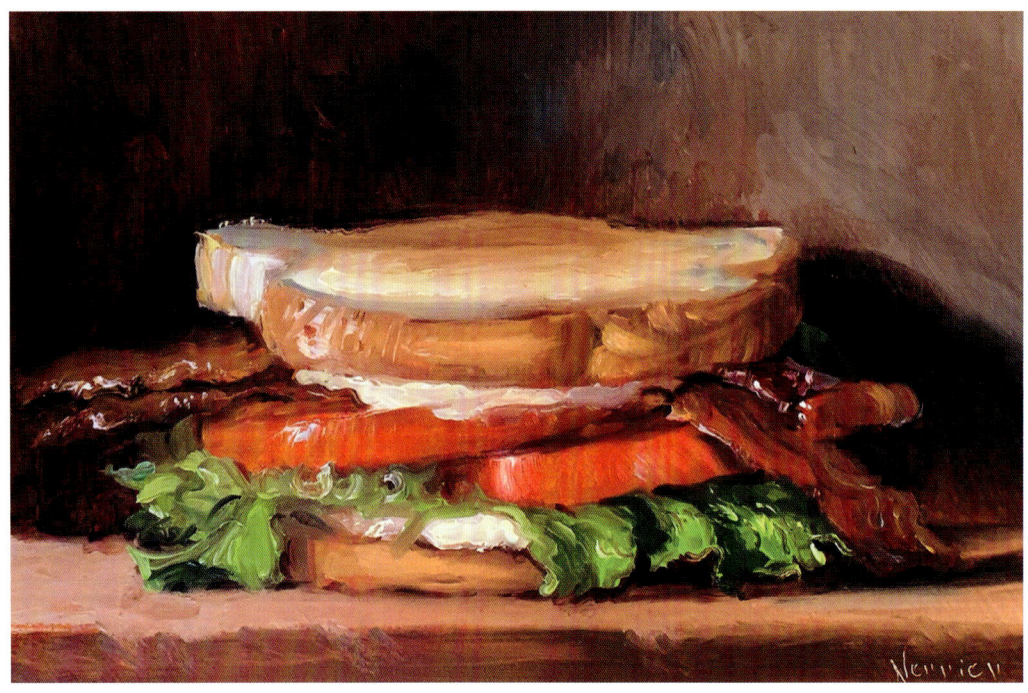

BLT
10 x 8 in.

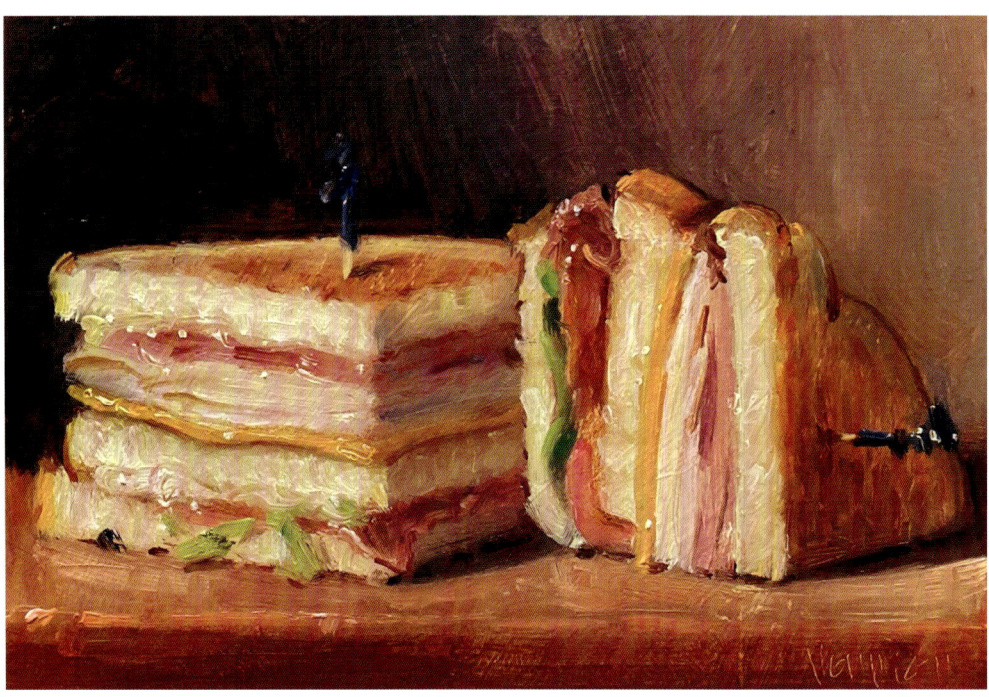

Club Sandwich
10 x 8 in.

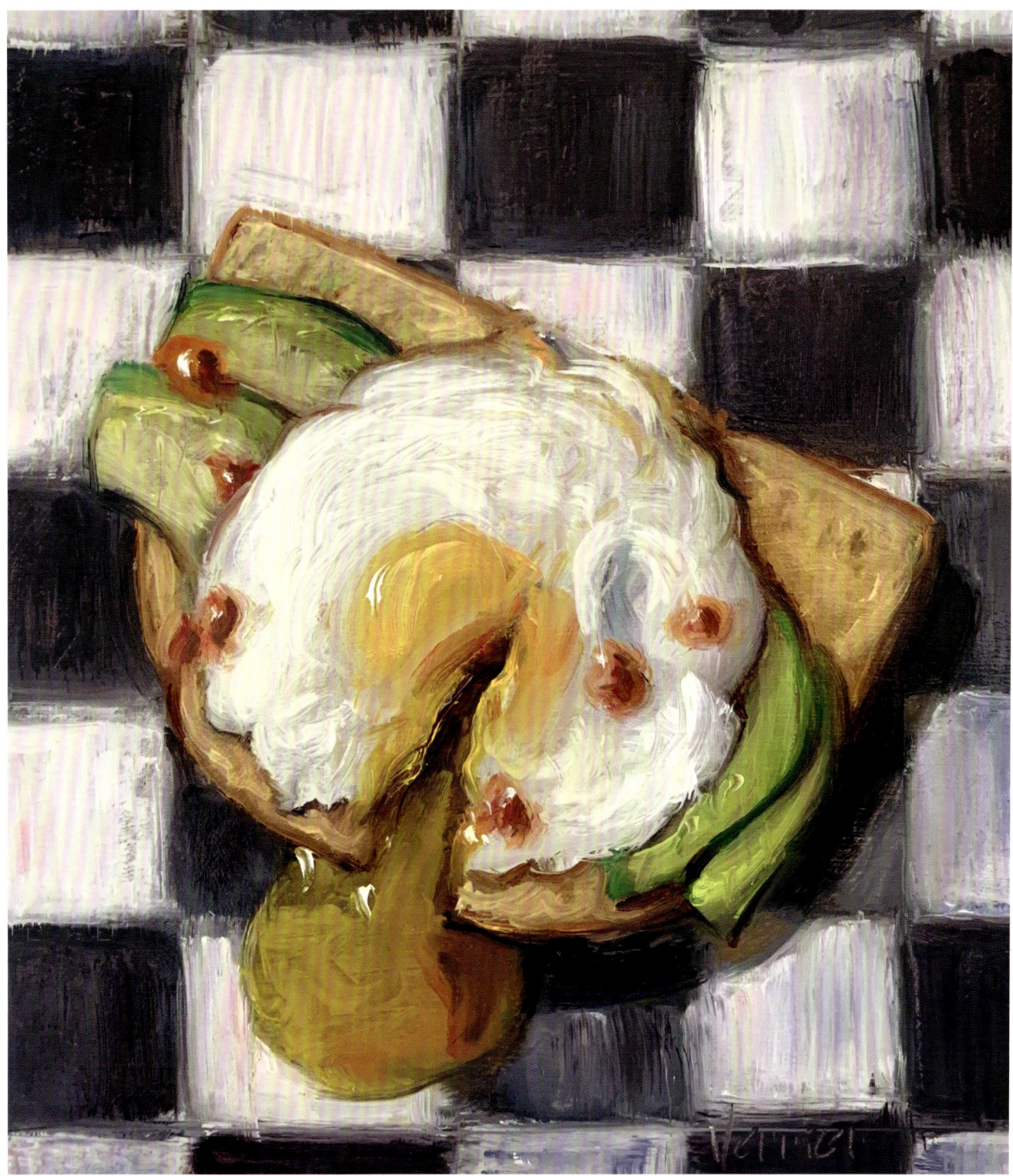

Avocado Toast

9 x 9 in.

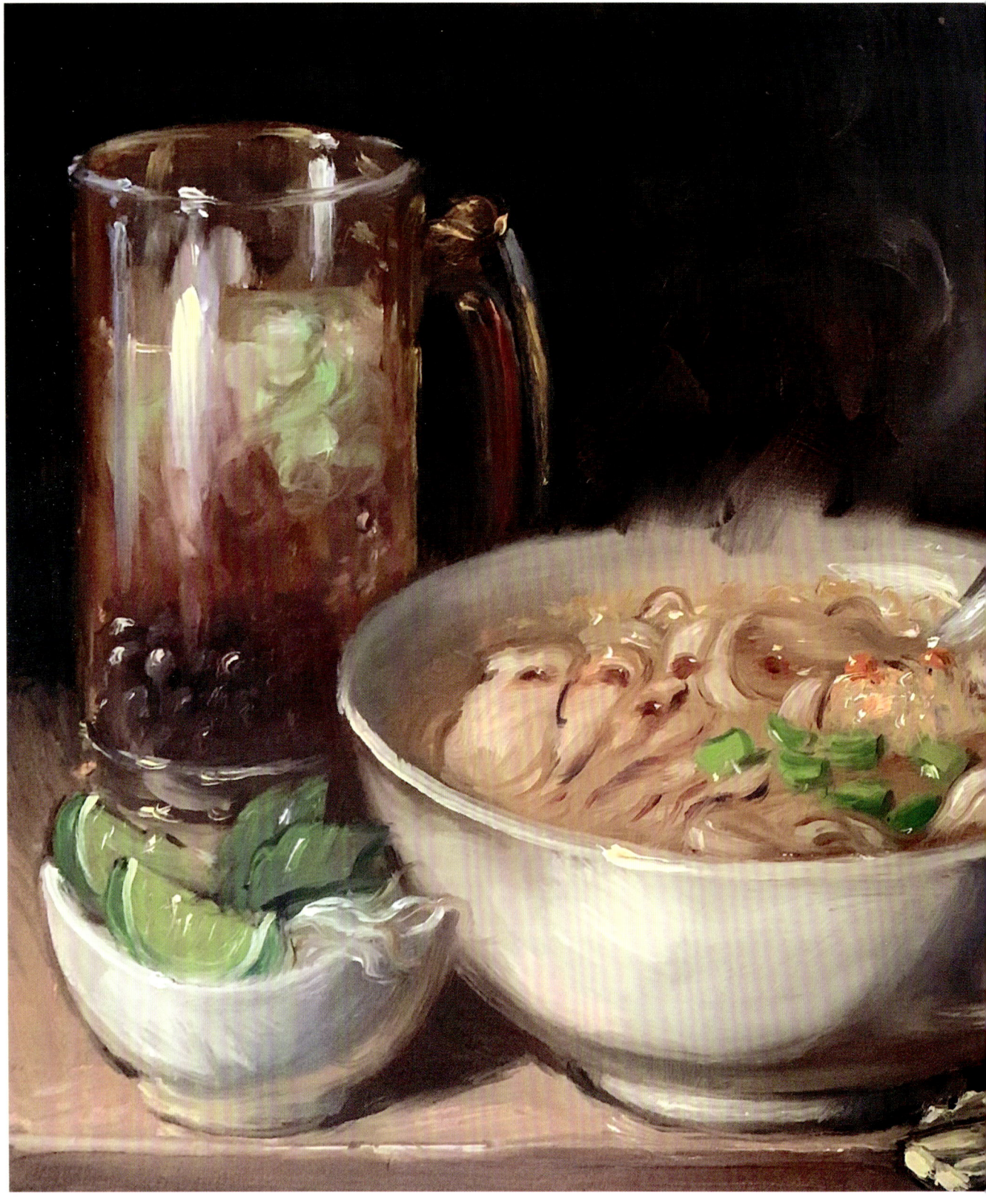

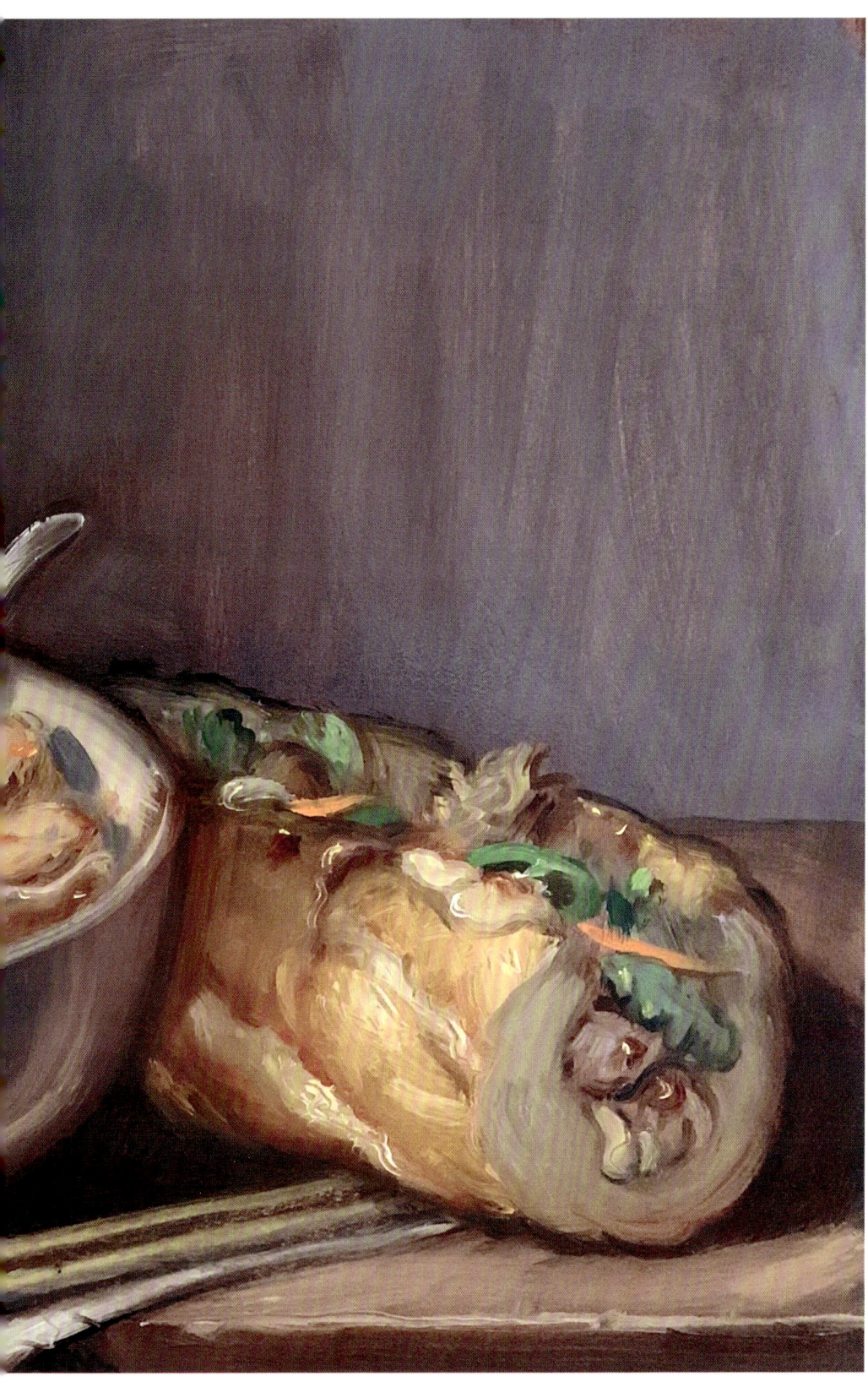

**Pho, Banh Mi, &
Boba Tea**

14 x 7 in.

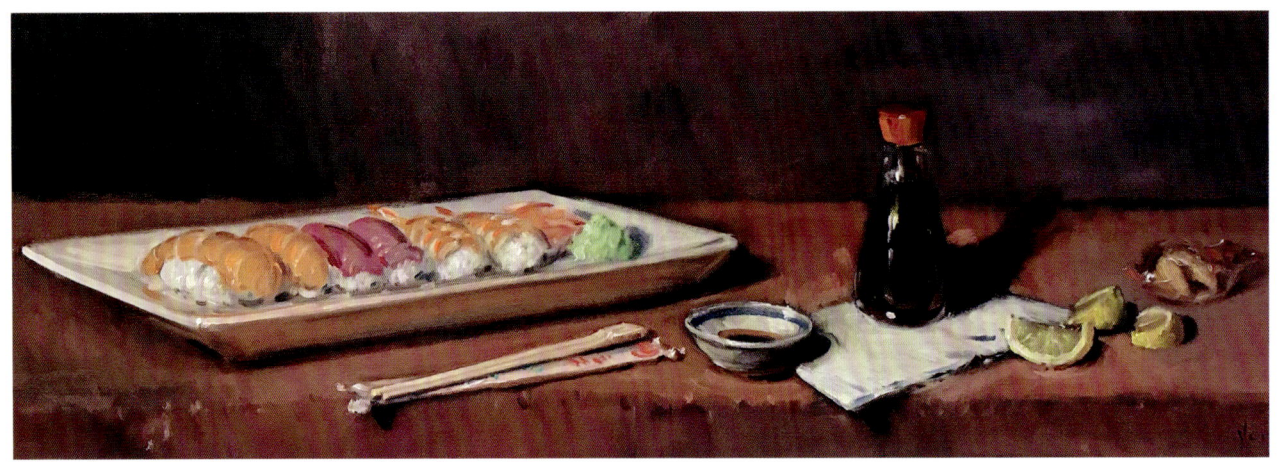

Nigiri Sushi
14 x 7 in.

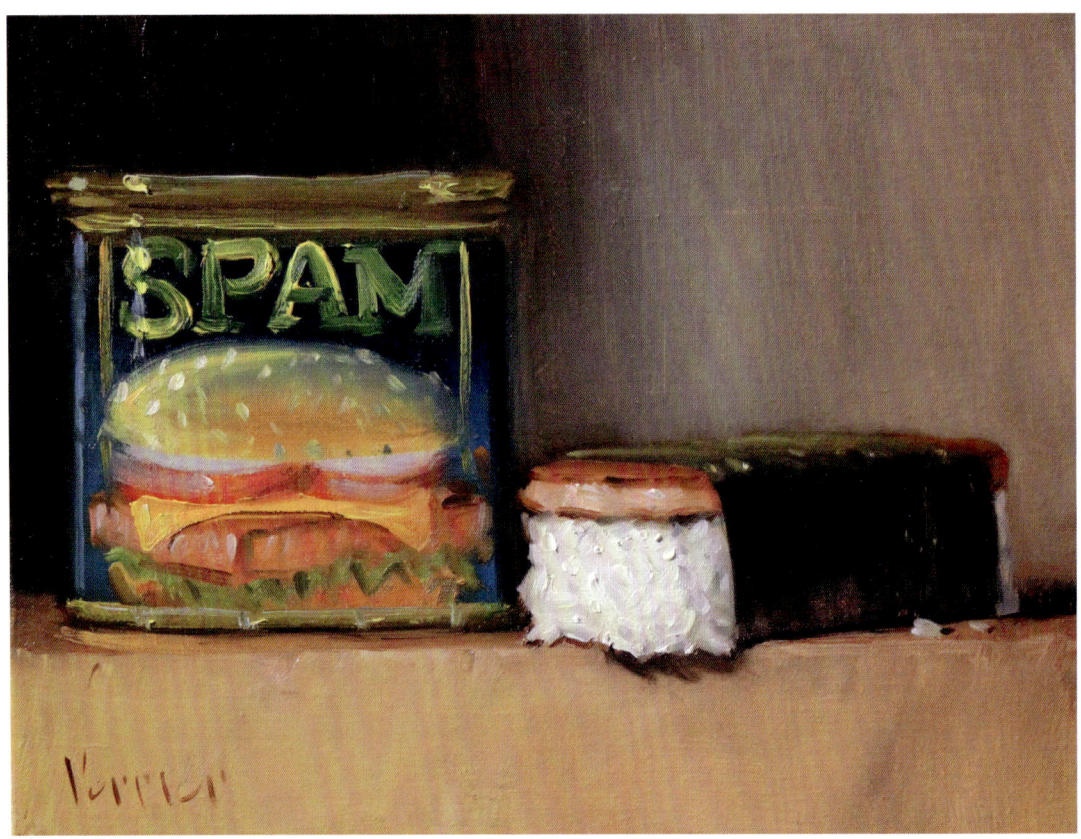

Spam Musubi
10 x 8 in.

OPPOSITE PAGE:
Espresso Martini & Uncrustable
9 x 12 in.

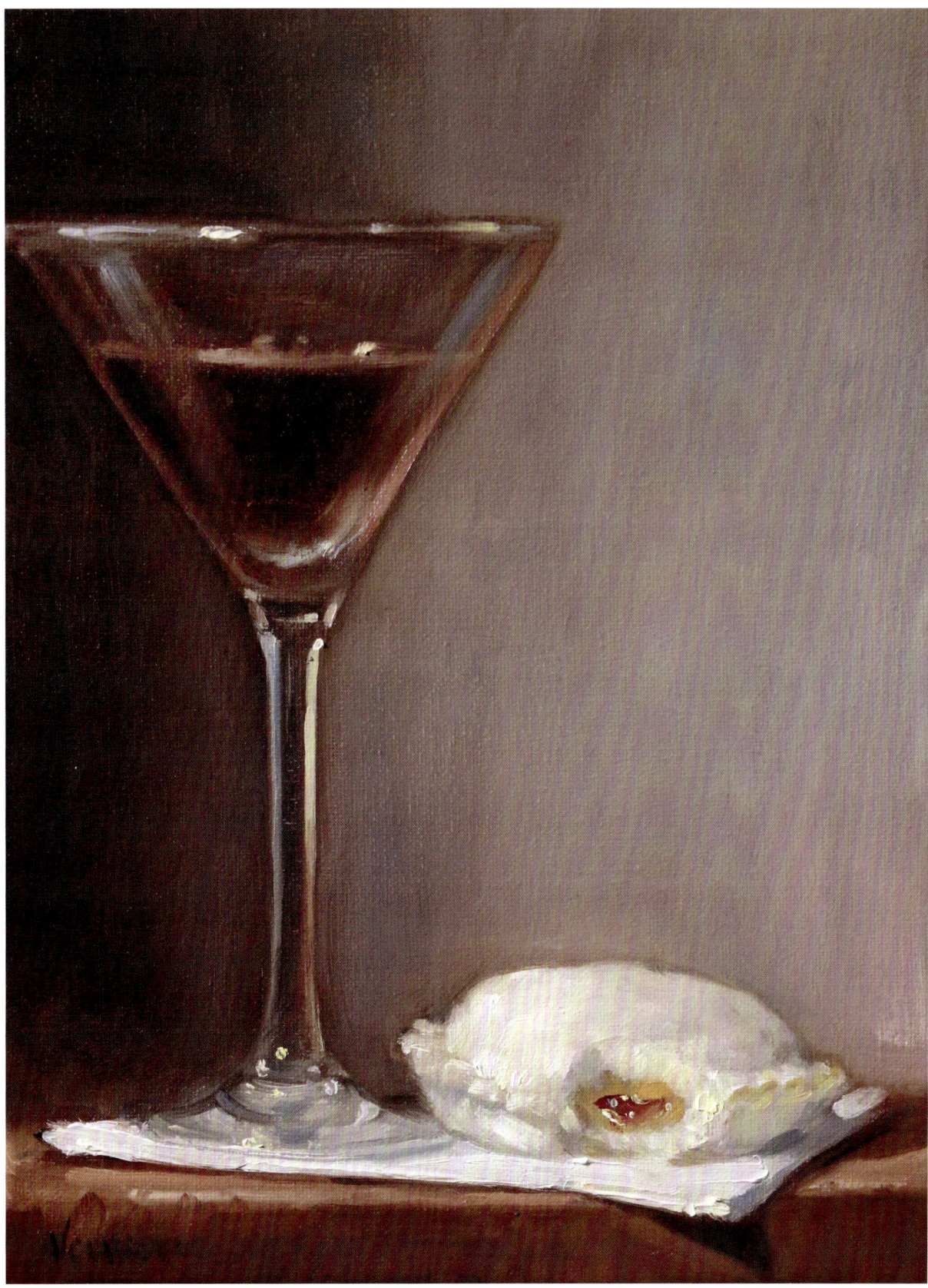

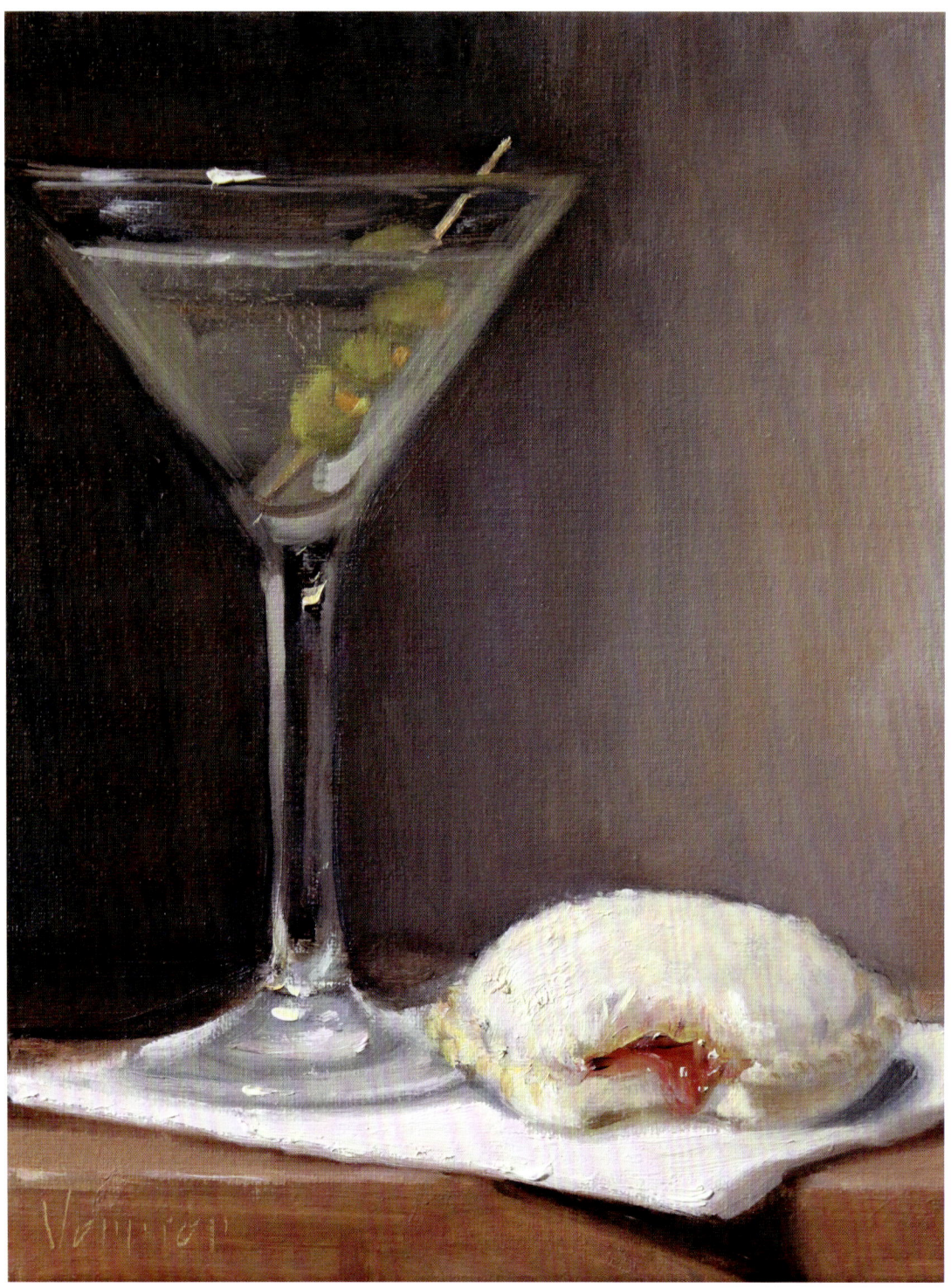

Dirty Martini & Uncrustable
9 x 12 in.

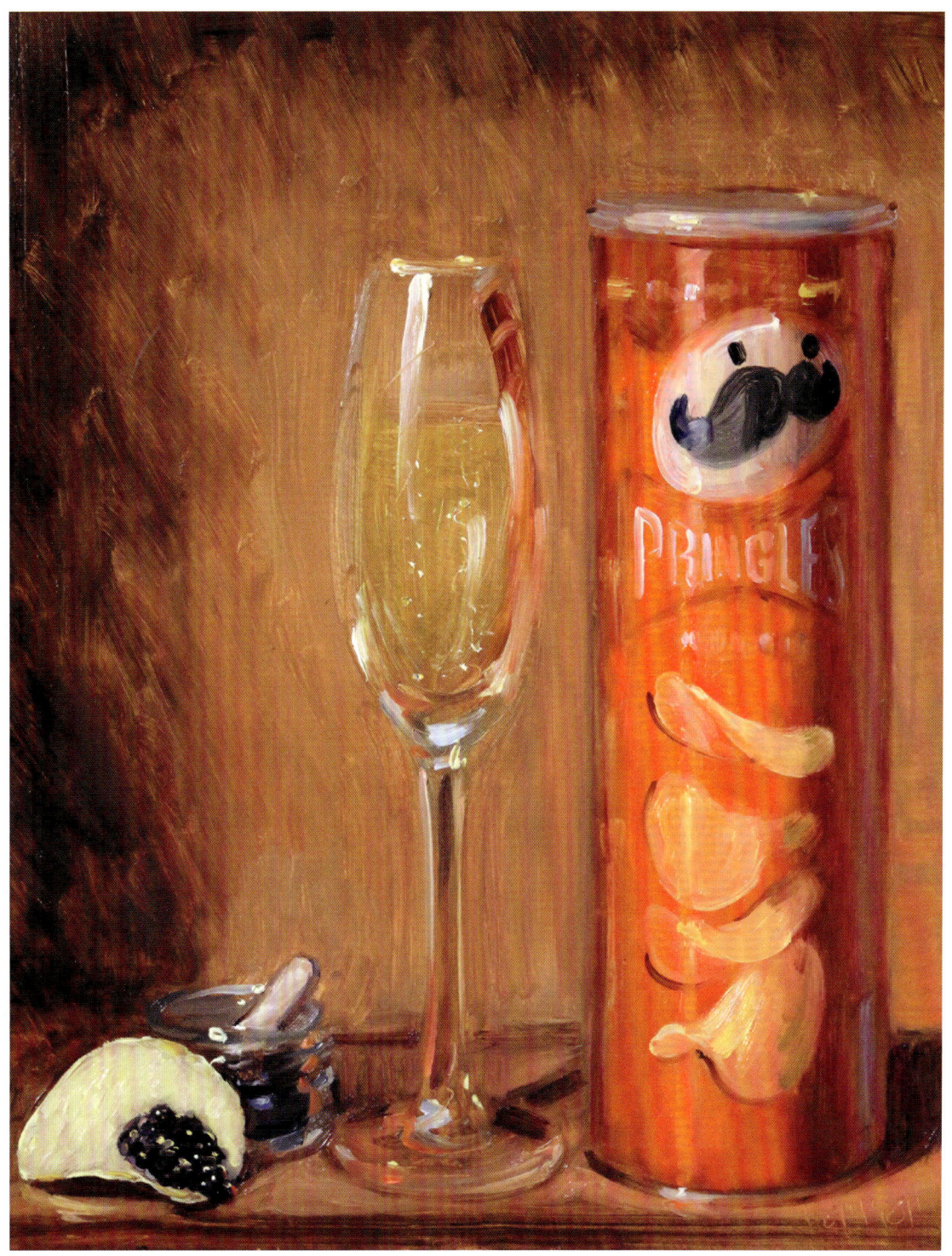

Caviar, Champagne, & Pringles

11 x 14 in.

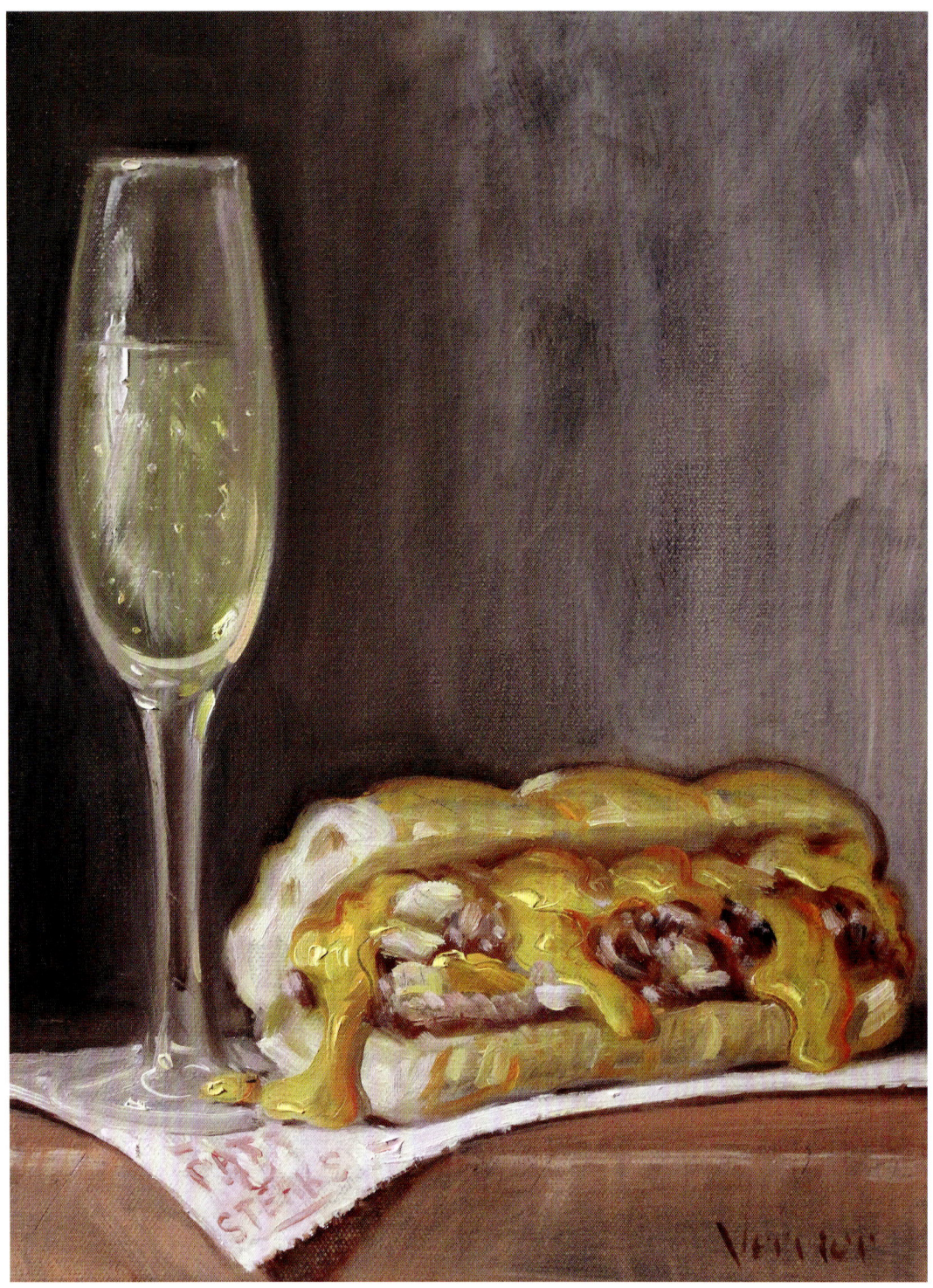

Champagne & Cheesesteak

9 x 12 in.

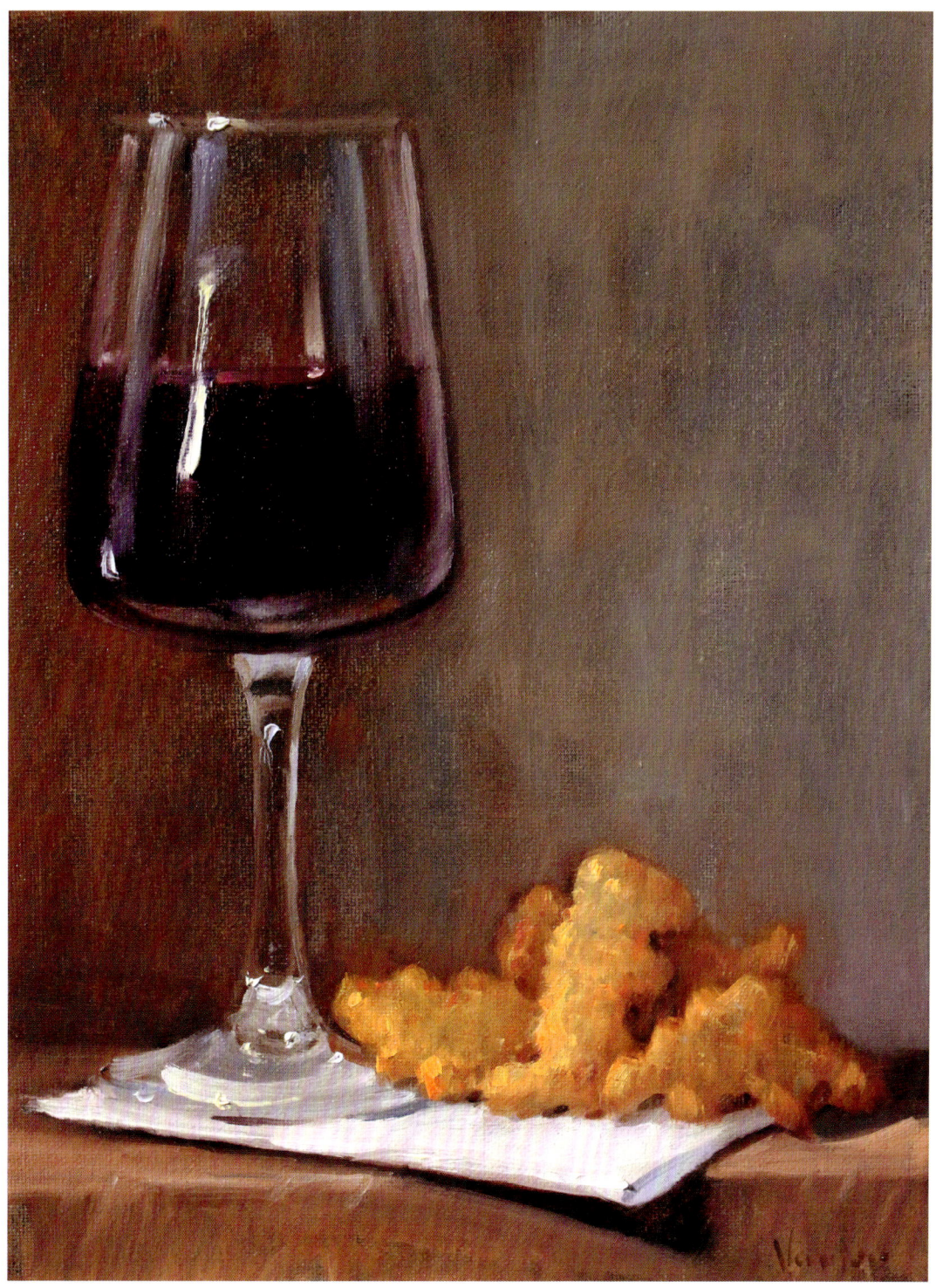

Wine & Dino Nuggets

9 x 12 in.

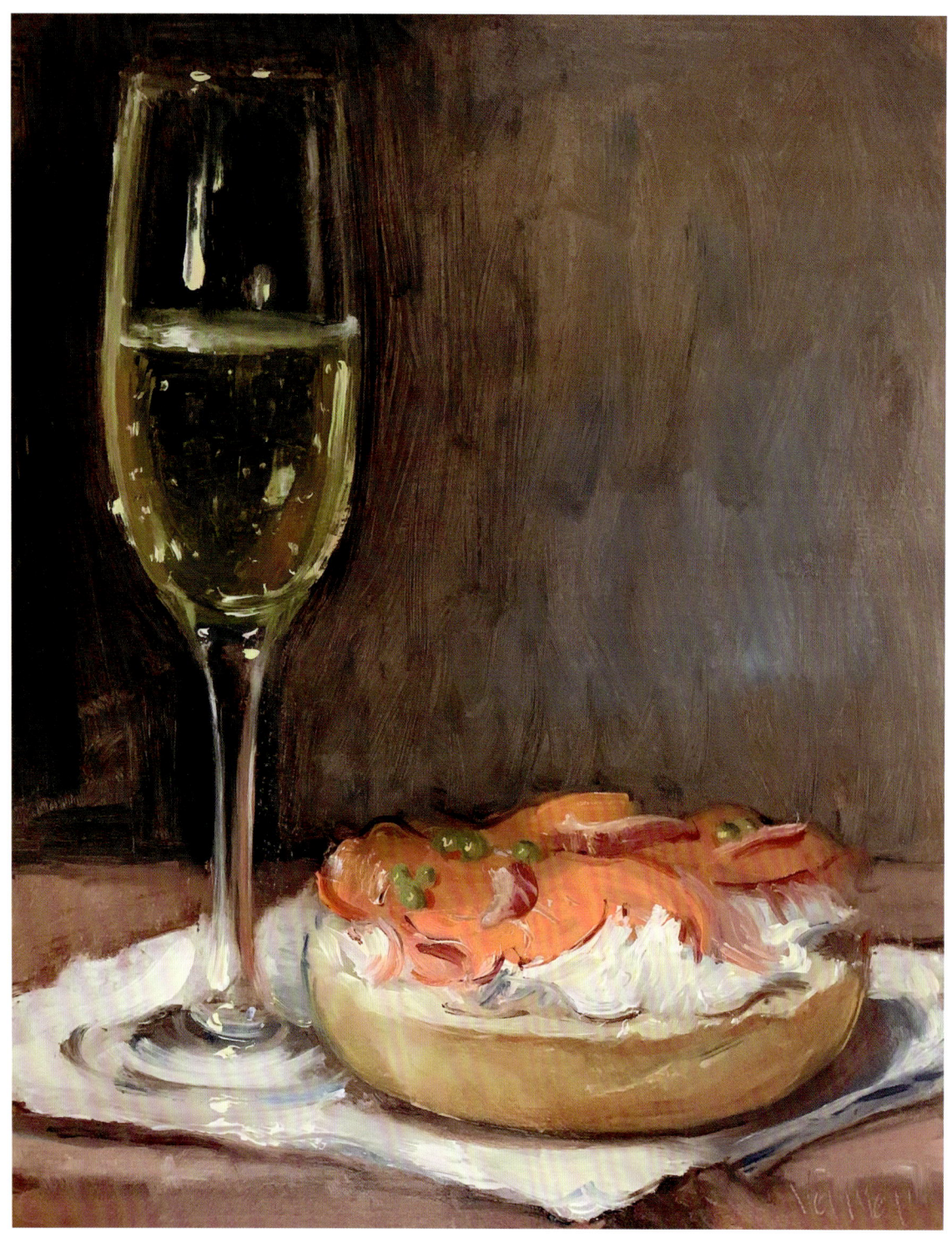

Champagne & Bagel with Lox

9 x 12 in.

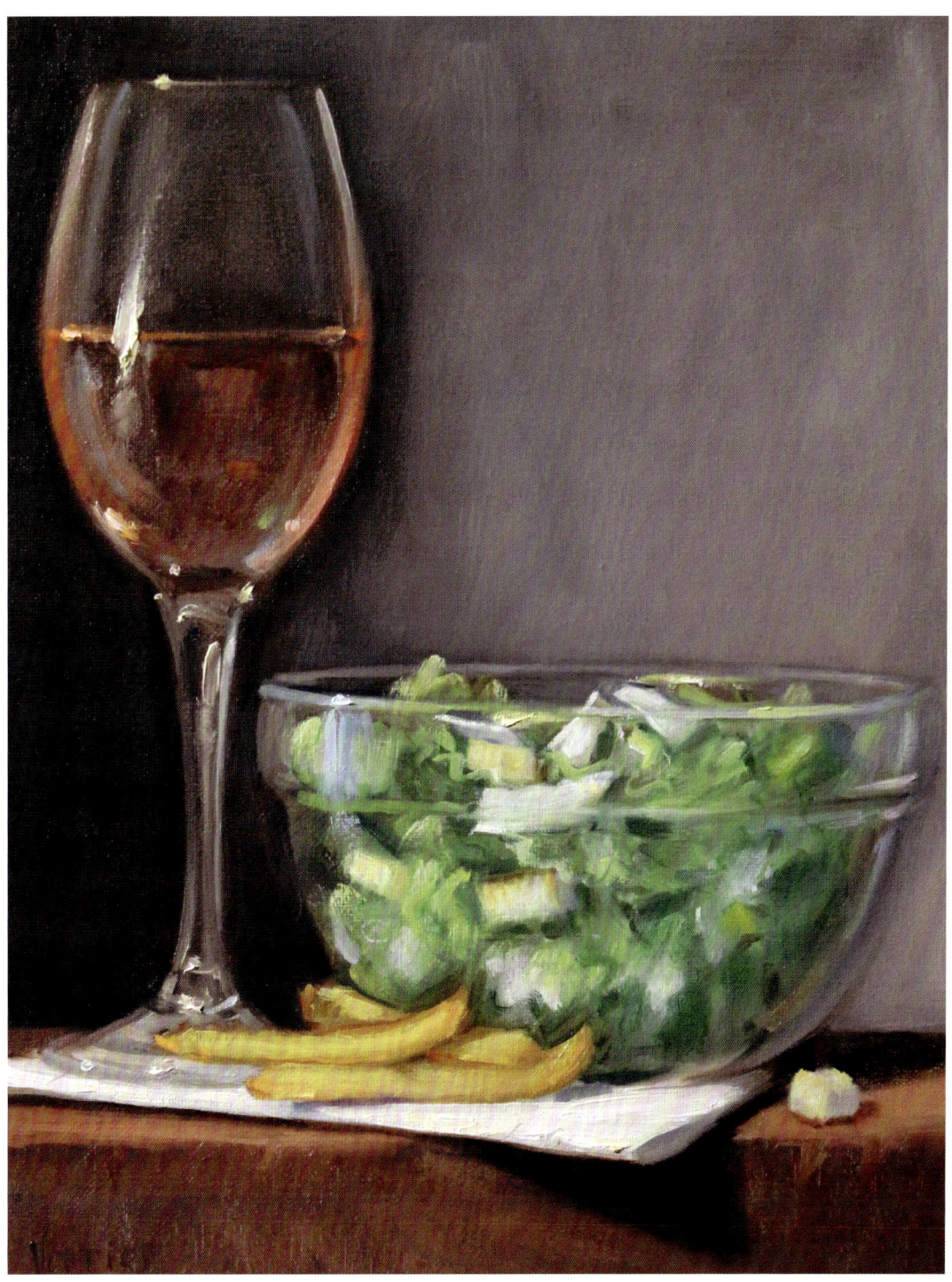

Rosé, Caesar Salad, & Fries

11 x 14 in.

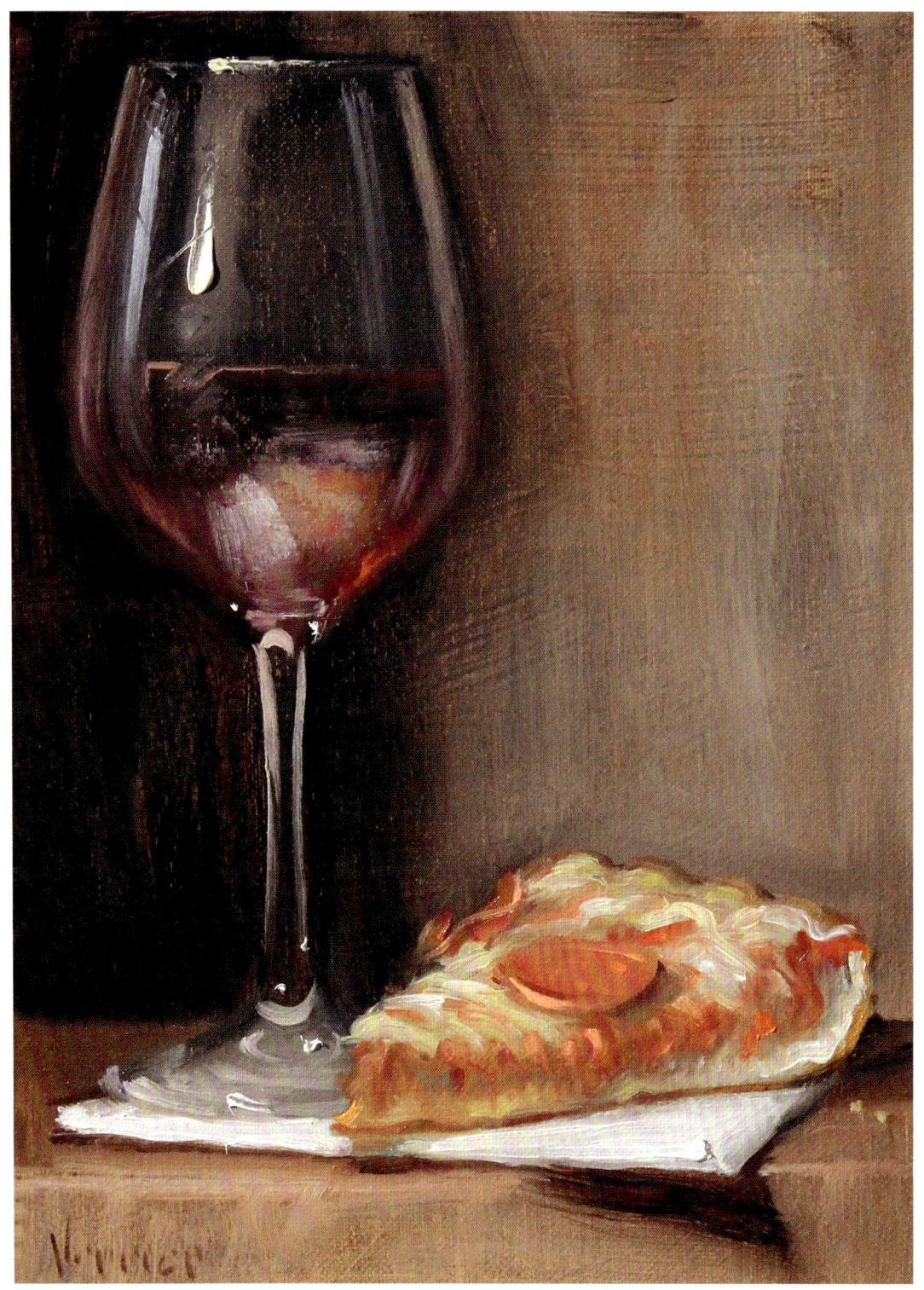

Wine & DiGiorno

9 x 12 in.

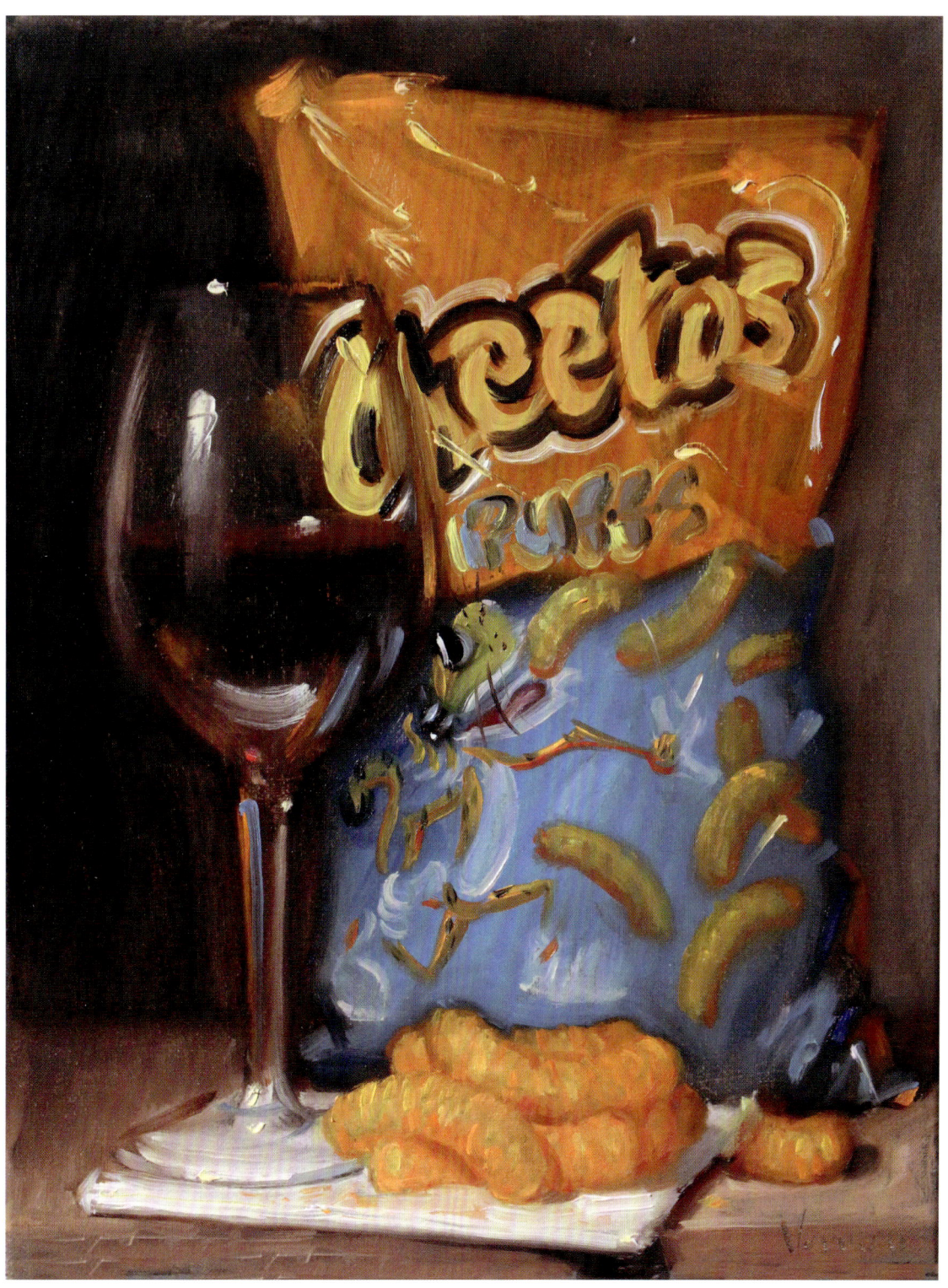

Wine & Cheetos

11 x 14 in.

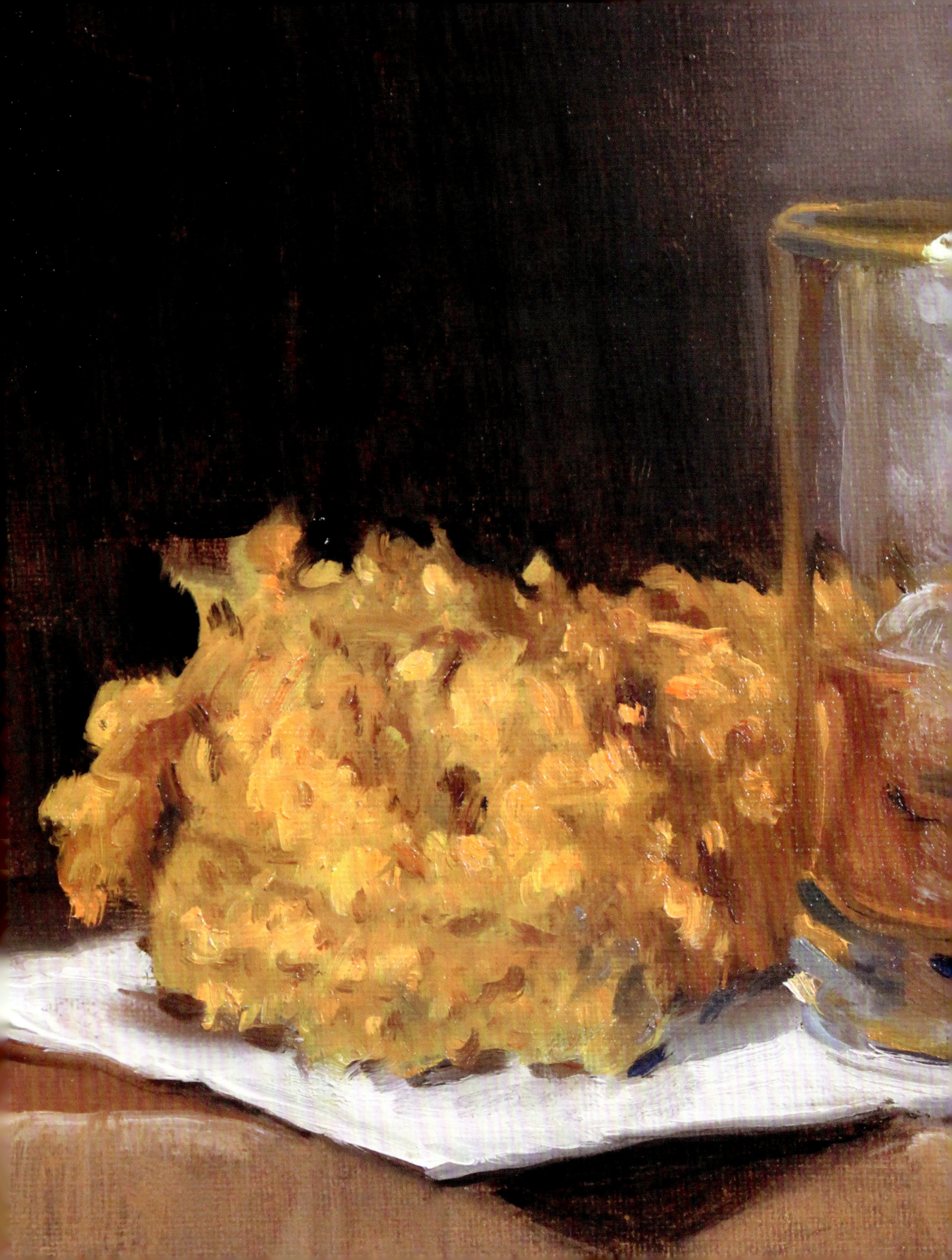

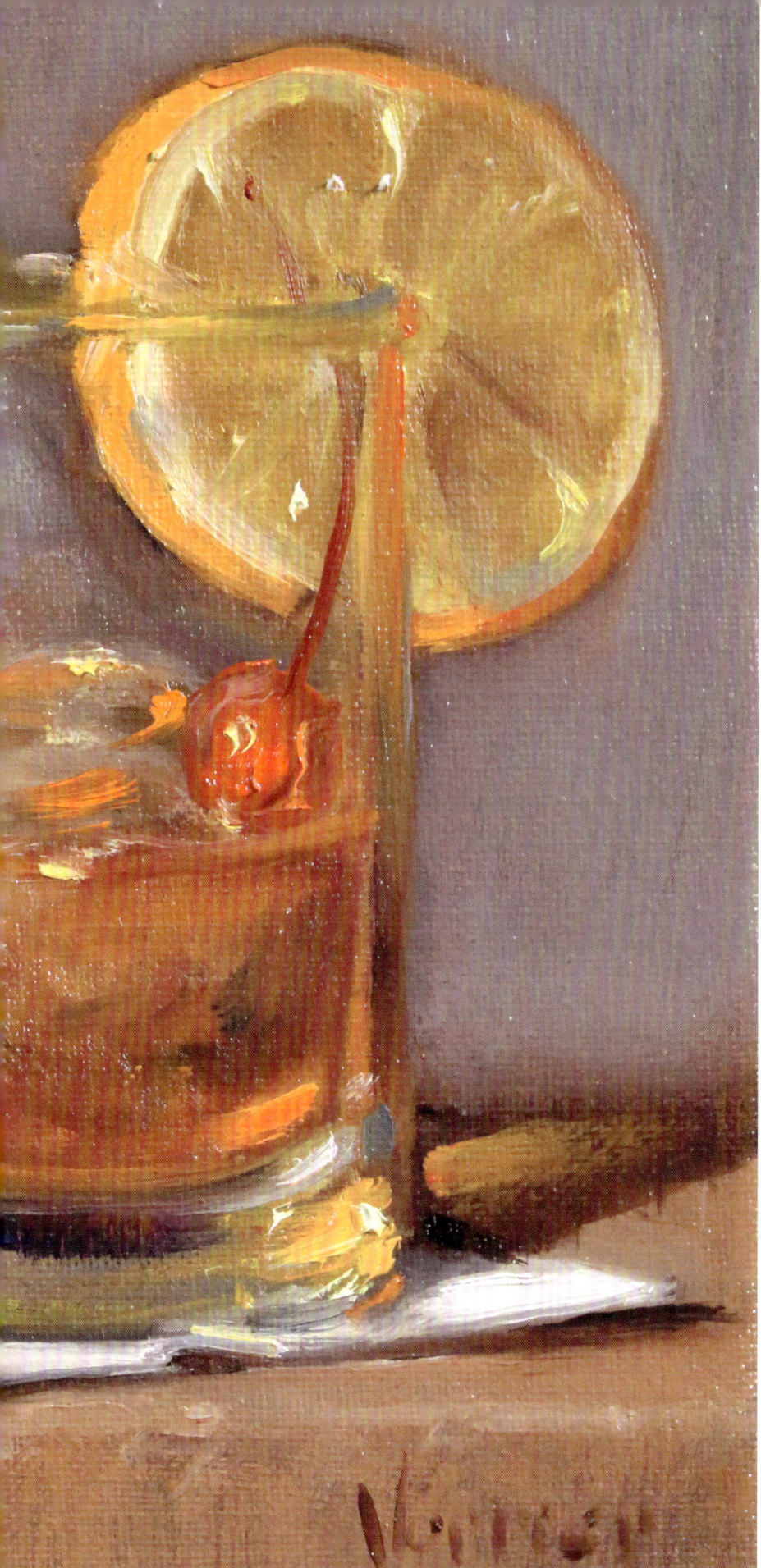

Fried Chicken & Old Fashioned
12 x 9 in.

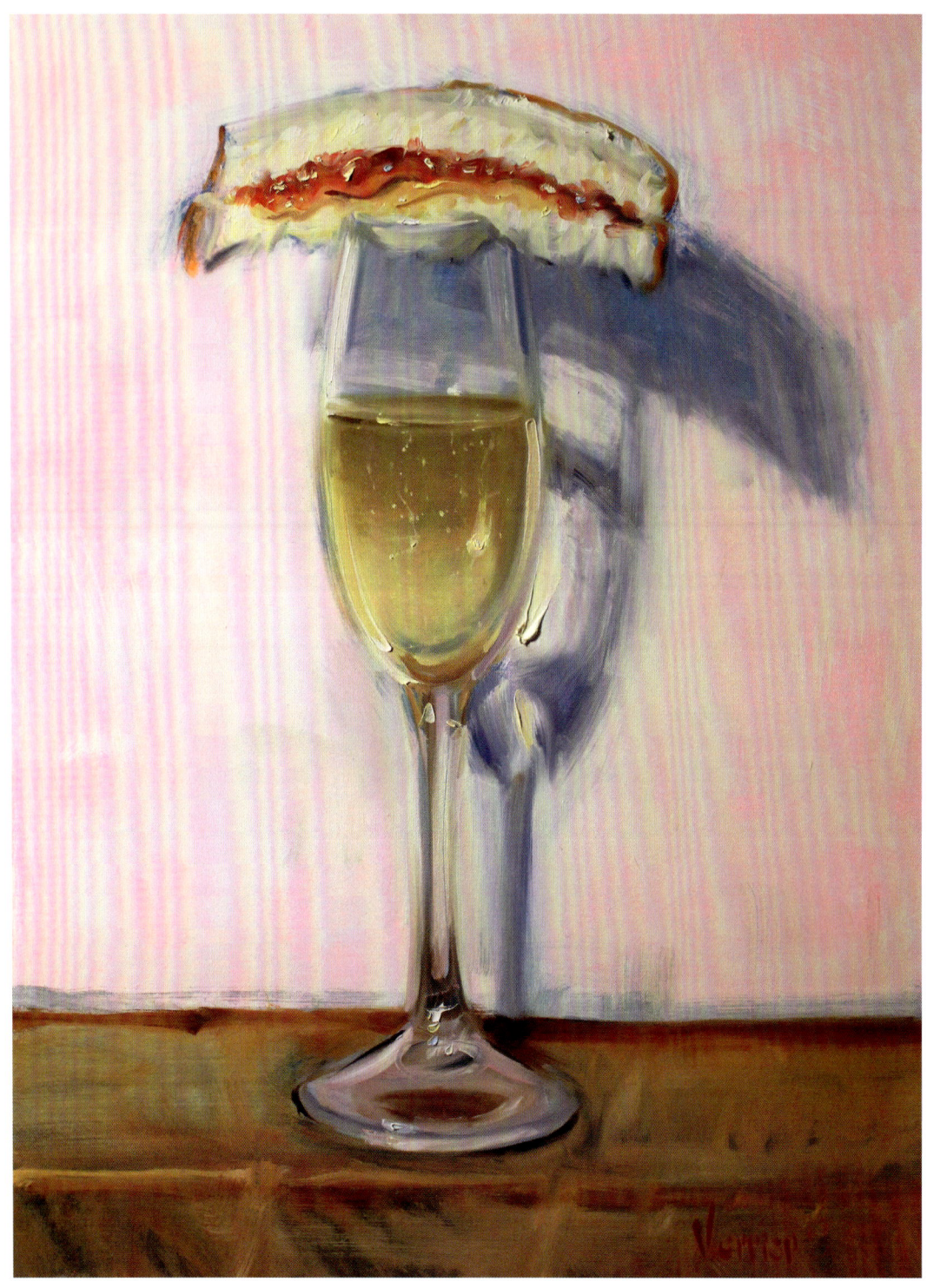

Champagne & PB&J
30 x 40 in.

OPPOSITE PAGE:
Beer & Hot Dog
8 x 10 in.

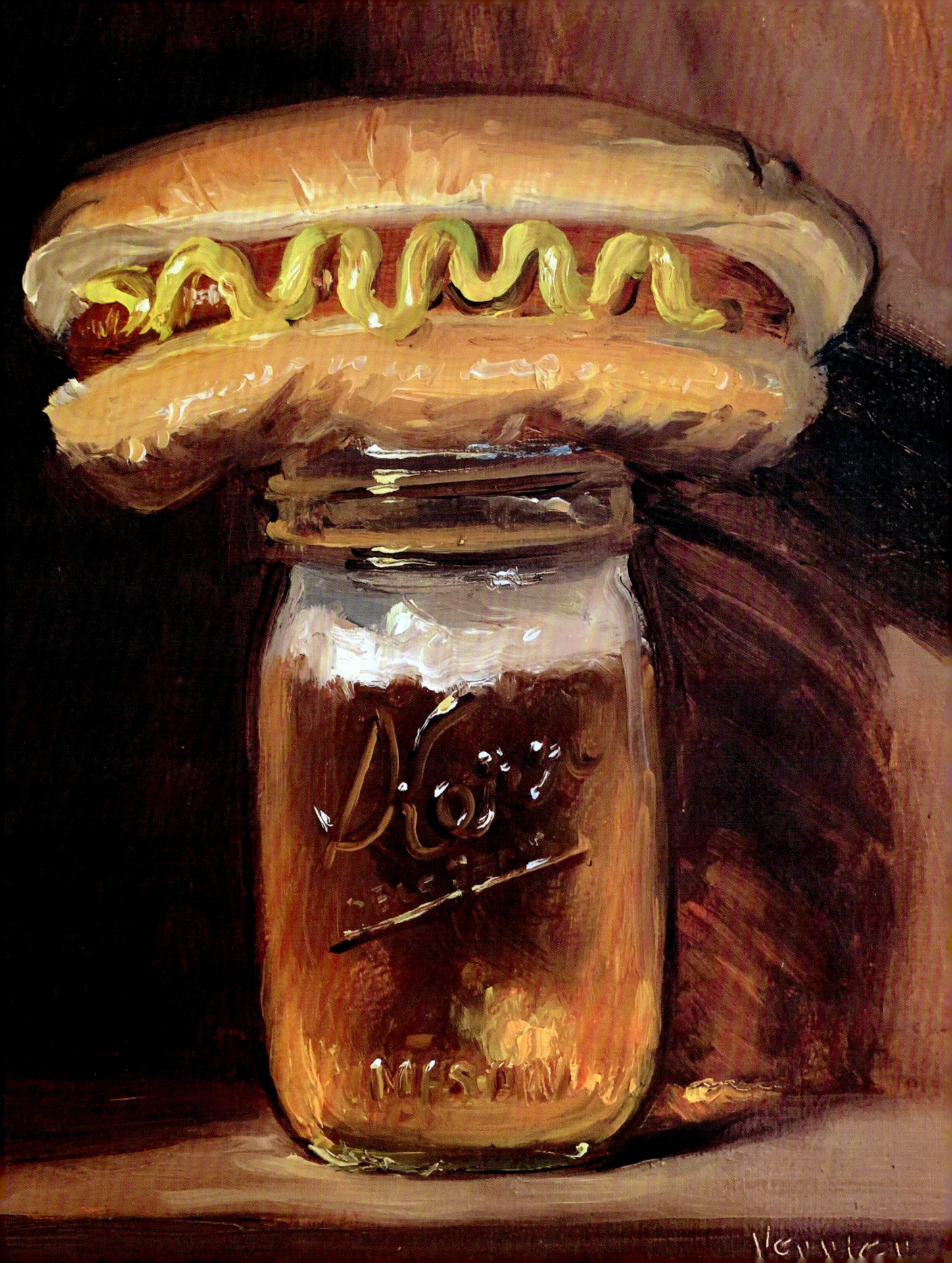

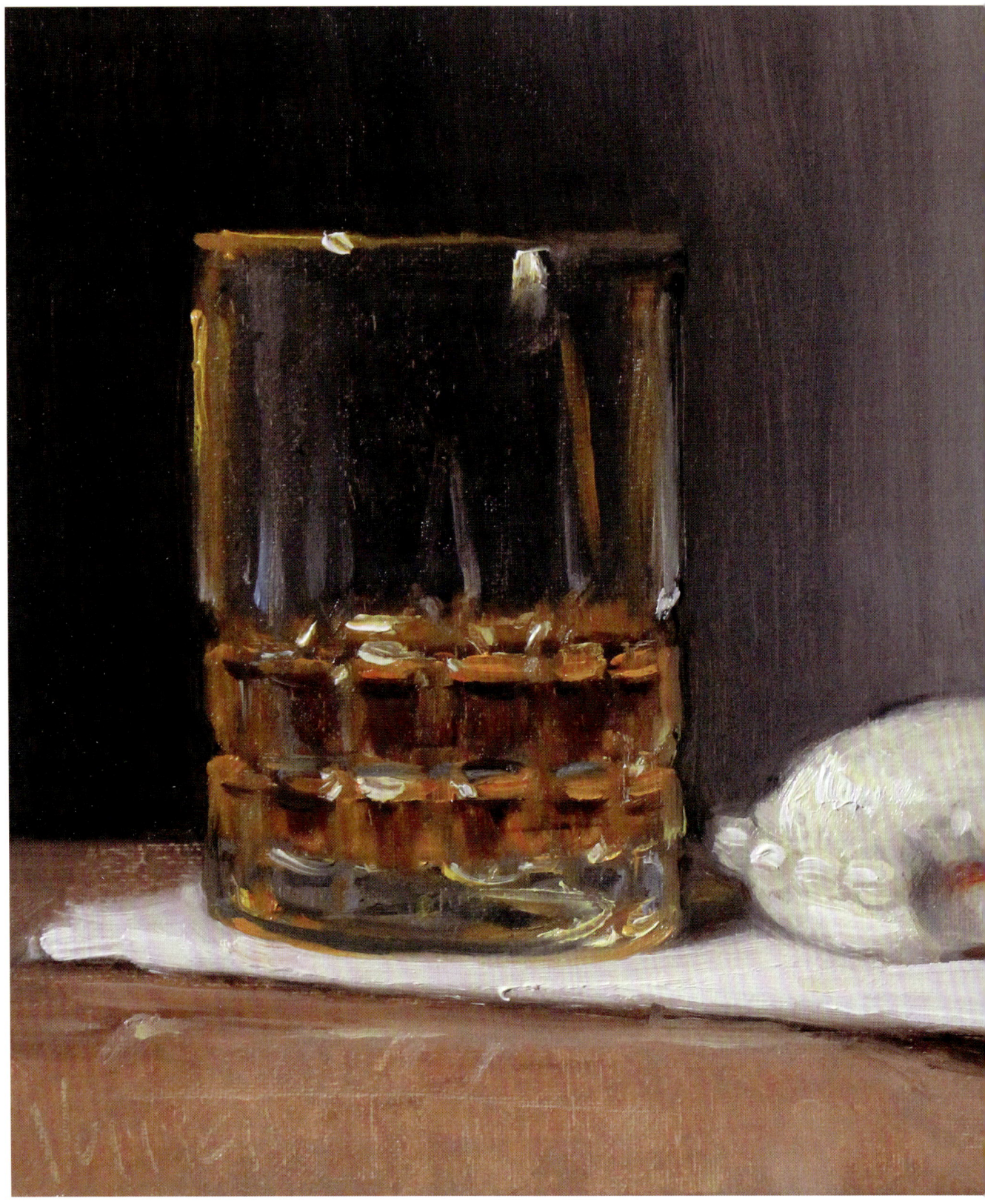

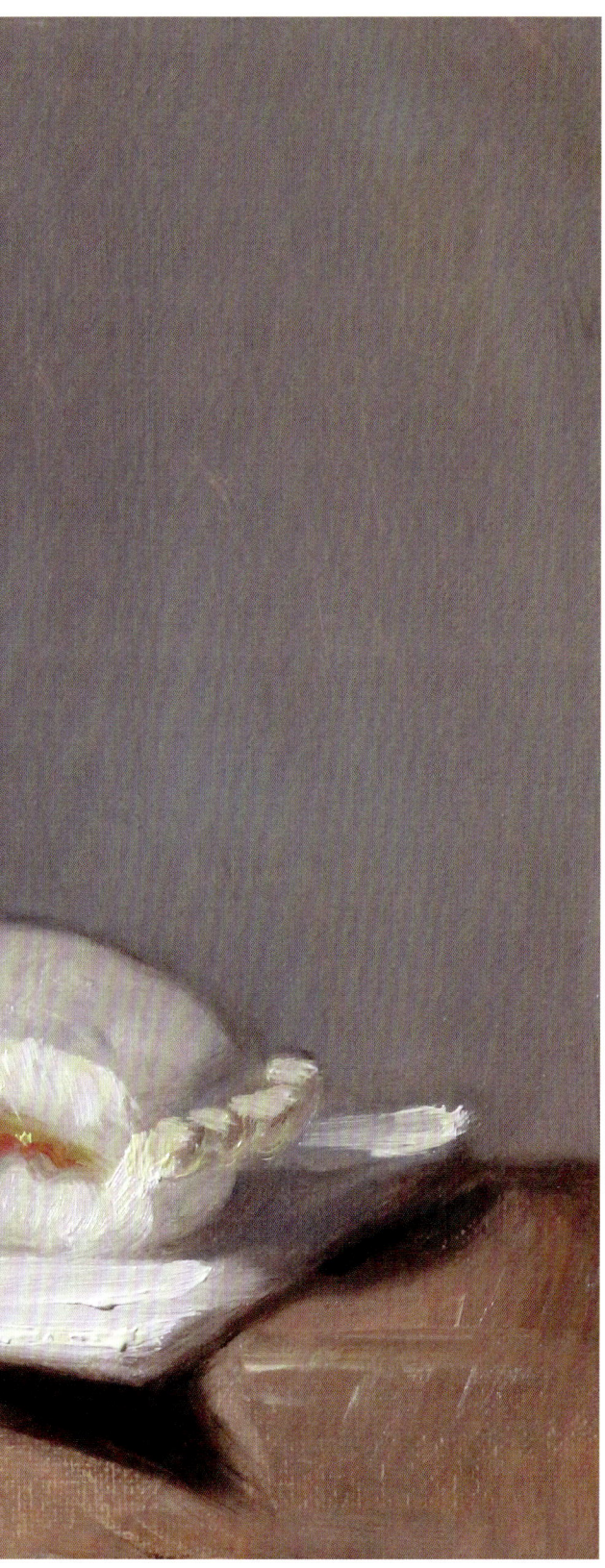

Whiskey & Uncrustable
12 x 9 in.

Whiskey & Uncrustables Sandwich
by Heather Beaupre

I consider this piece my version of girl dinner. The high and low of a great whiskey and an Uncrustables sandwich is exactly what I want after a long day. The slight bite taken out where you can see the gooey jelly inside is absolute perfection. It's just what a teacher deserves at the end of the year when I'm too tired to cook and just need something quick to eat.

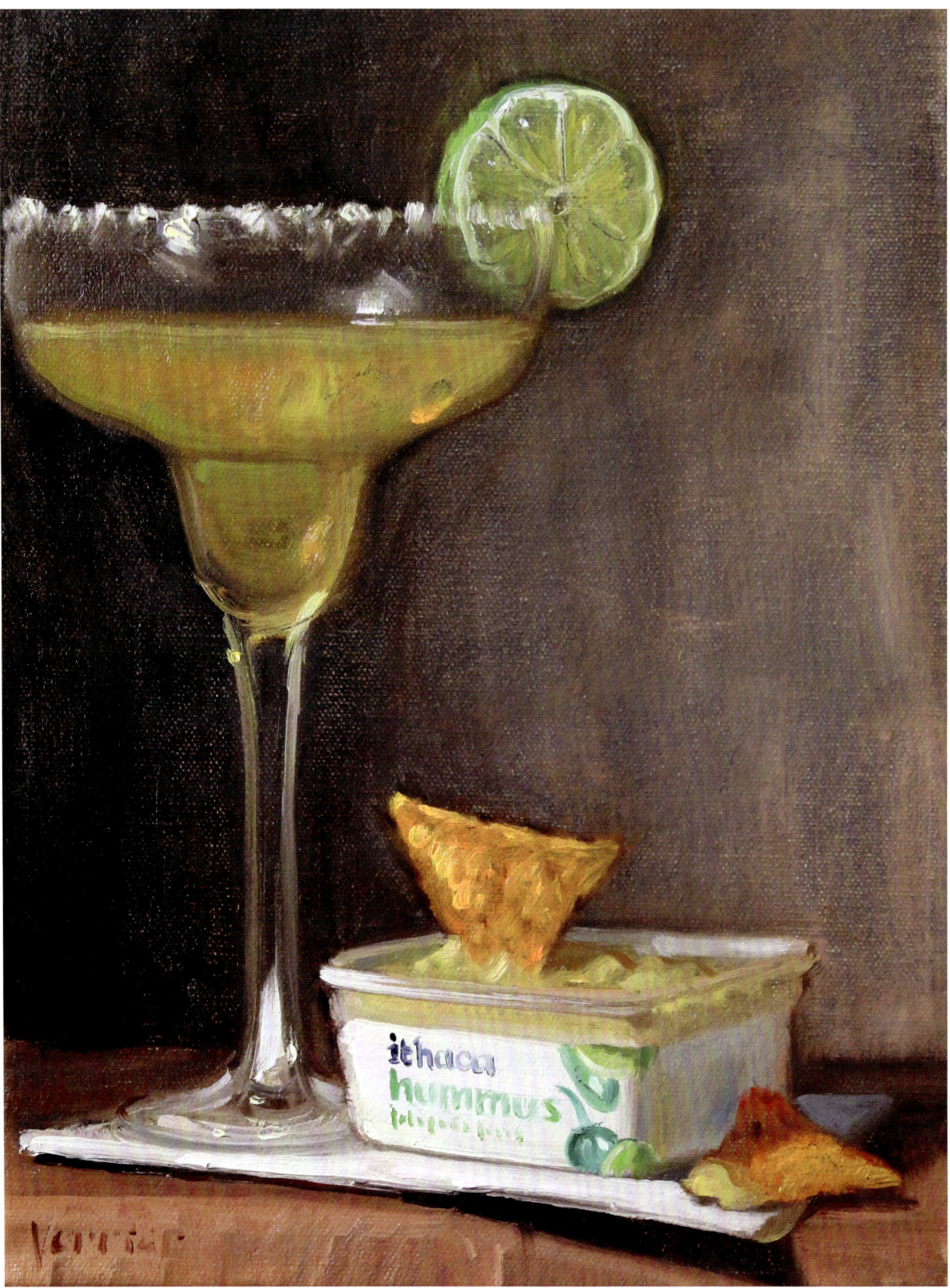

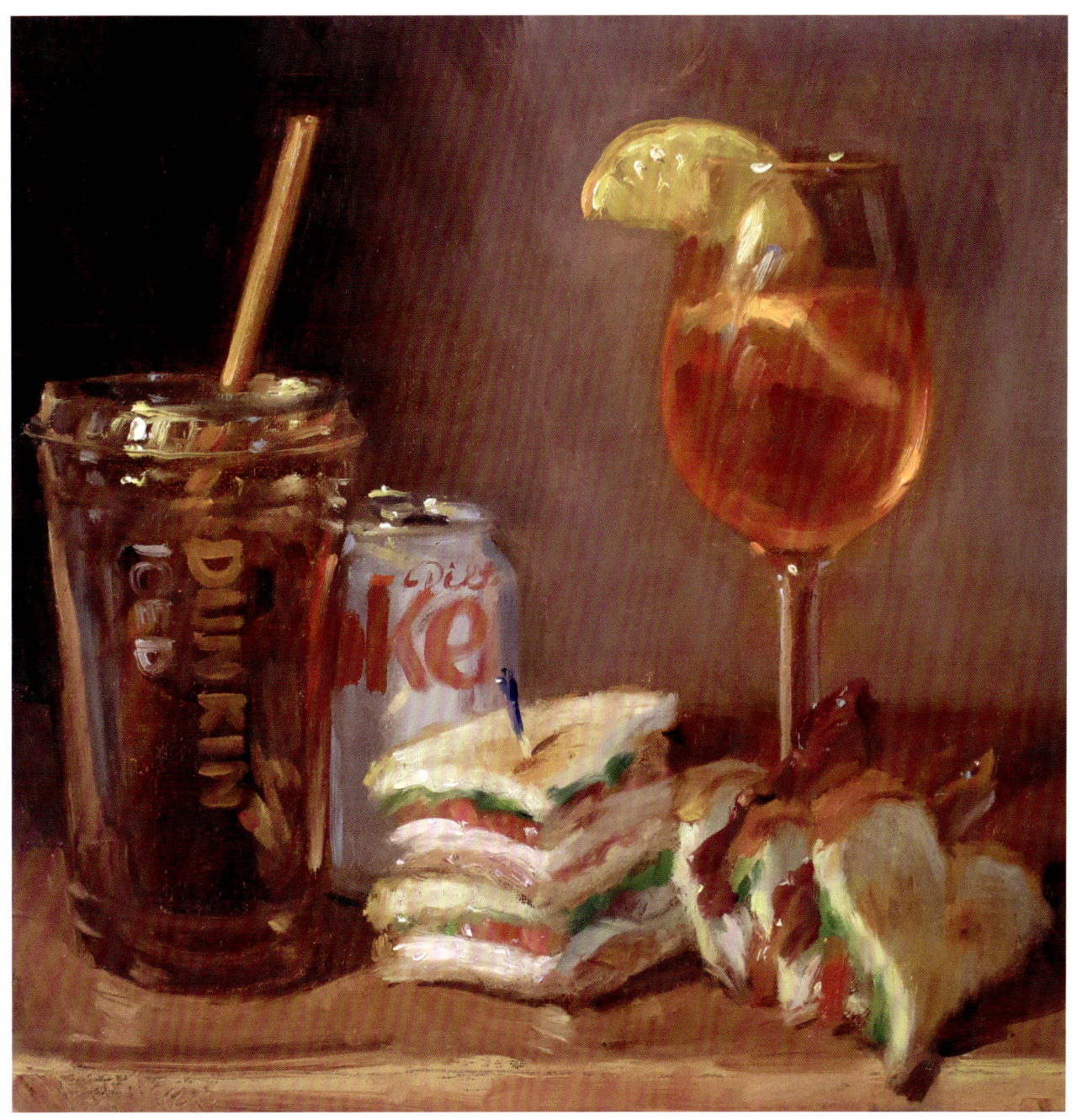

OPPOSITE PAGE:

Margaritas & Hummus

12 x 9 in.

Club & Drinks

14 x 14 in.

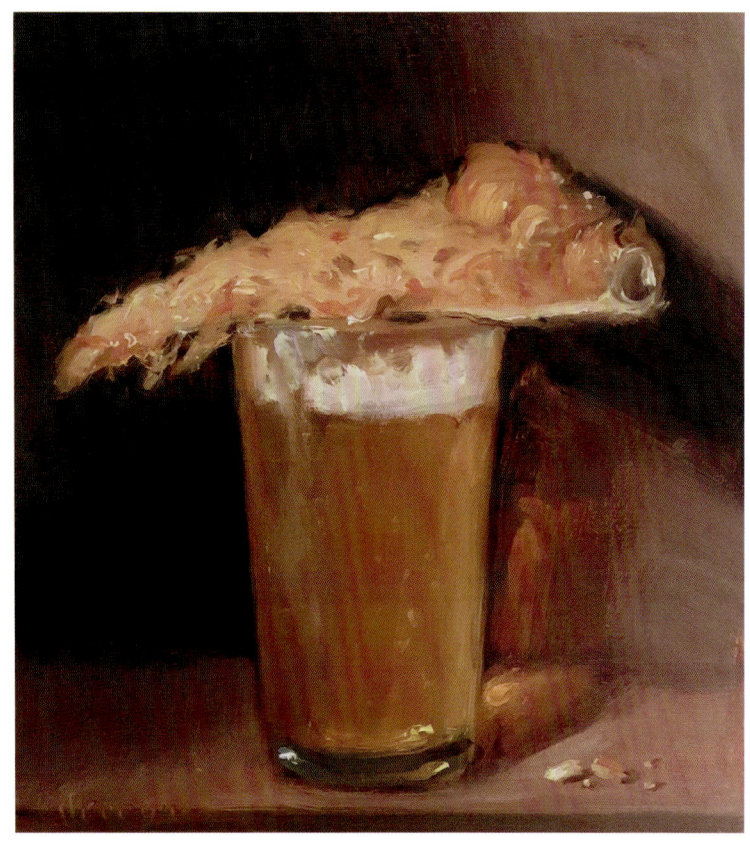

Pizza & Beer
8 x 10 in.

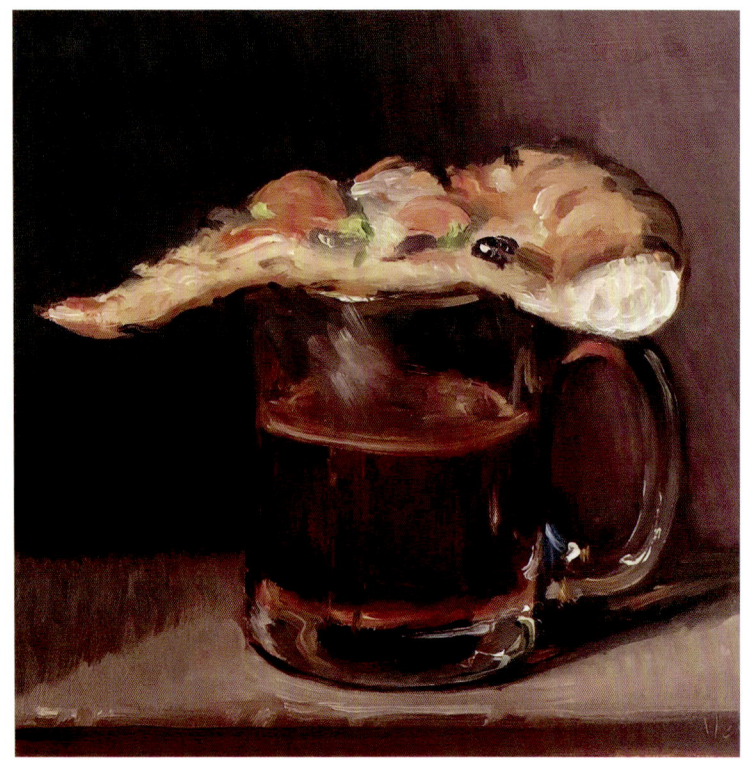

Pizza & Coffee
9 x 8 in.

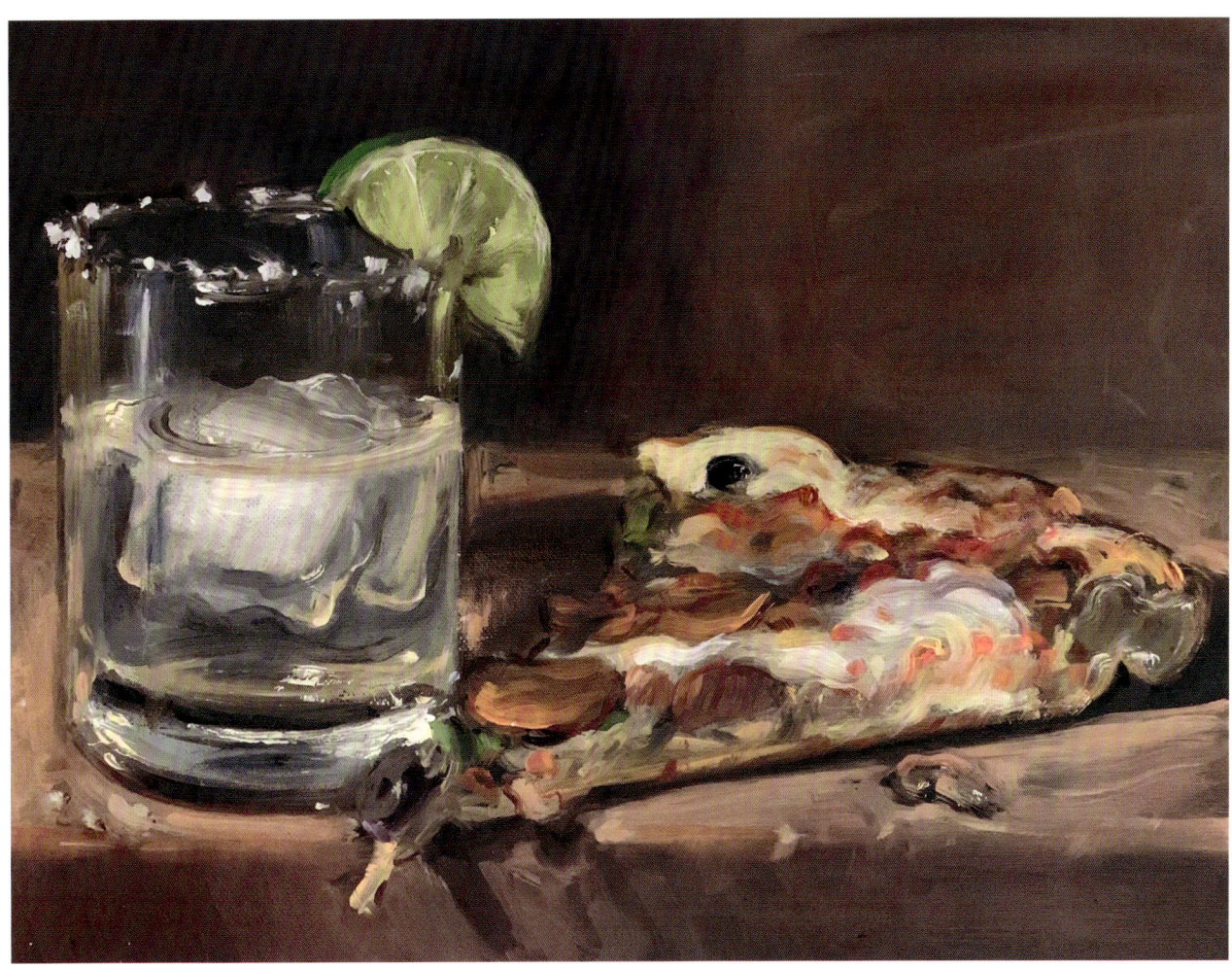

Pizza & Tequila
14 x 11 in.

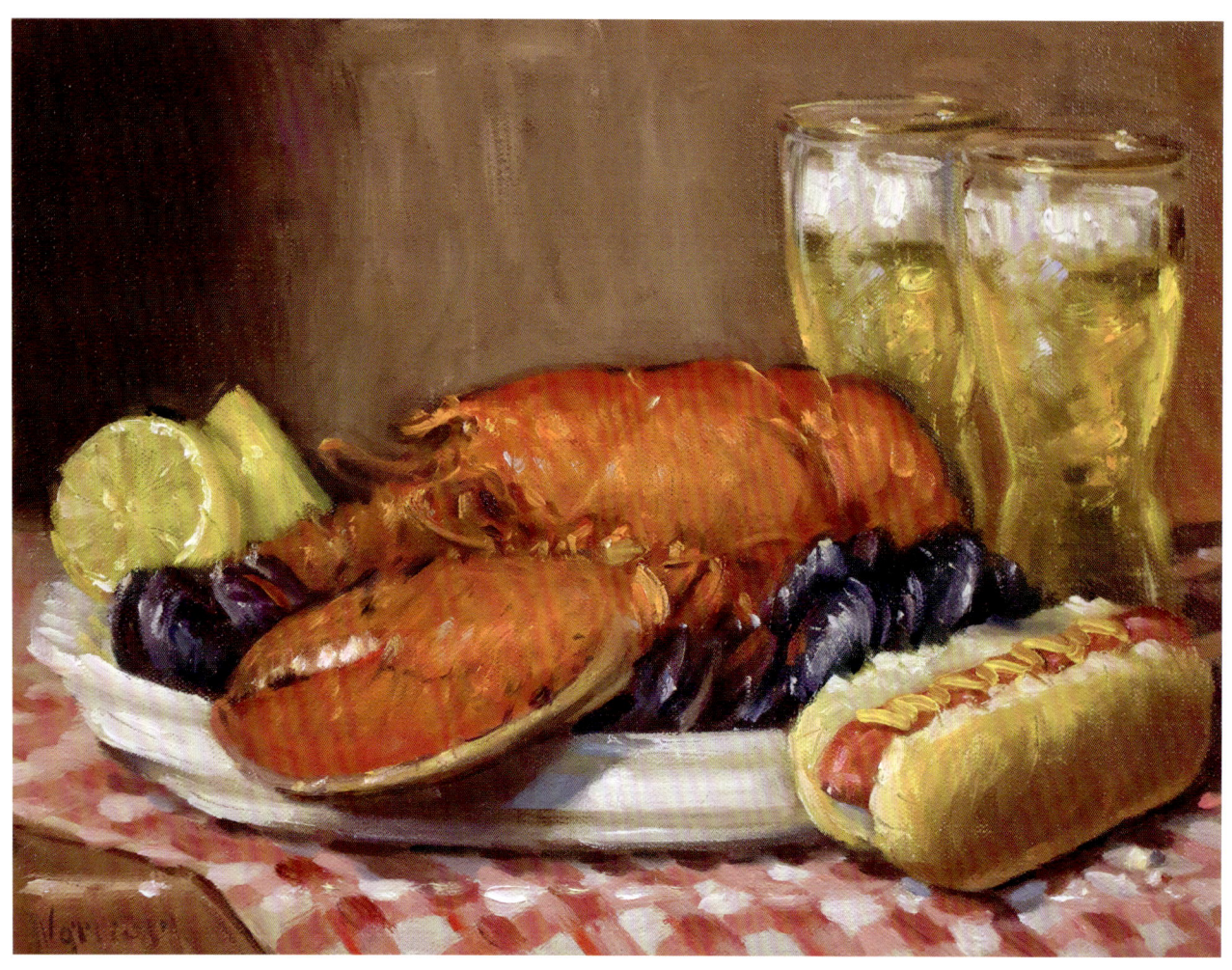

Lobster, Mussels, & Hot Dog
20 x 16 in.

OPPOSITE PAGE:
Crawfish
8 x 9 in.

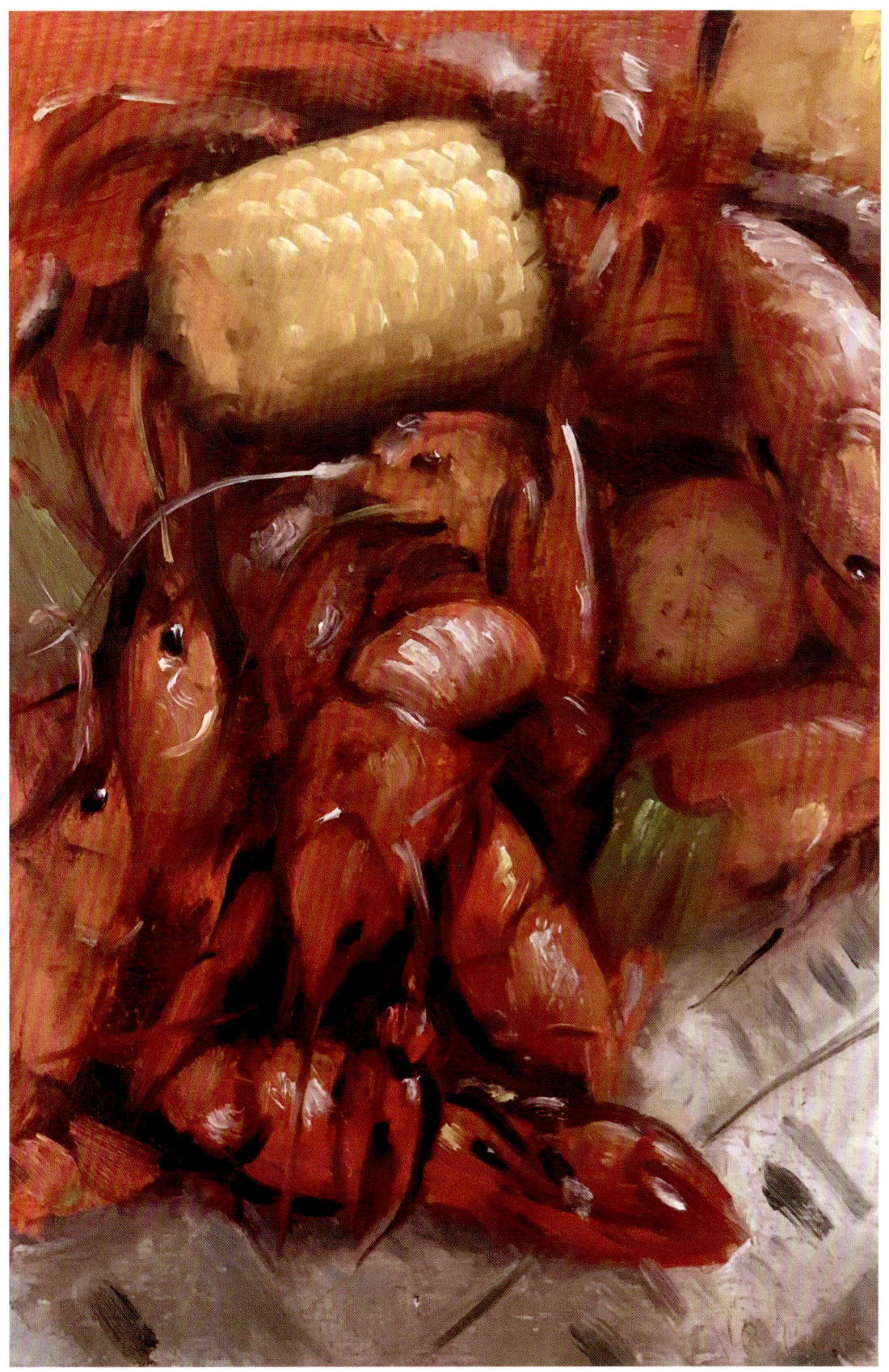

COMFORT FOOD

*Classical-looking paintings of familiar things we all **know** and love are so interesting to me. And an oil painting has less calories.*

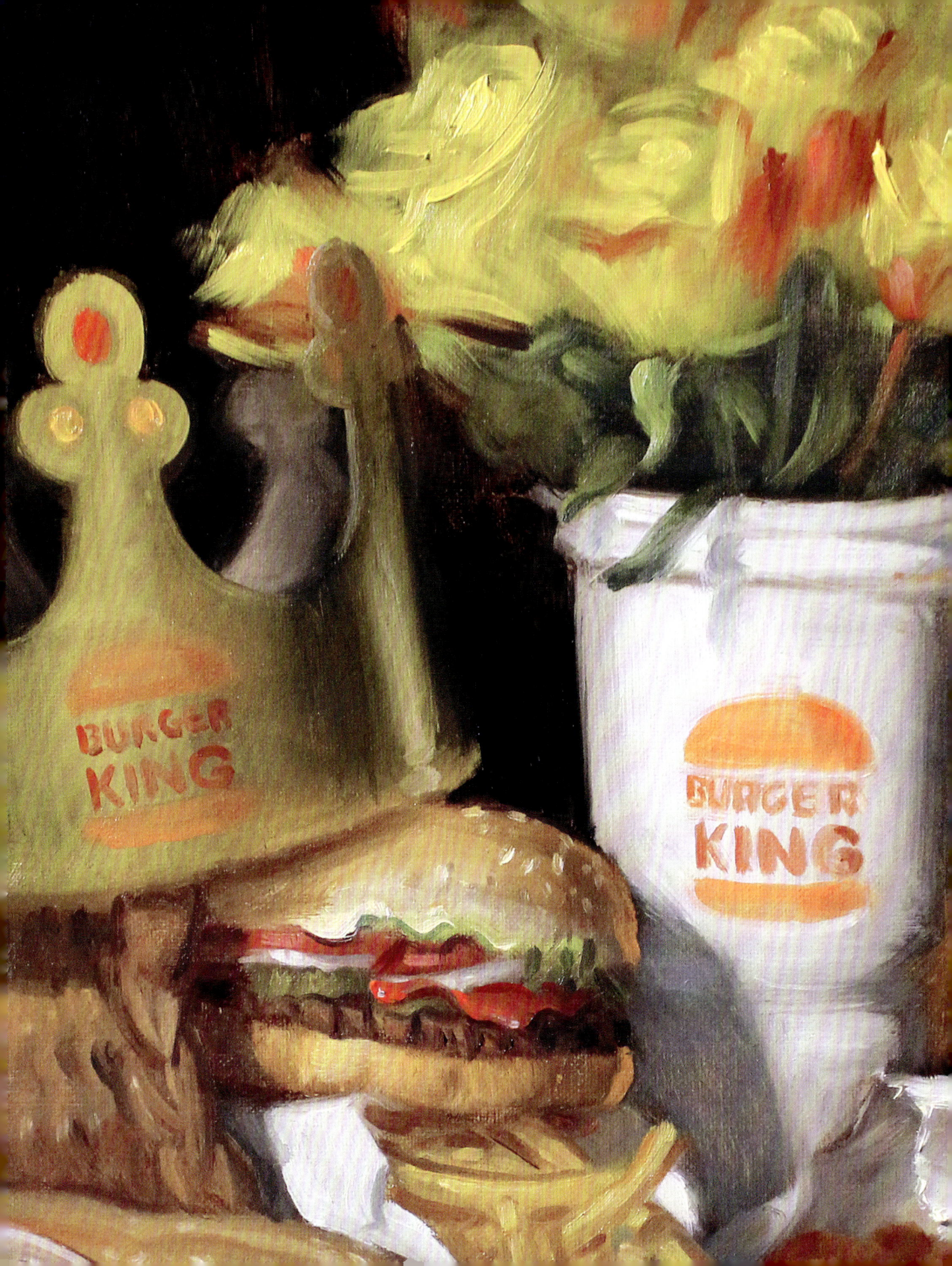

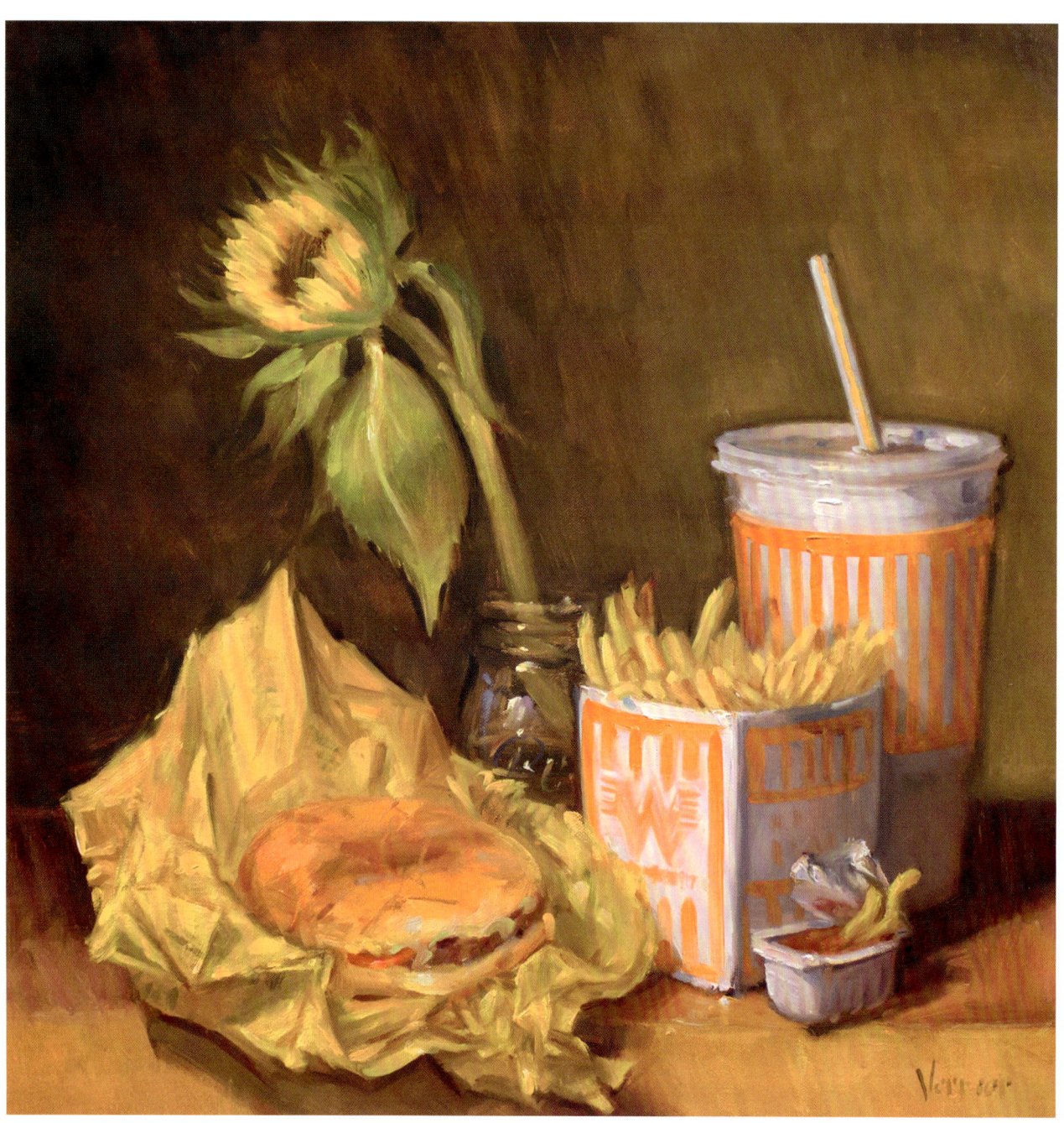

Whataburger
20 x 20 in.

OPPOSITE PAGE:
Taco Bell
18 x 24 in.

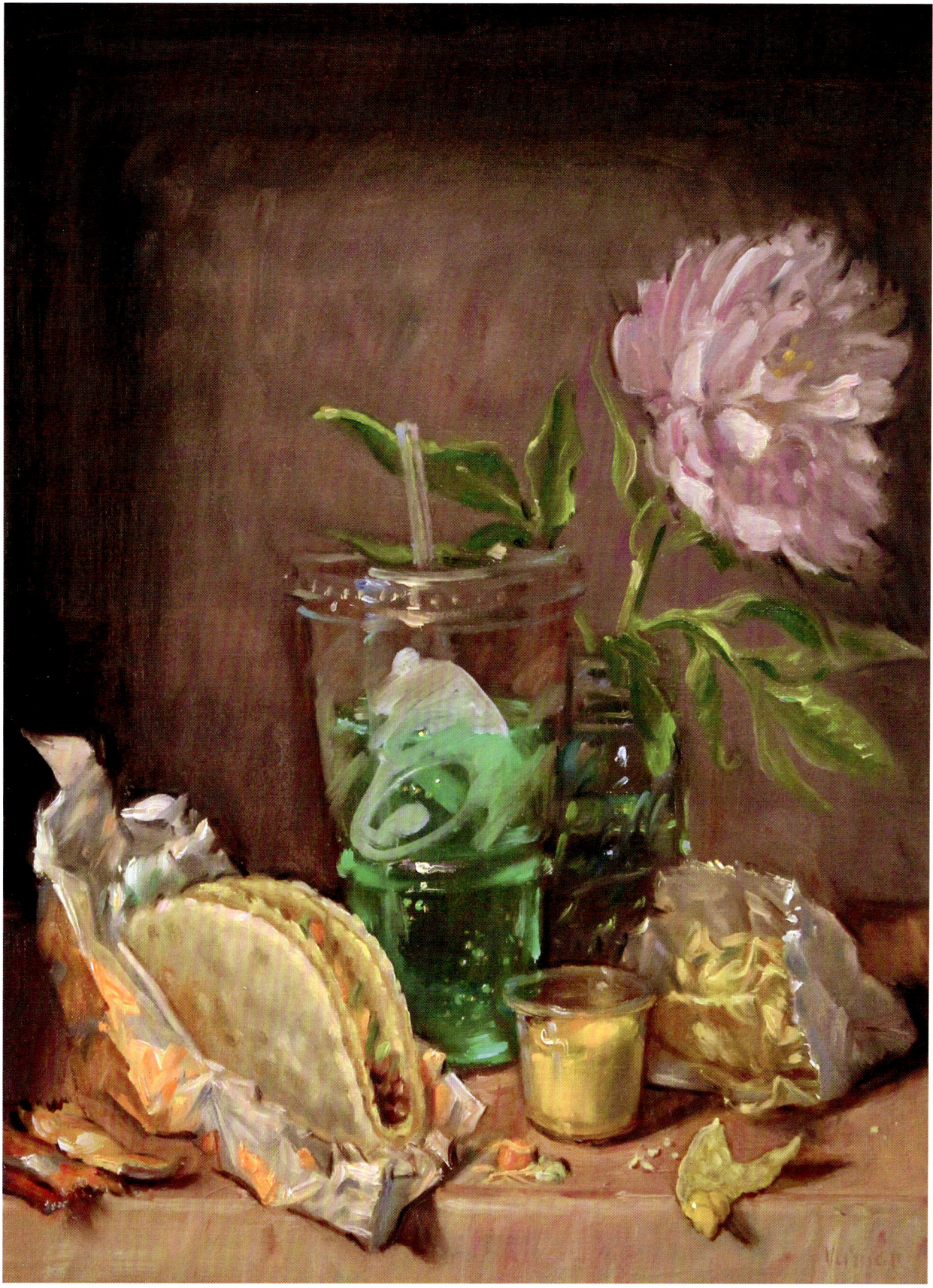

Big Mac by Conor Demmett

It takes me back to childhood, when McDonald's was for special occasions, maybe after a big test or on birthdays. Just looking at Noah's painting, I can taste the sweetness of the pickles, onions, and ketchup. All that's missing is that crisp, ice-cold, refreshing Sprite.

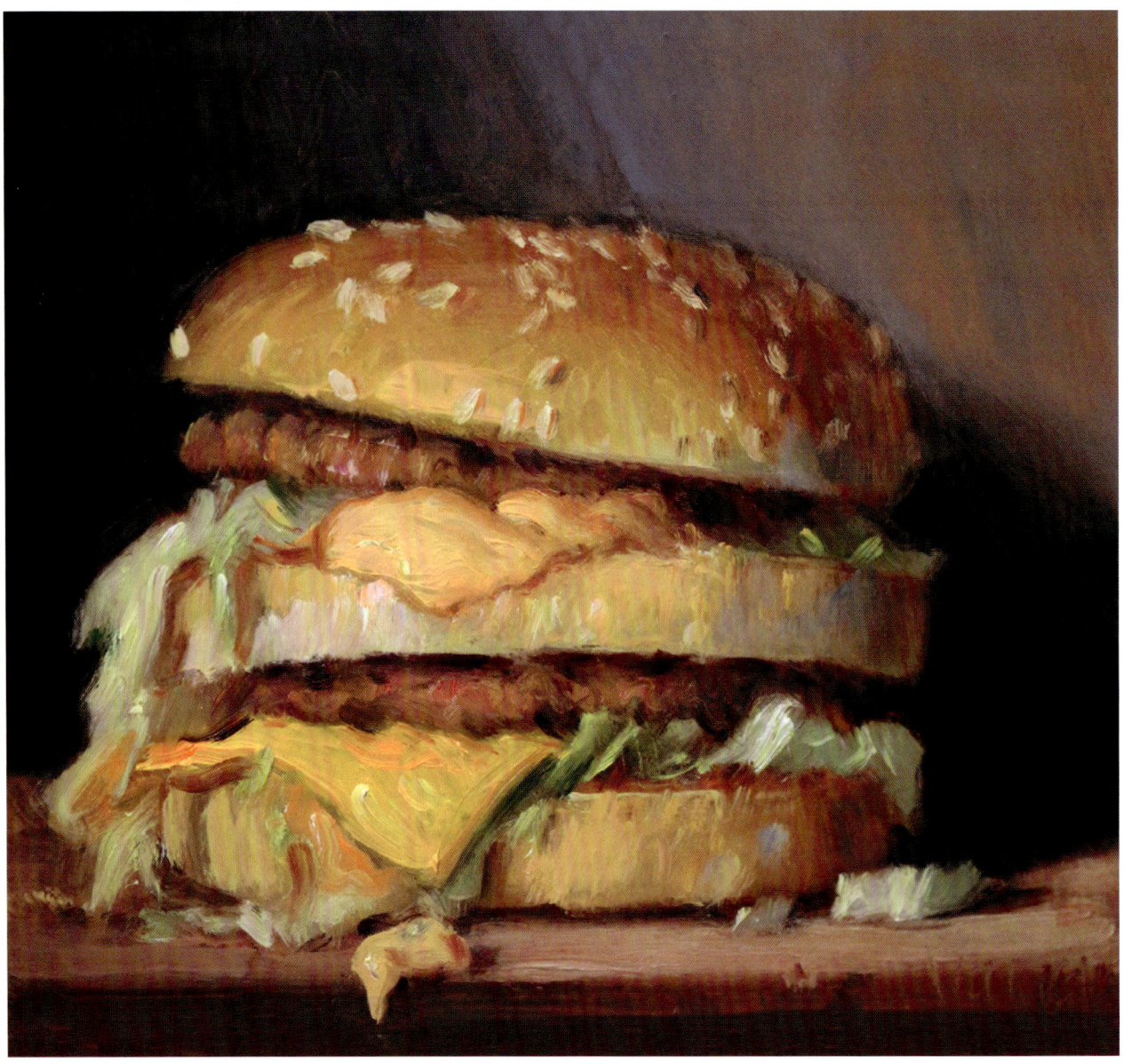

Big Mac
9 x 8 in.

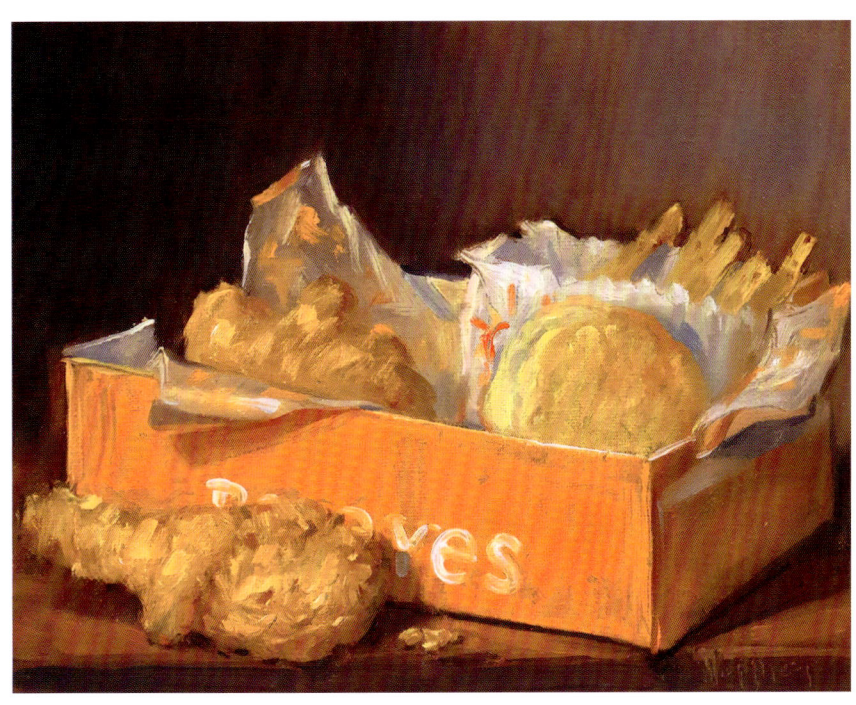

Popeyes
11 x 14 in.

No.7 Combo
16 x 20 in.

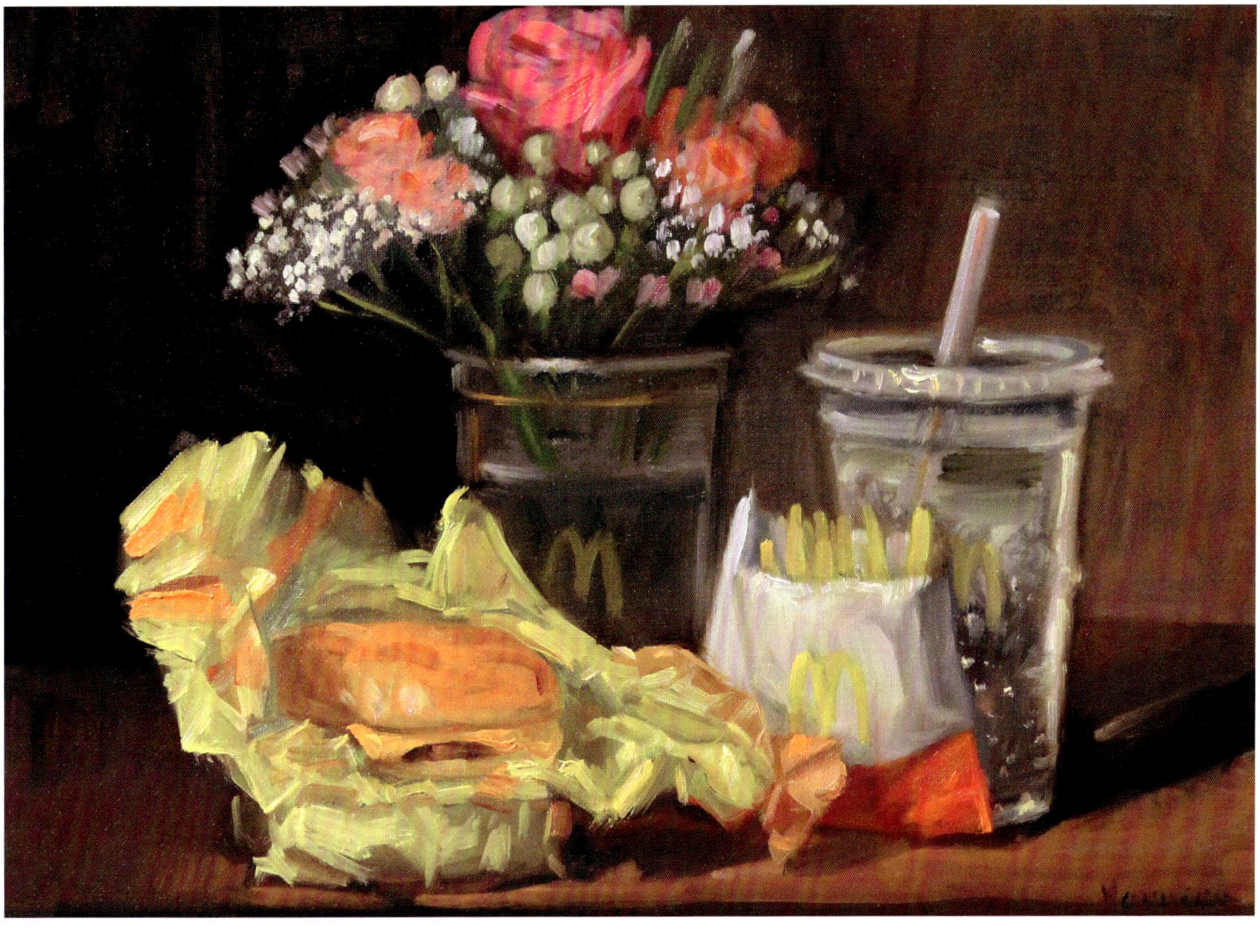

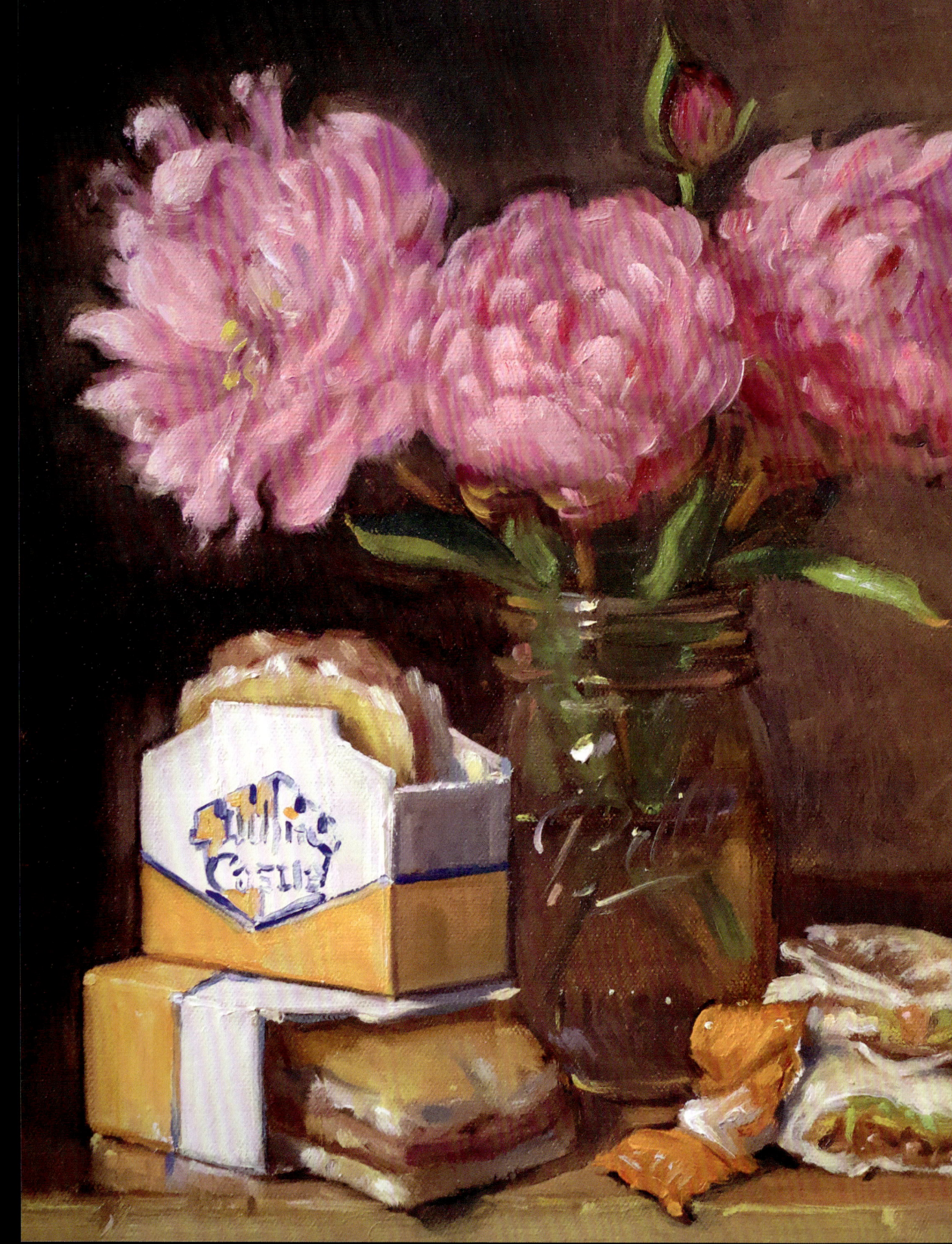

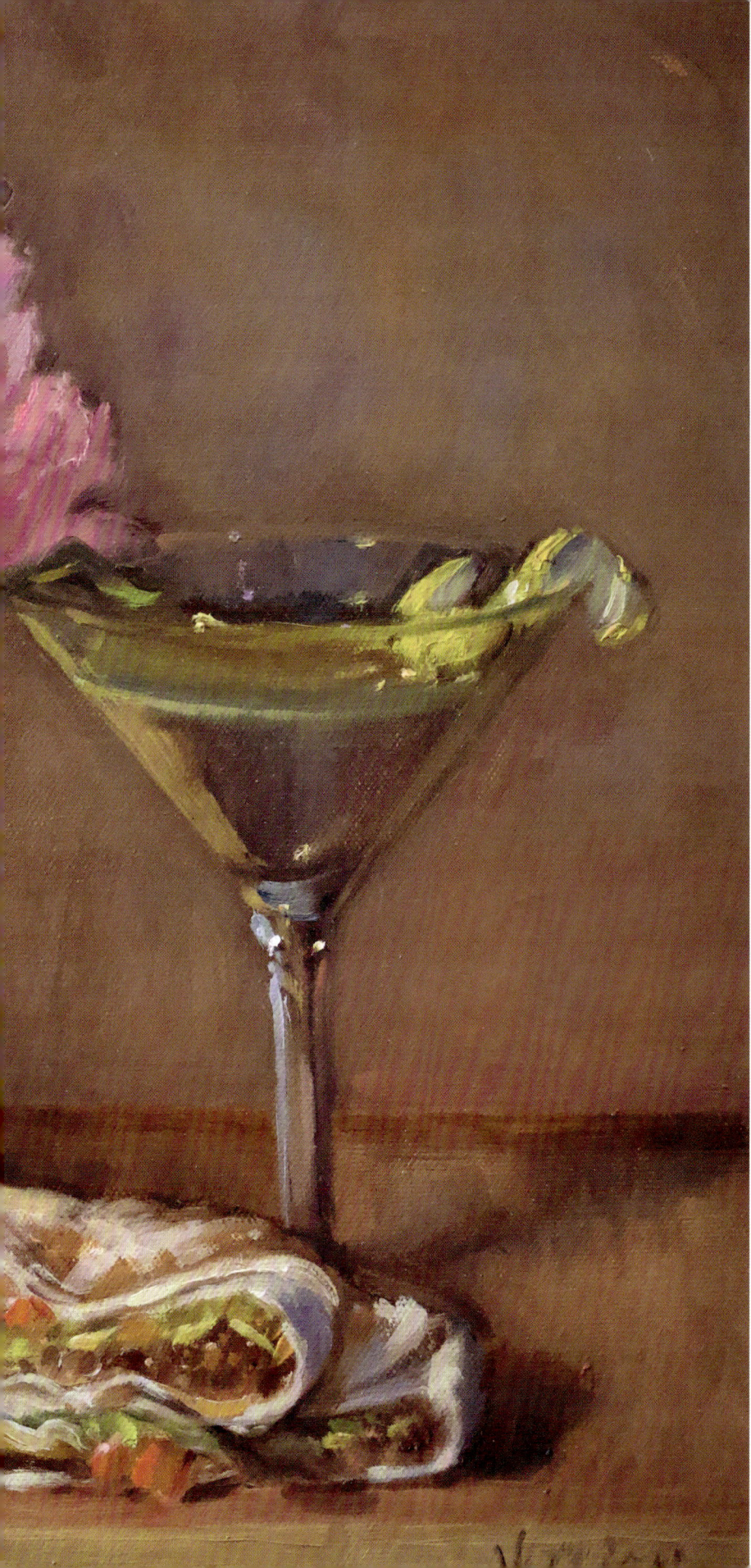

White Castle, Taco Bell, & Martini

16 x 20 in.

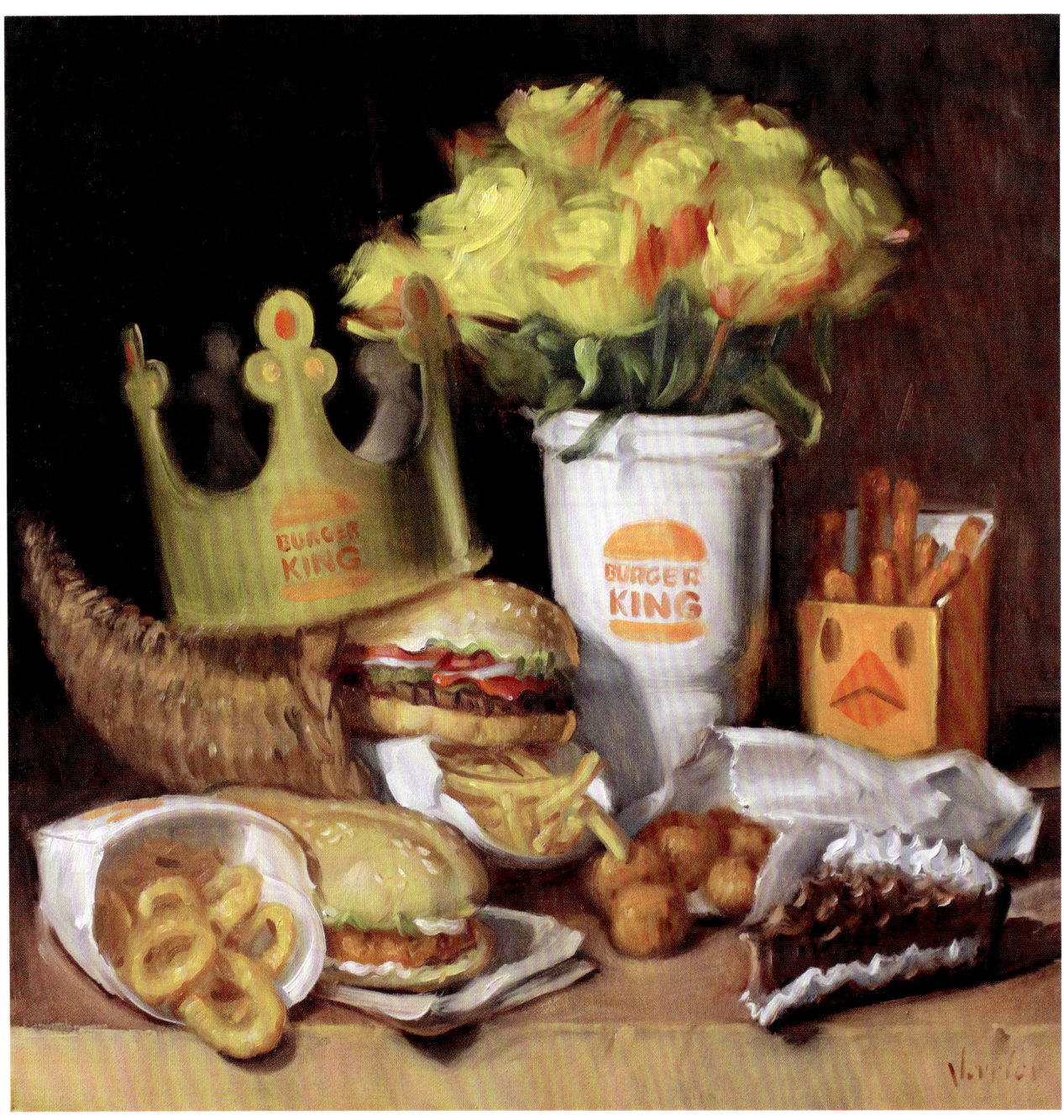

Burger King
20 x 20 in.

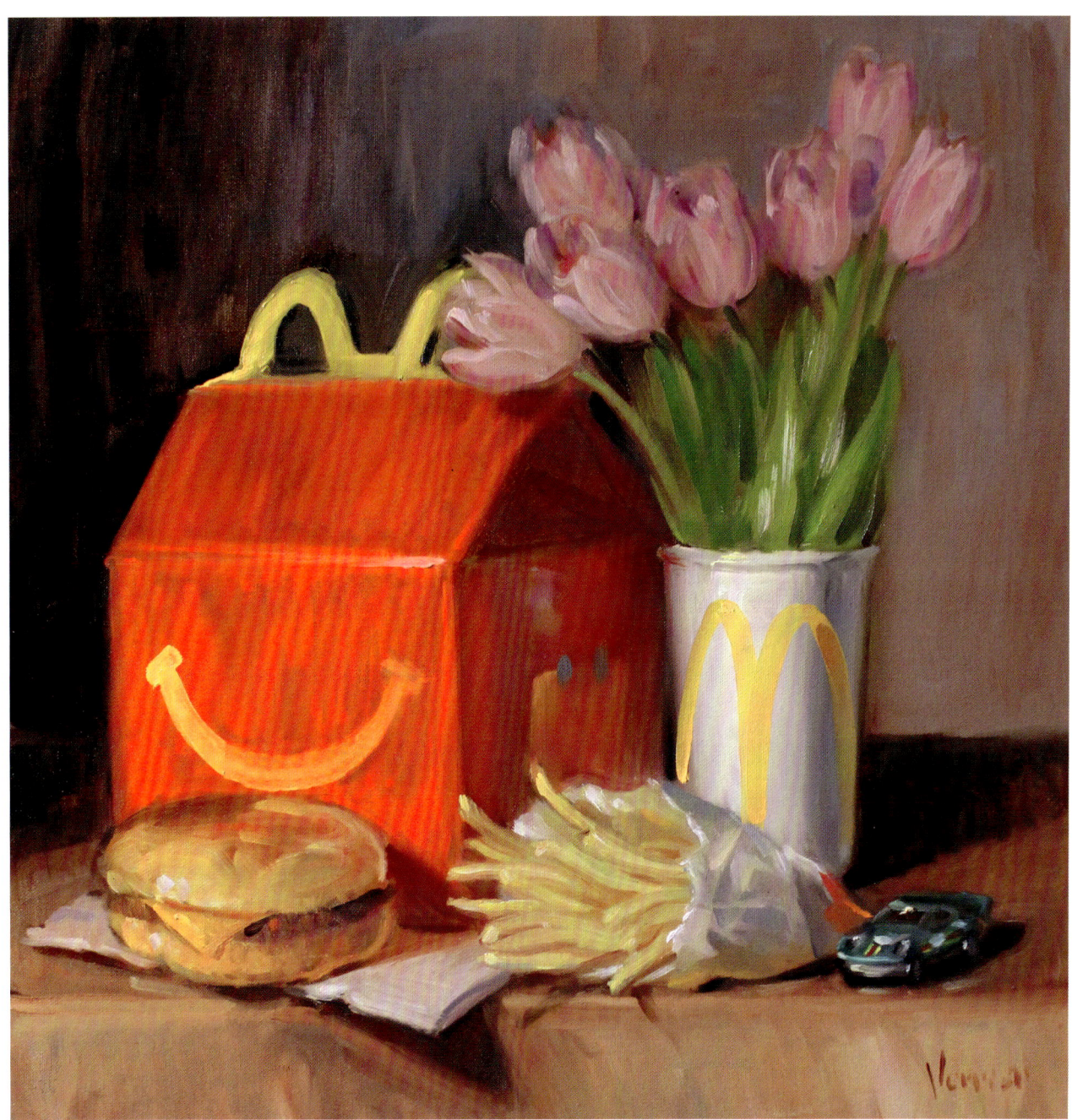

Happy Meal
20 x 20 in.

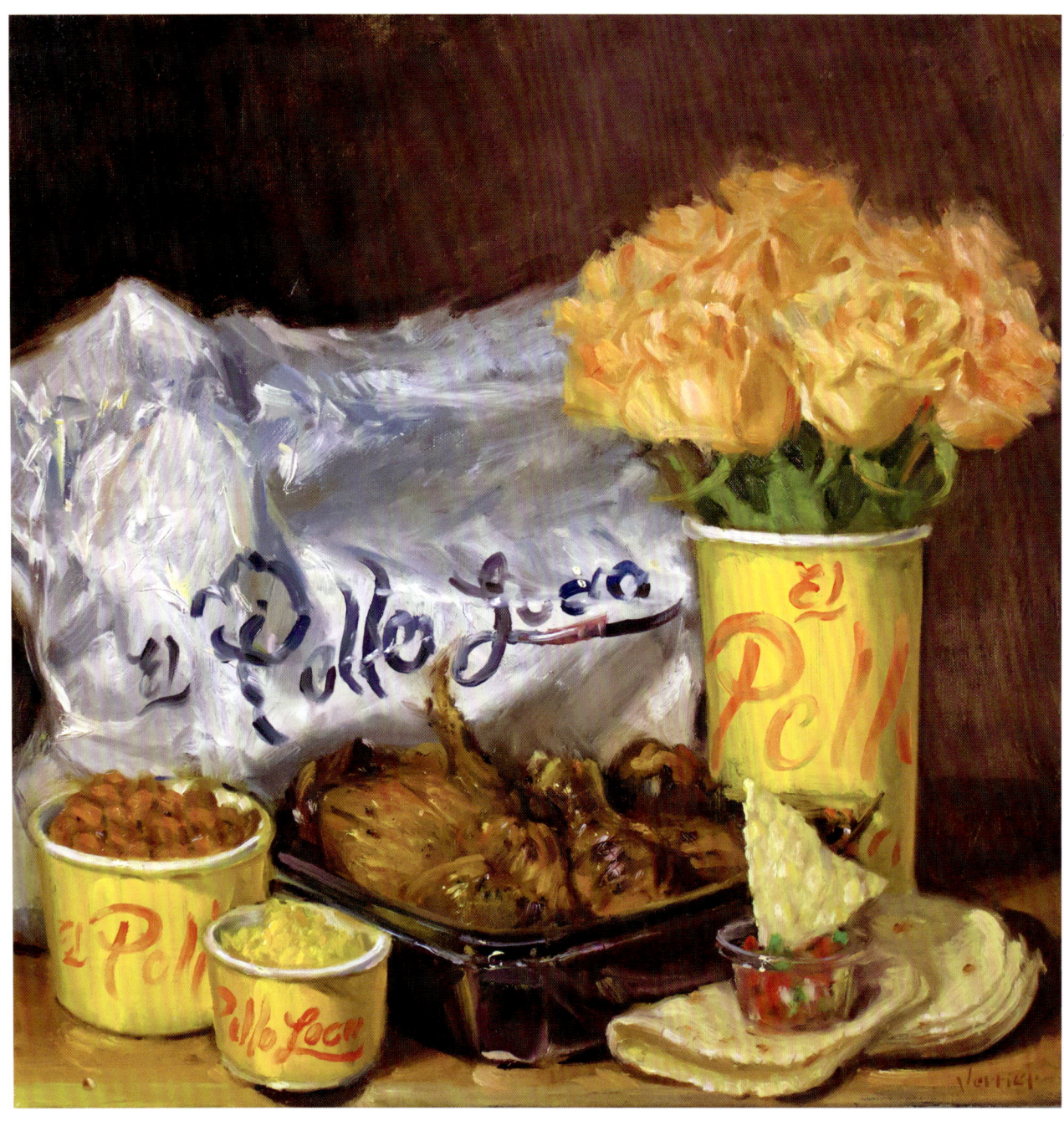

El Pollo Loco
20 x 20 in.

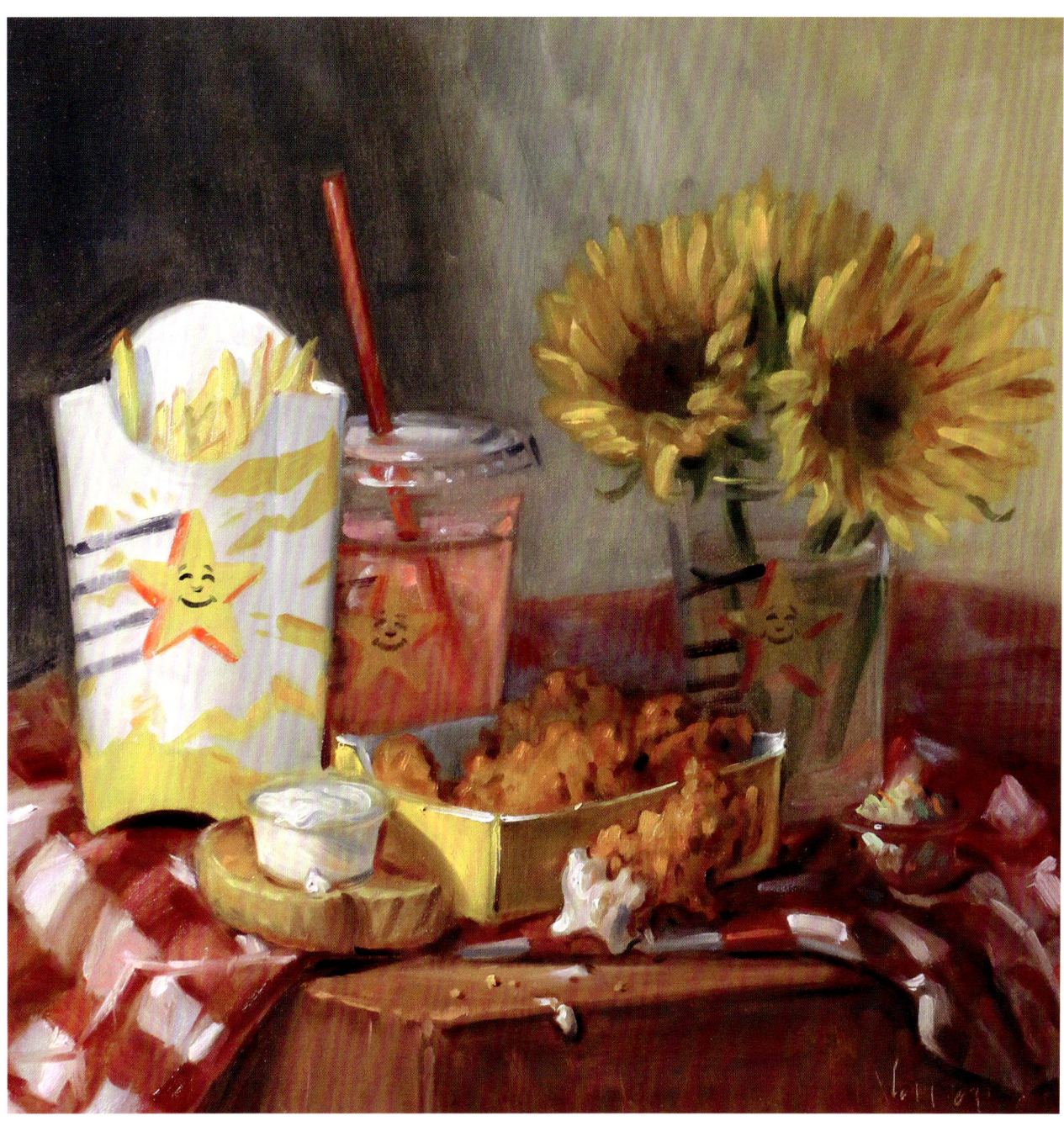

Hardee's
20 x 20 in.

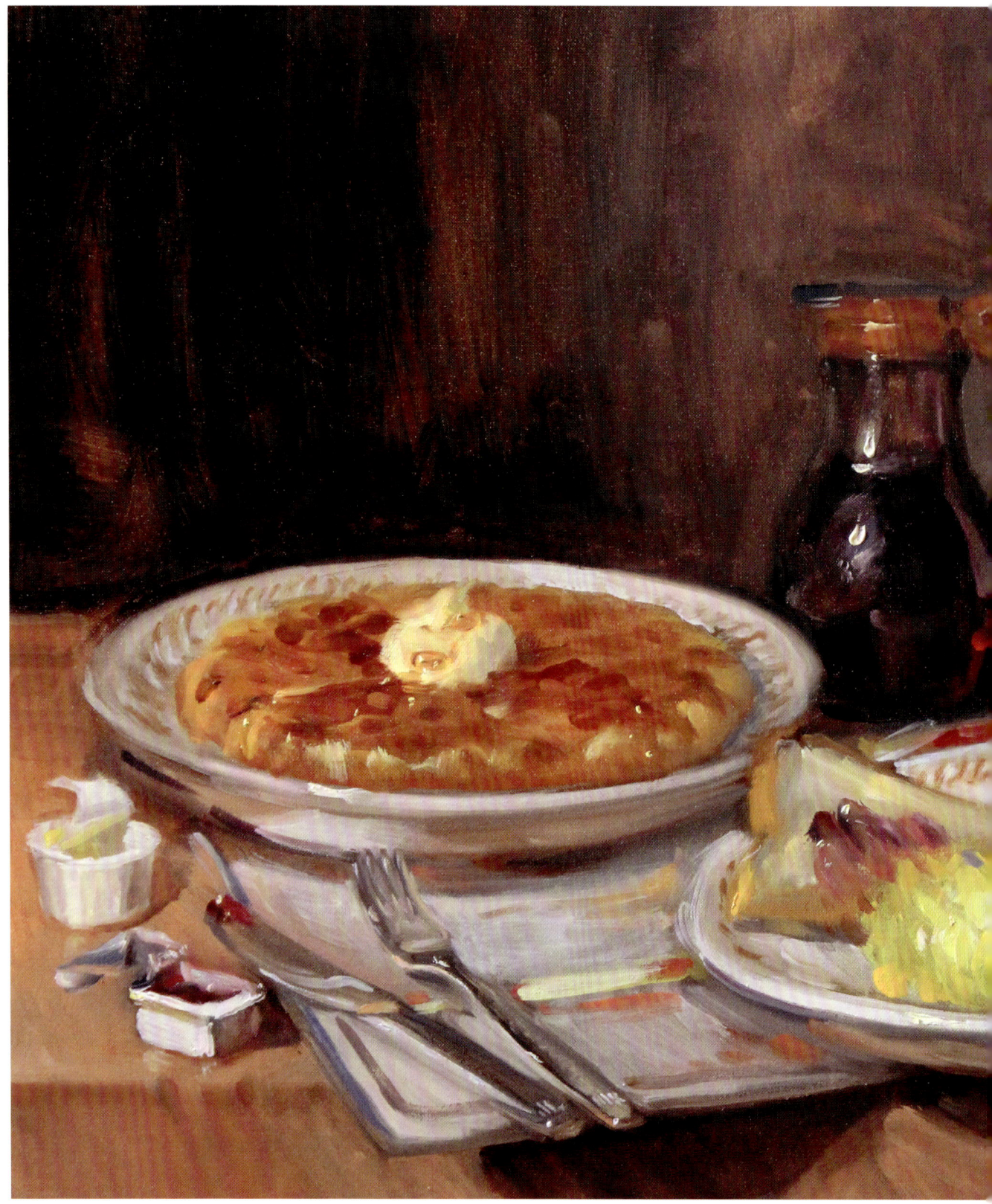

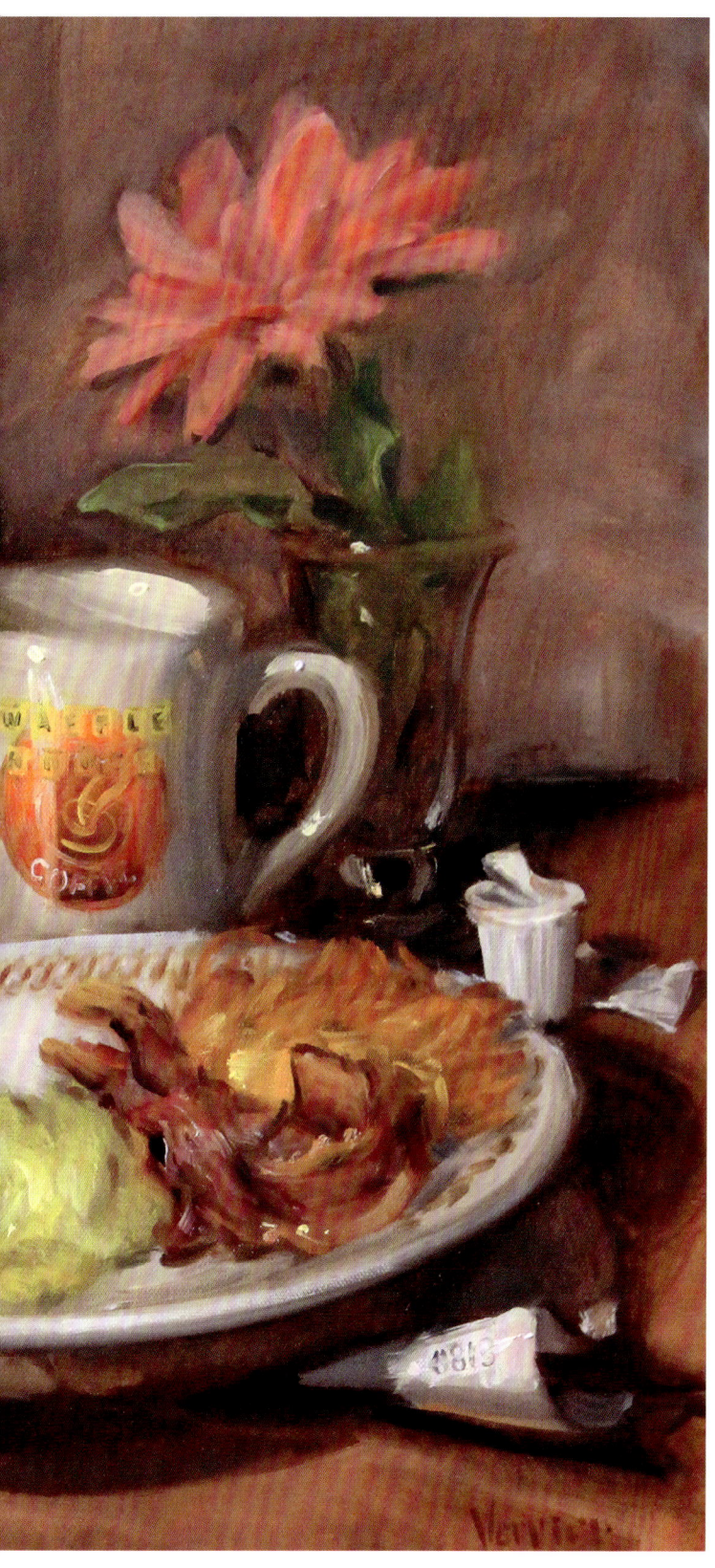

Waffle House
24 x 18 in.

Waffle House by Beatriz A Santana Ramirez

From the perspective of someone who lives nowhere near a Waffle House, there's truly something special about the mediocre yet memorable first taste of grits. The classic metal chairs that sat high against the countertop next to the plastic booths, surrounded by the white checkered walls, the aroma of breakfast danced in the air.

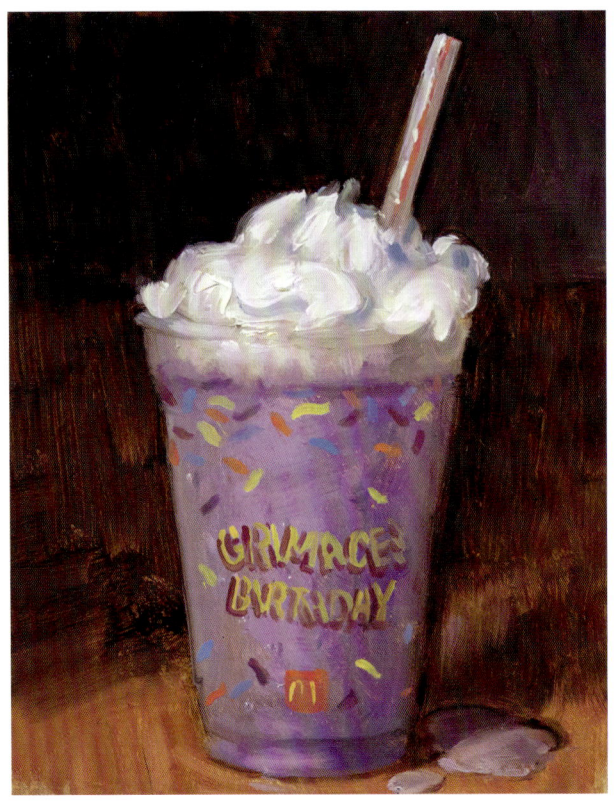

Grimace Shake
8 x 10 in.

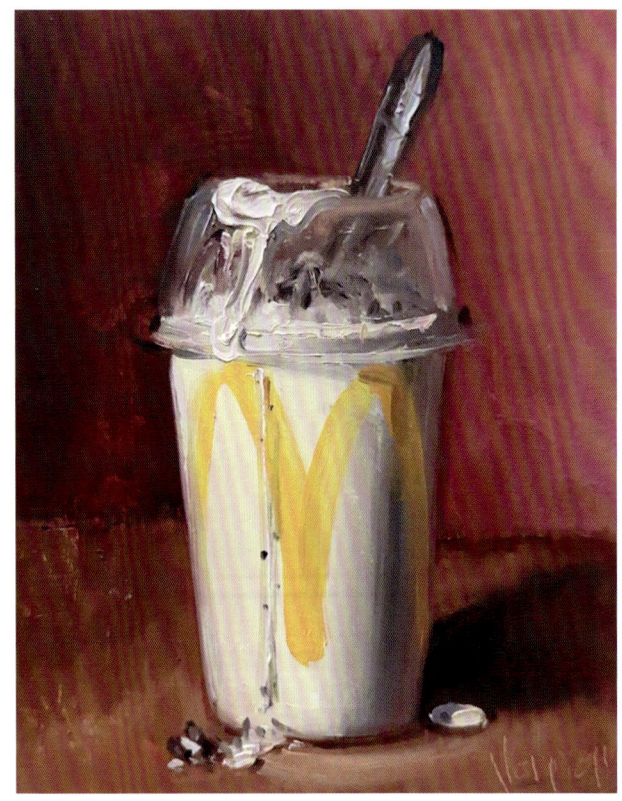

McFlurry
8 x 10 in.

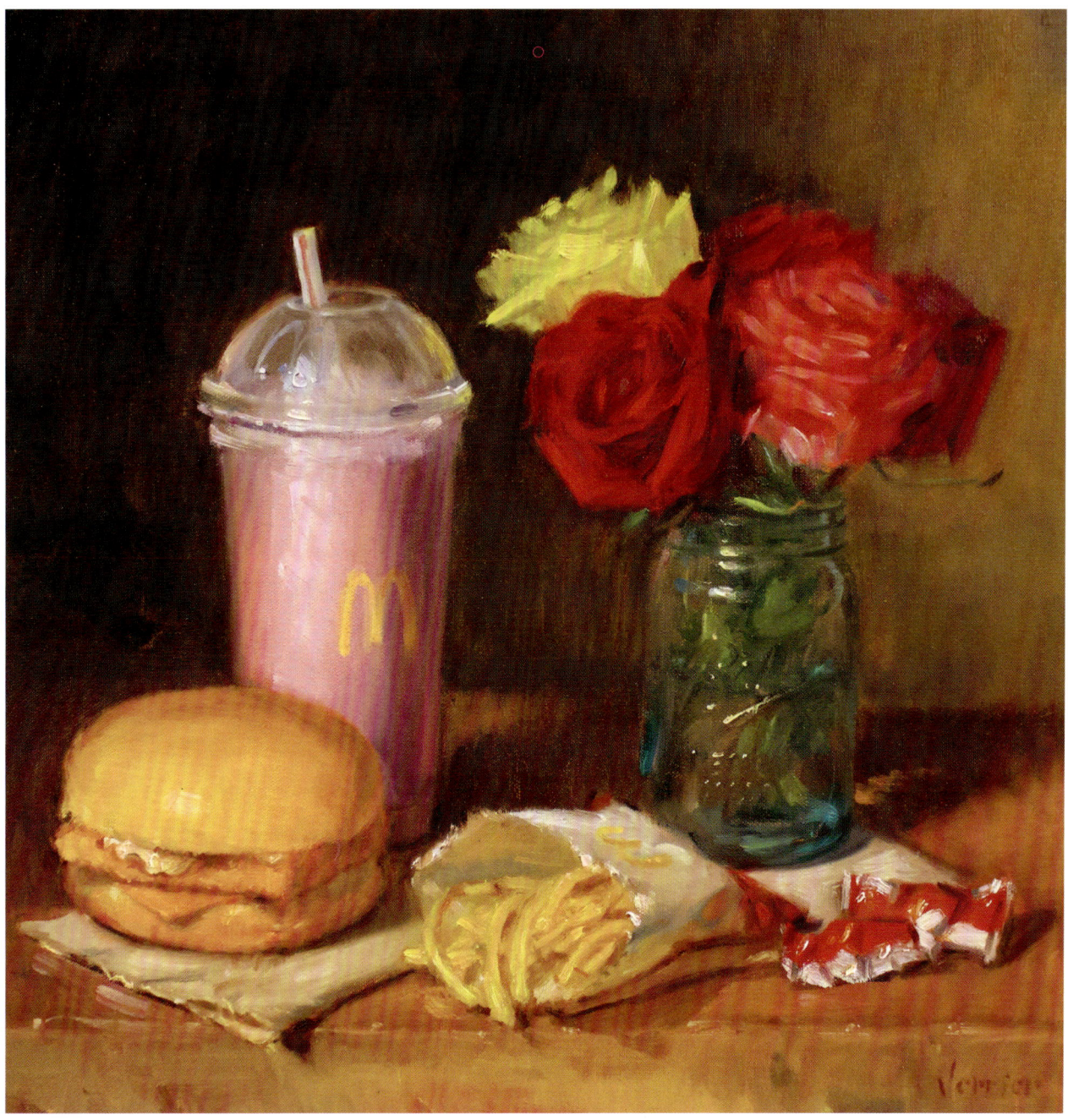

Filet-O-Fish & Strawberry Milkshake
20 x 20 in.

Filet-O-Fish & Strawberry Milkshake
by Noah Verrier

I painted this one as a commission for a lovely lady from Europe who wanted to honor the memory of going to McDonald's with her grandmother. Soon after I shared it on social, Britney Spears saw it and re-posted it on her page. I was floored when I found out.

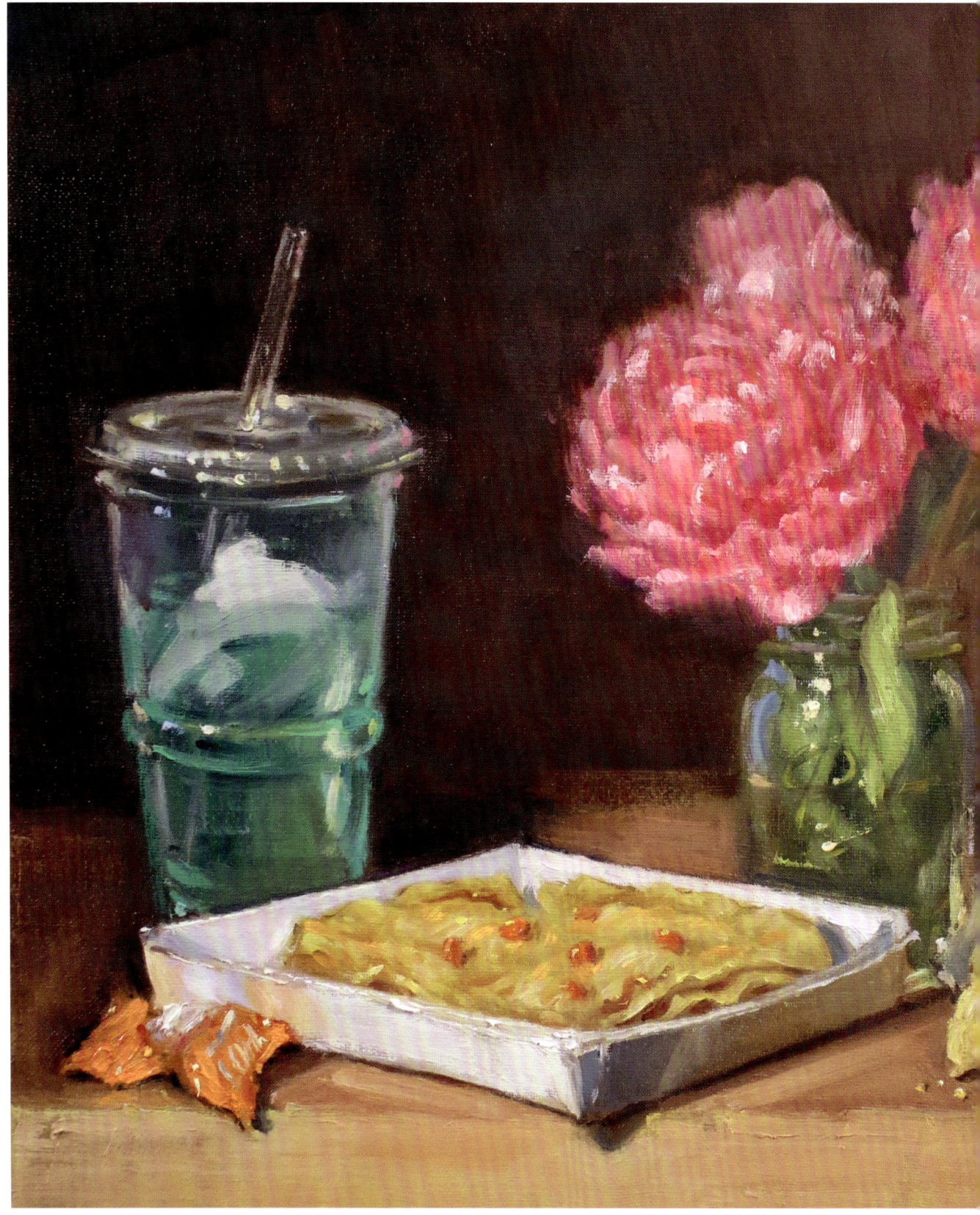

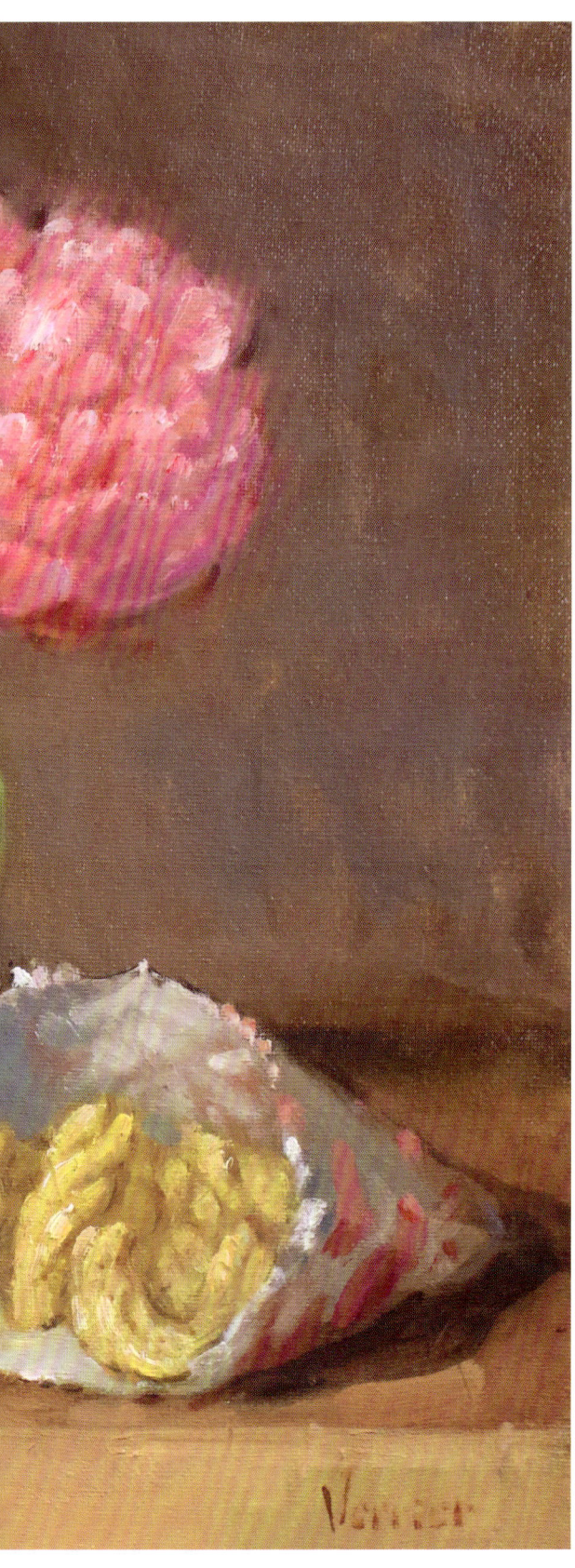

Taco Bell Mexican Pizza
20 x 16 in.

Taco Bell Mexican Pizza   by Dan Martine

My family and I would often take road trips throughout the year, and only on these trips would we get Taco Bell. At the time, nothing beat pulling up to the drive-thru, ordering a soft taco or Mexican pizza, and sipping on the Baja Blast as we listened to music and watched the California landscape pass by. The drip of the cheese and that crisp shine on the cup in the painting, I can taste it. It brings me back to the comfort of that simple family time.

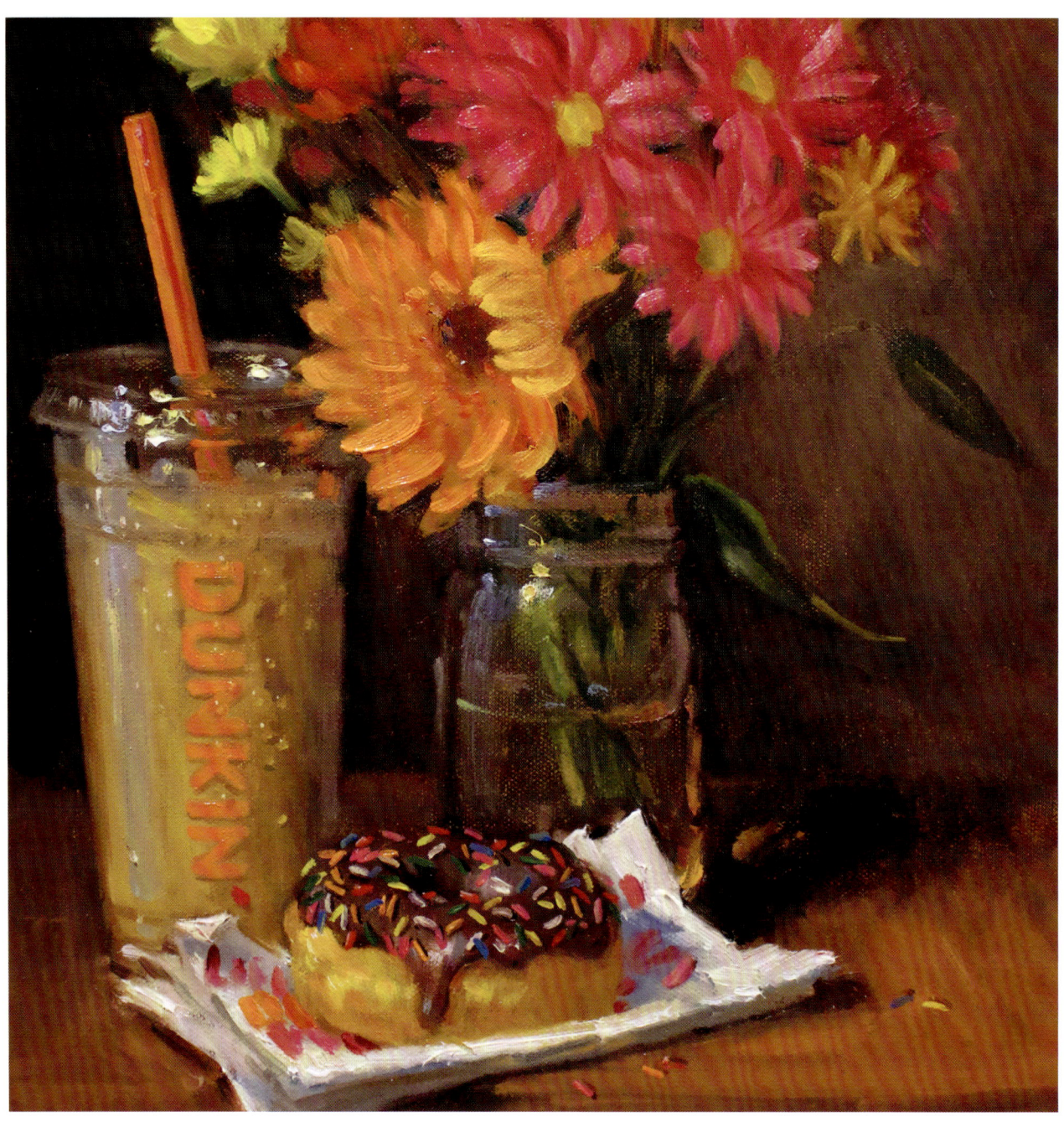

Dunkin'
18 x 24 in.

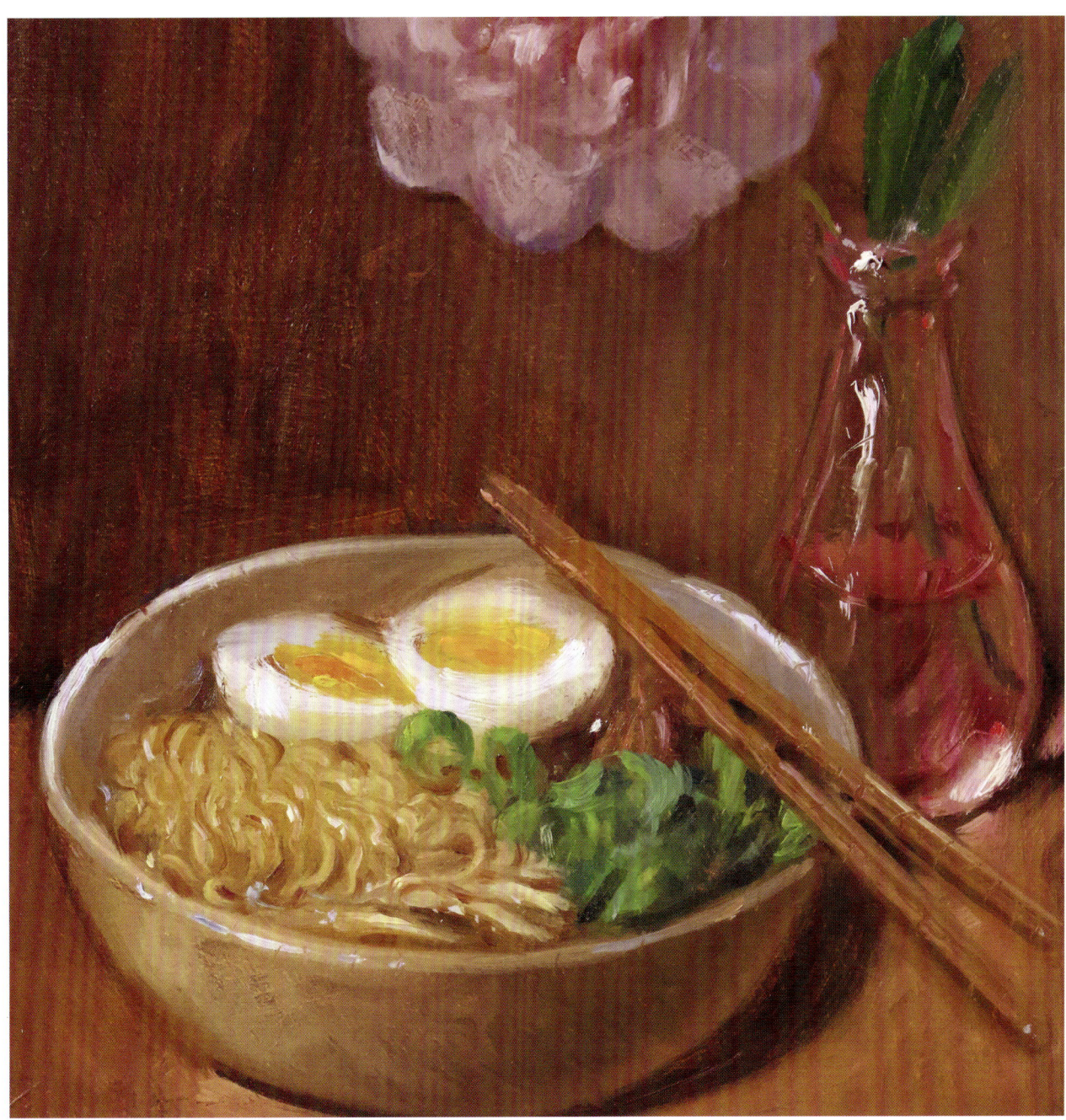

Ramen & Peony
11 x 14 in.

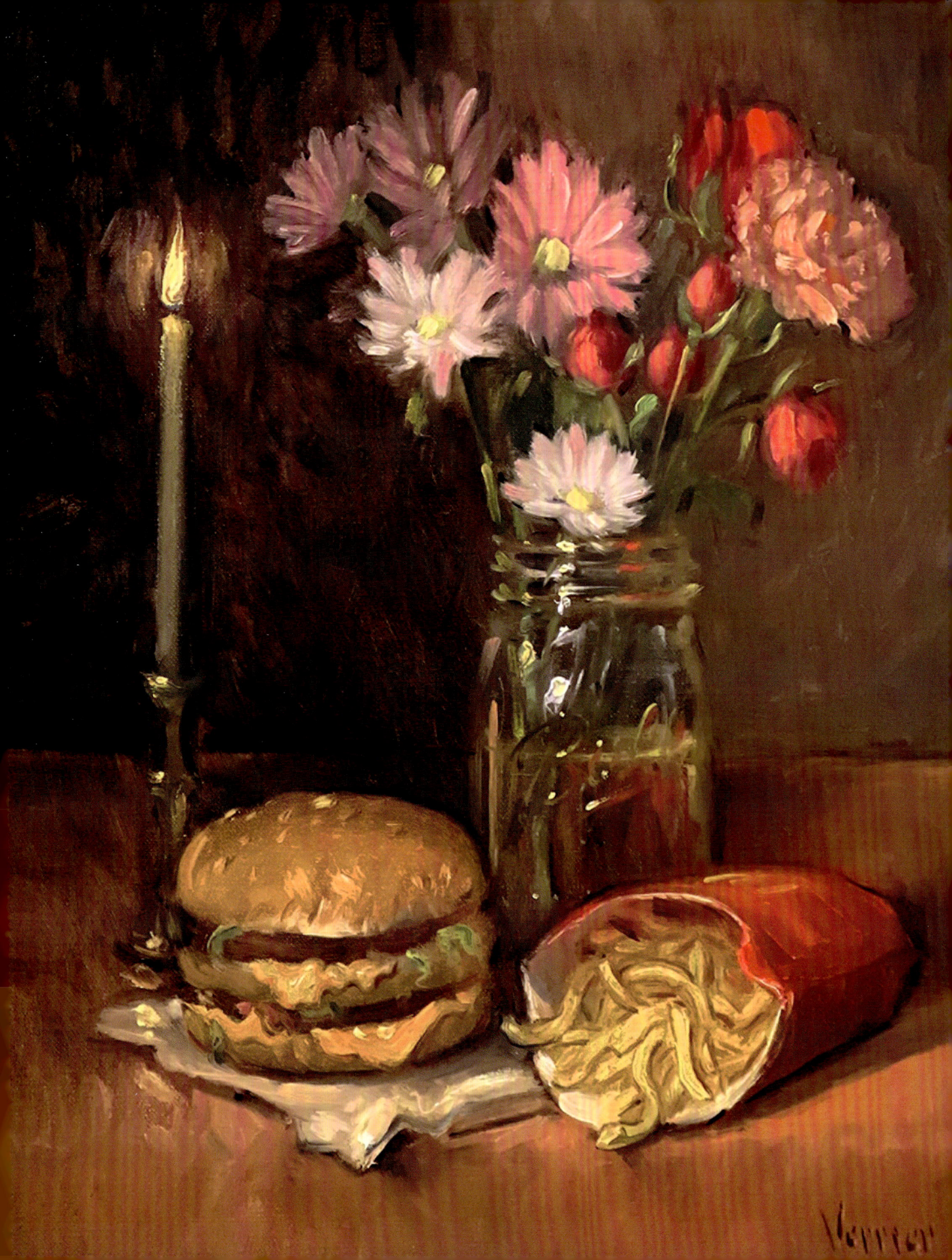

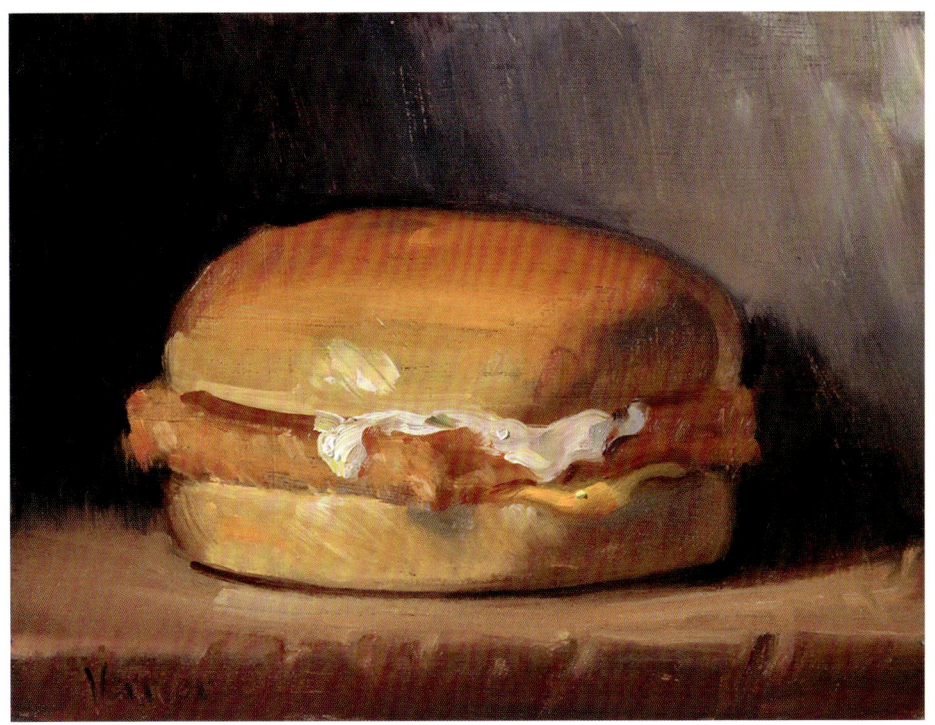

OPPOSITE PAGE:

McDonald's & Trader Joe's Bouquet
11 x 14 in.

Filet-O-Fish
10 x 8 in.

McChicken
12 x 9 in.

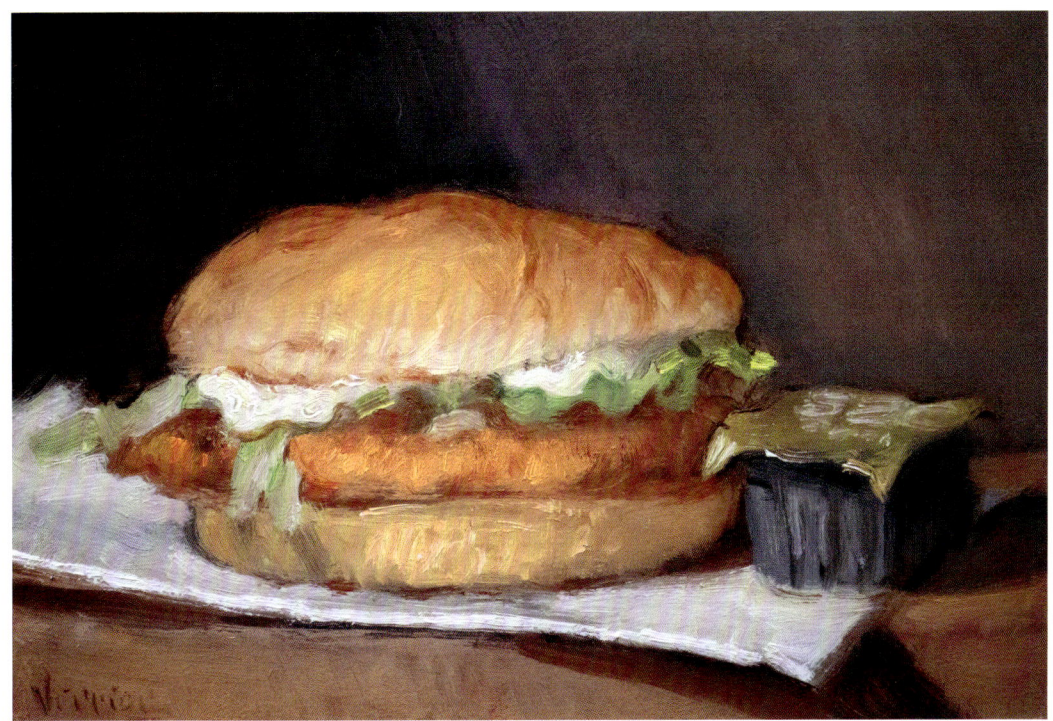

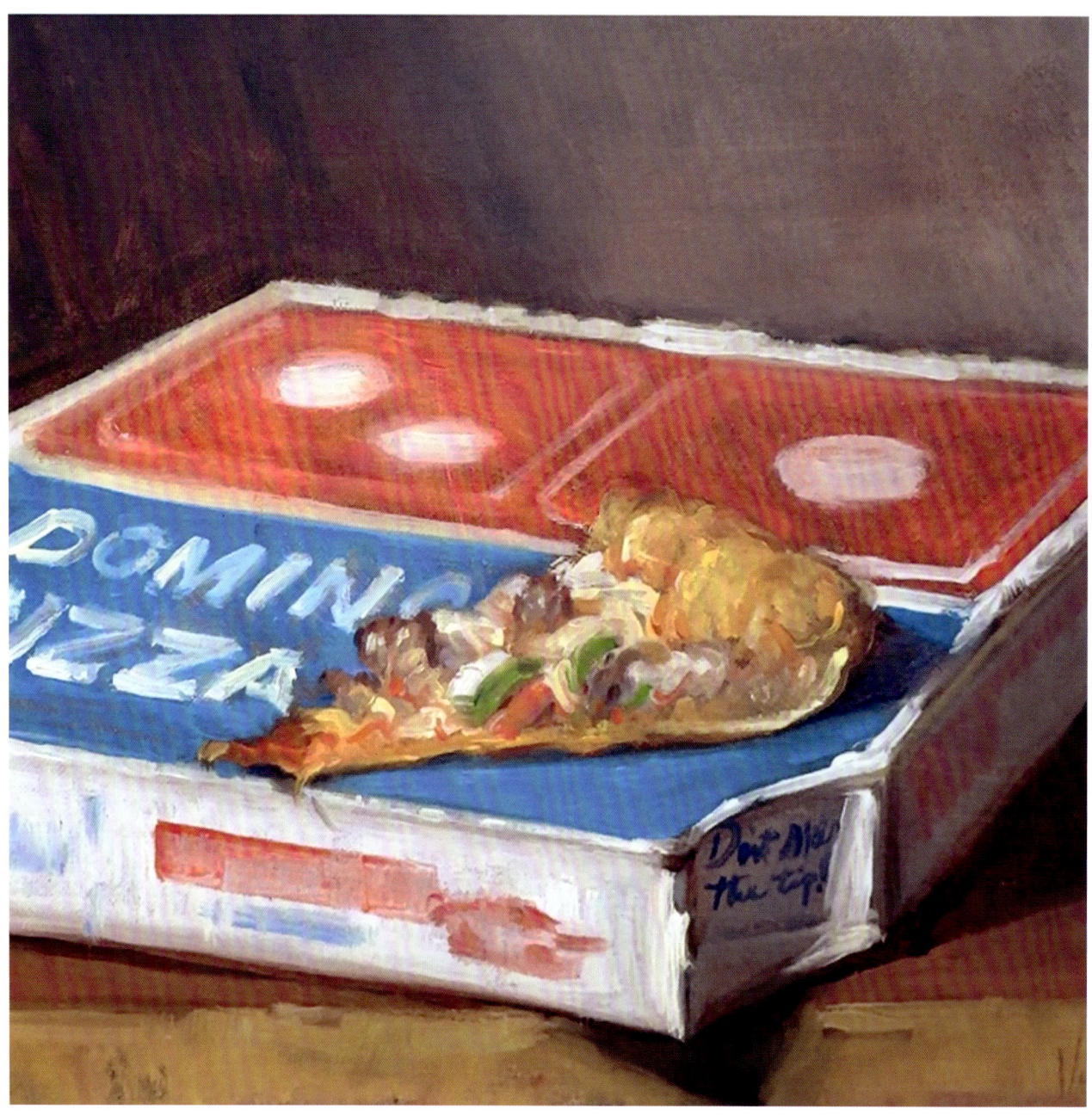

Domino's
16 x 20 in.

OPPOSITE PAGE:
Fried Rice
8 x 10 in.

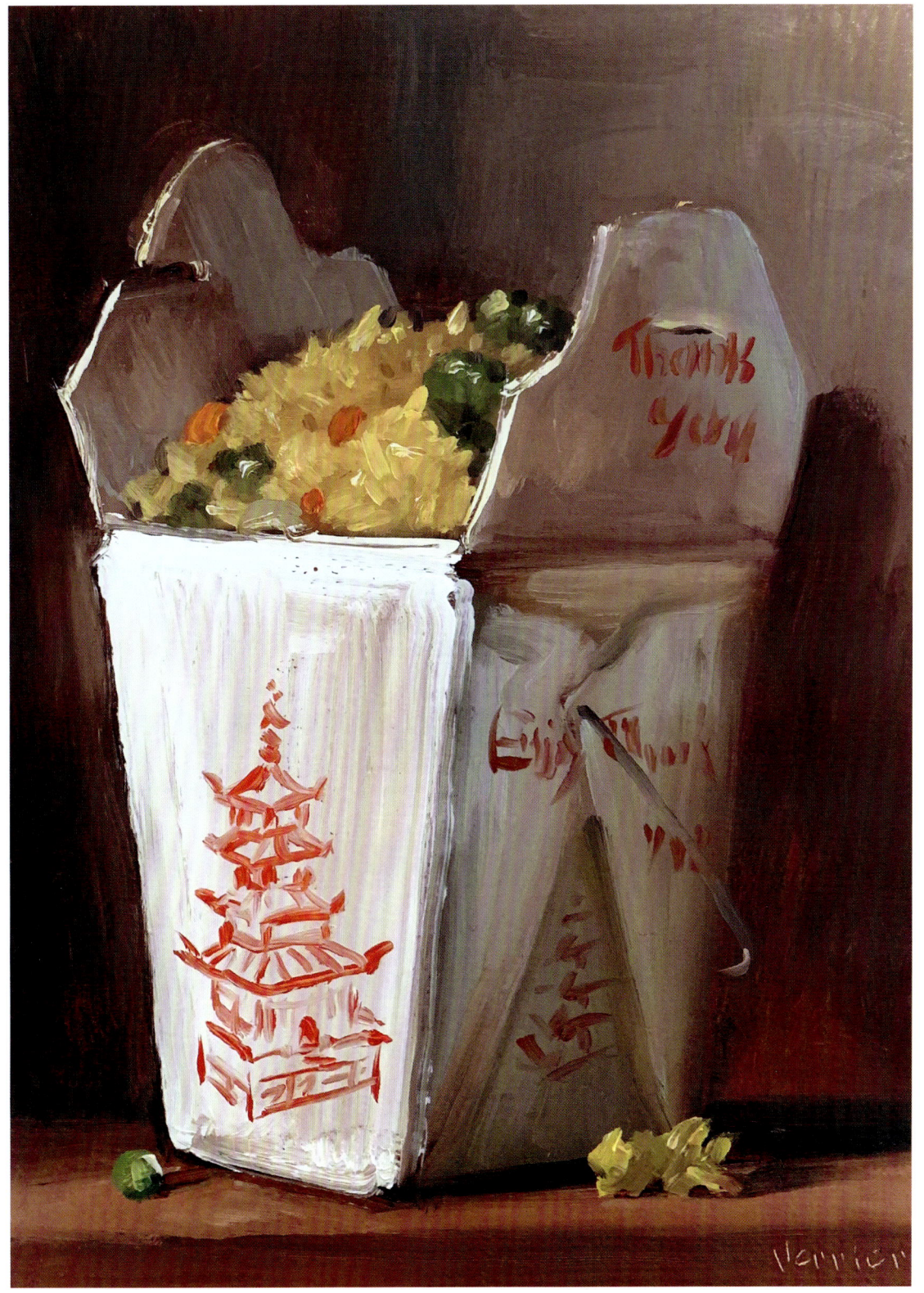

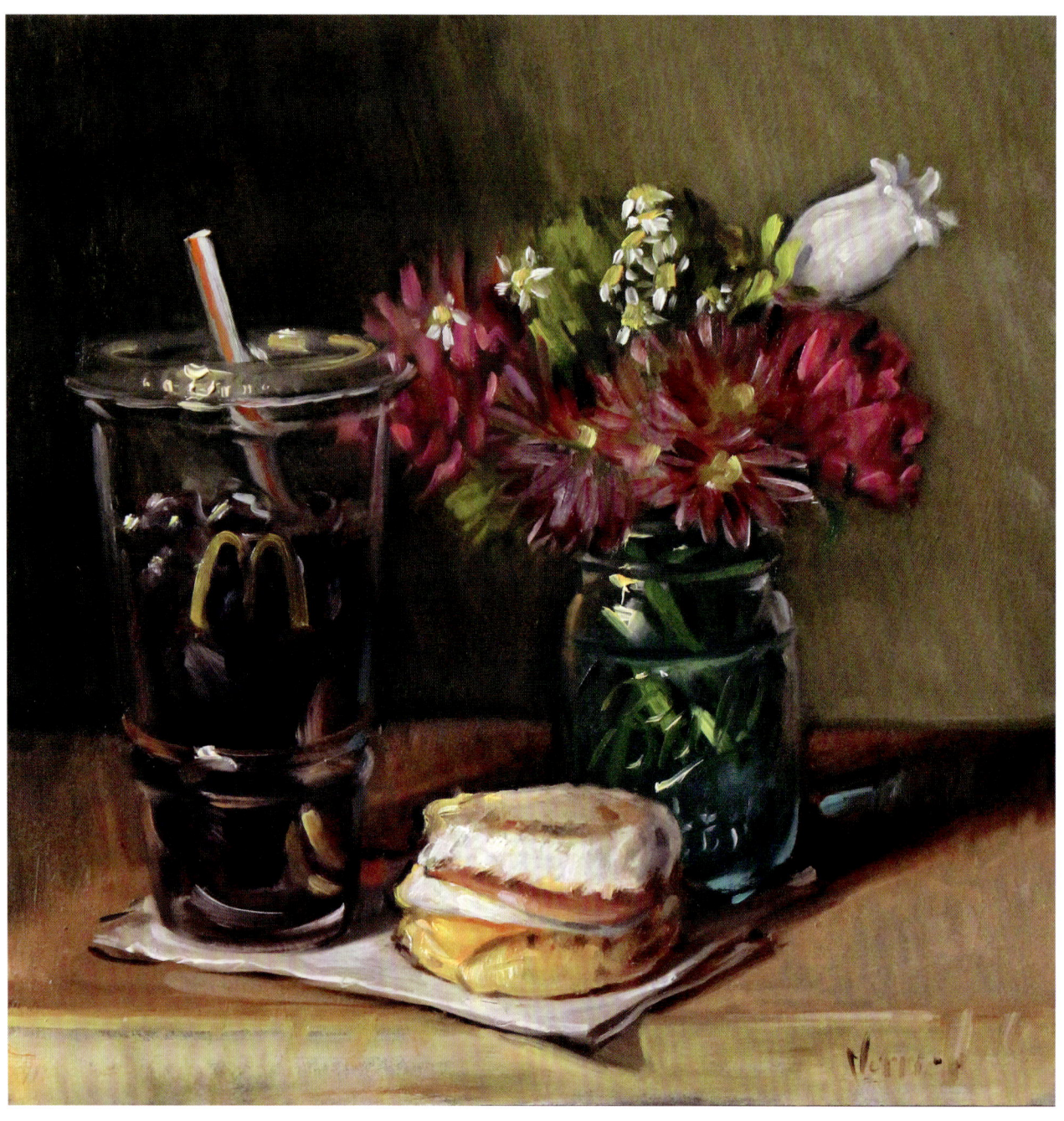

McDonald's Breakfast
20 x 20 in.

OPPOSITE PAGE:
McNuggets
8 x 10 in.

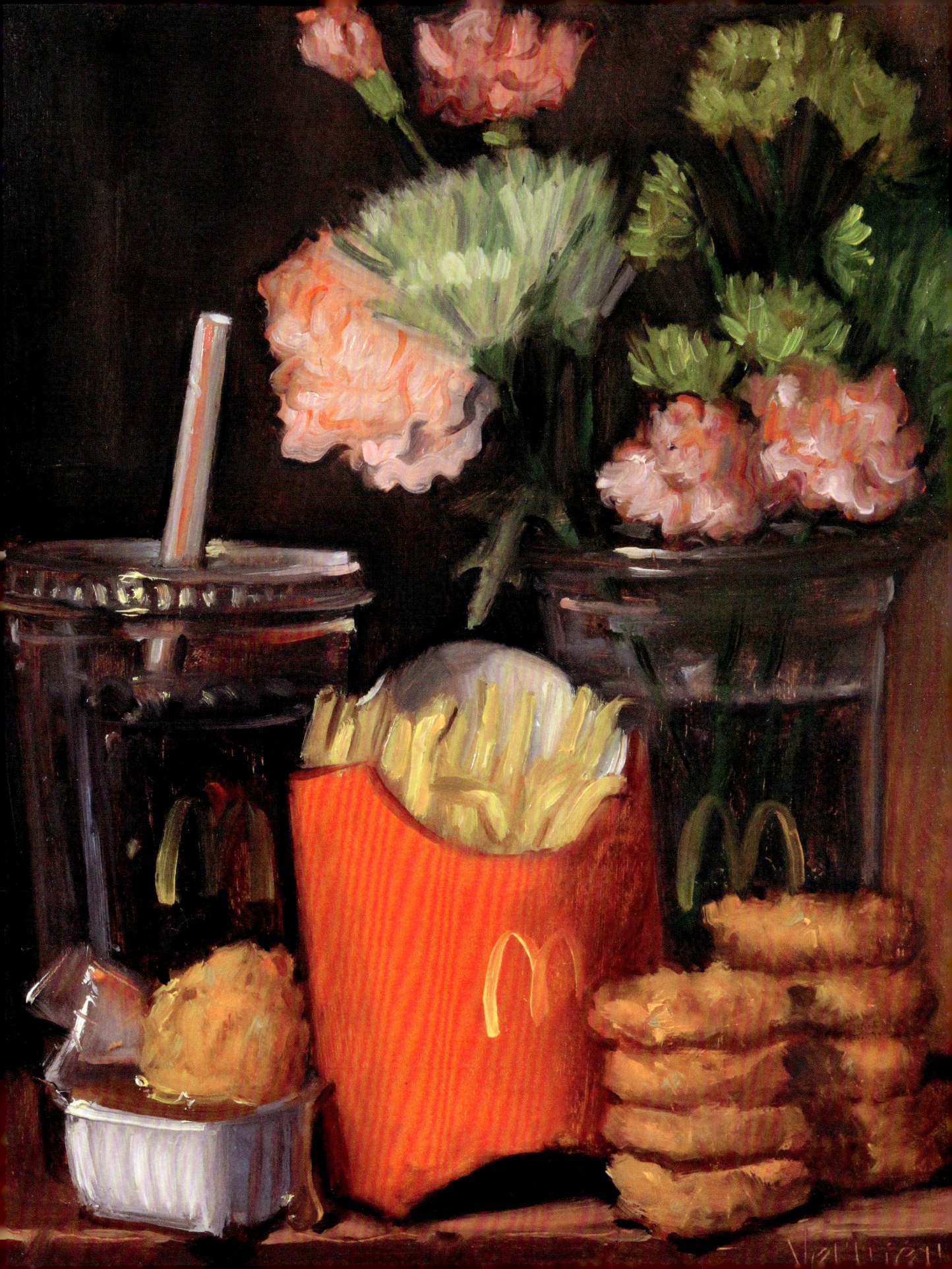

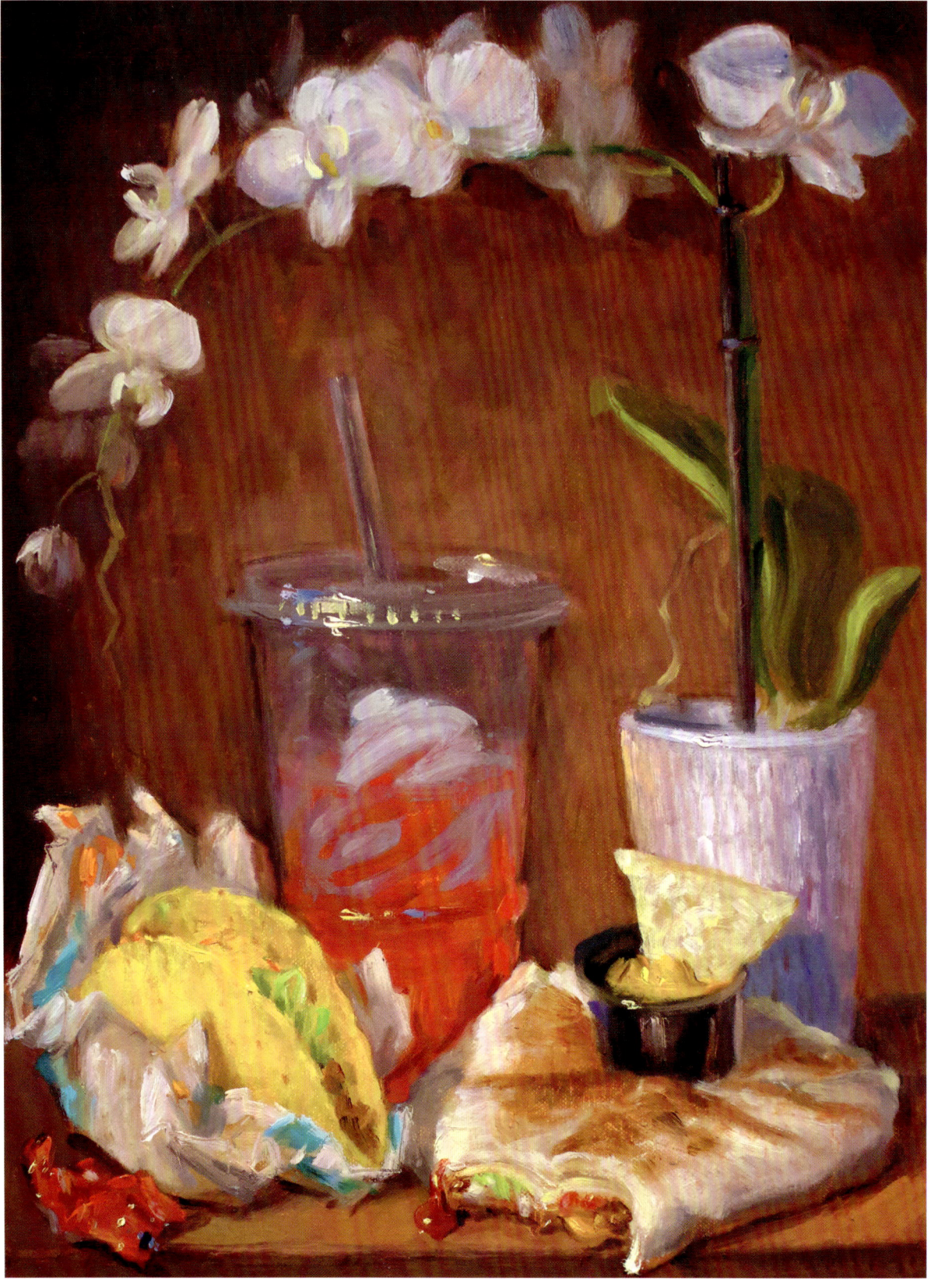

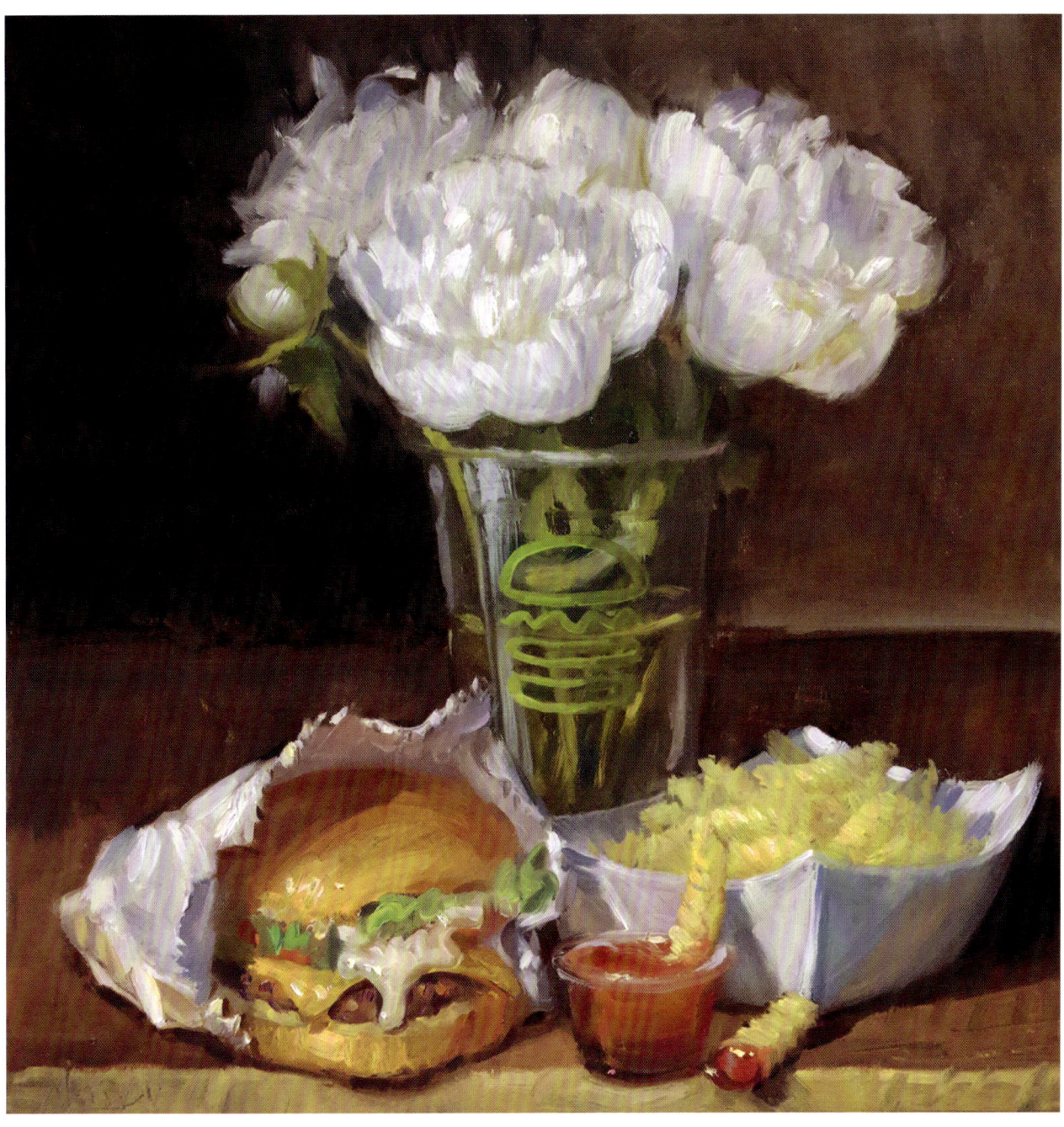

Taco Bell Crunchwrap Supreme
16 x 20 in.

Shake Shack
20 x 20 in.

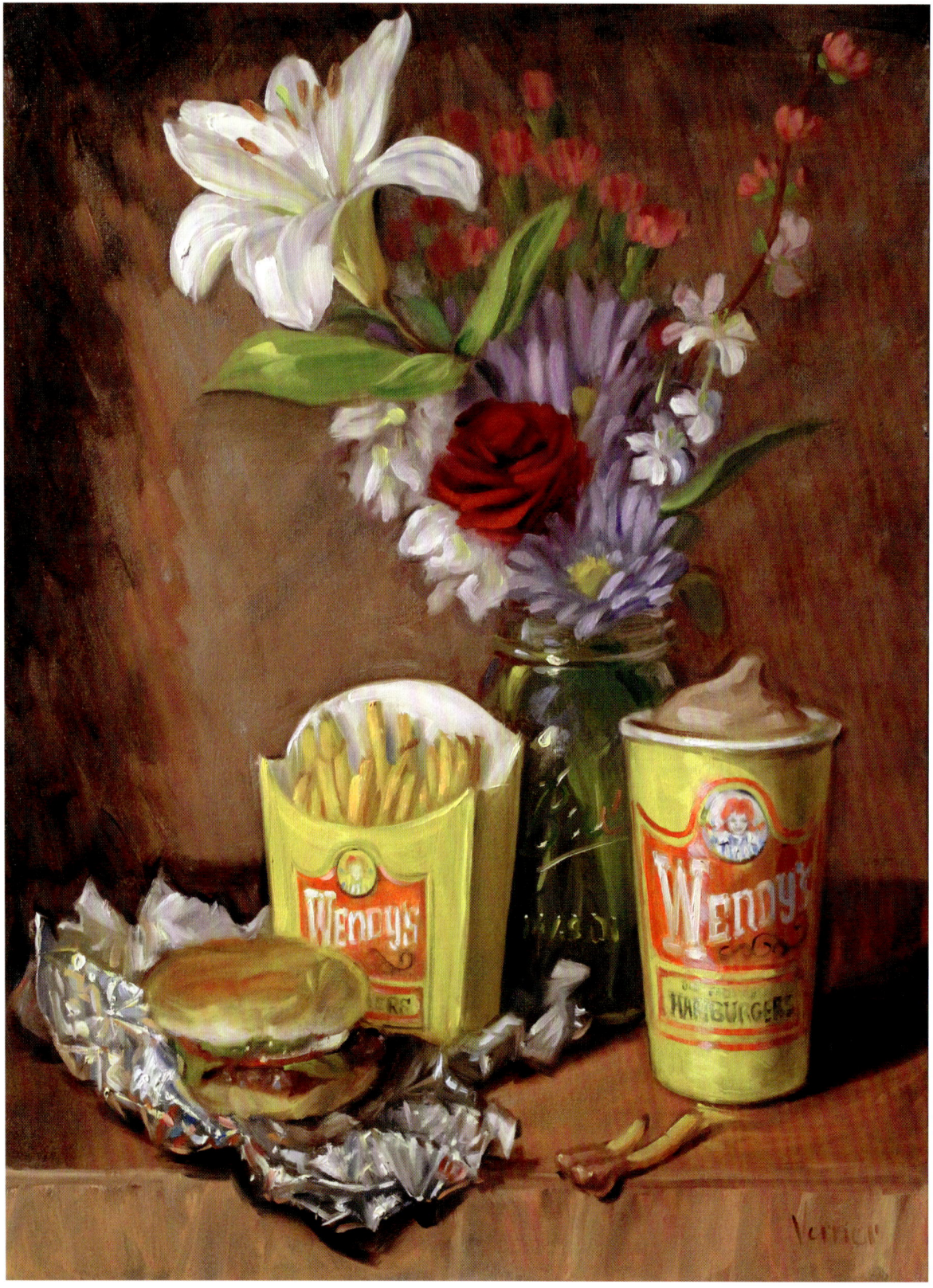

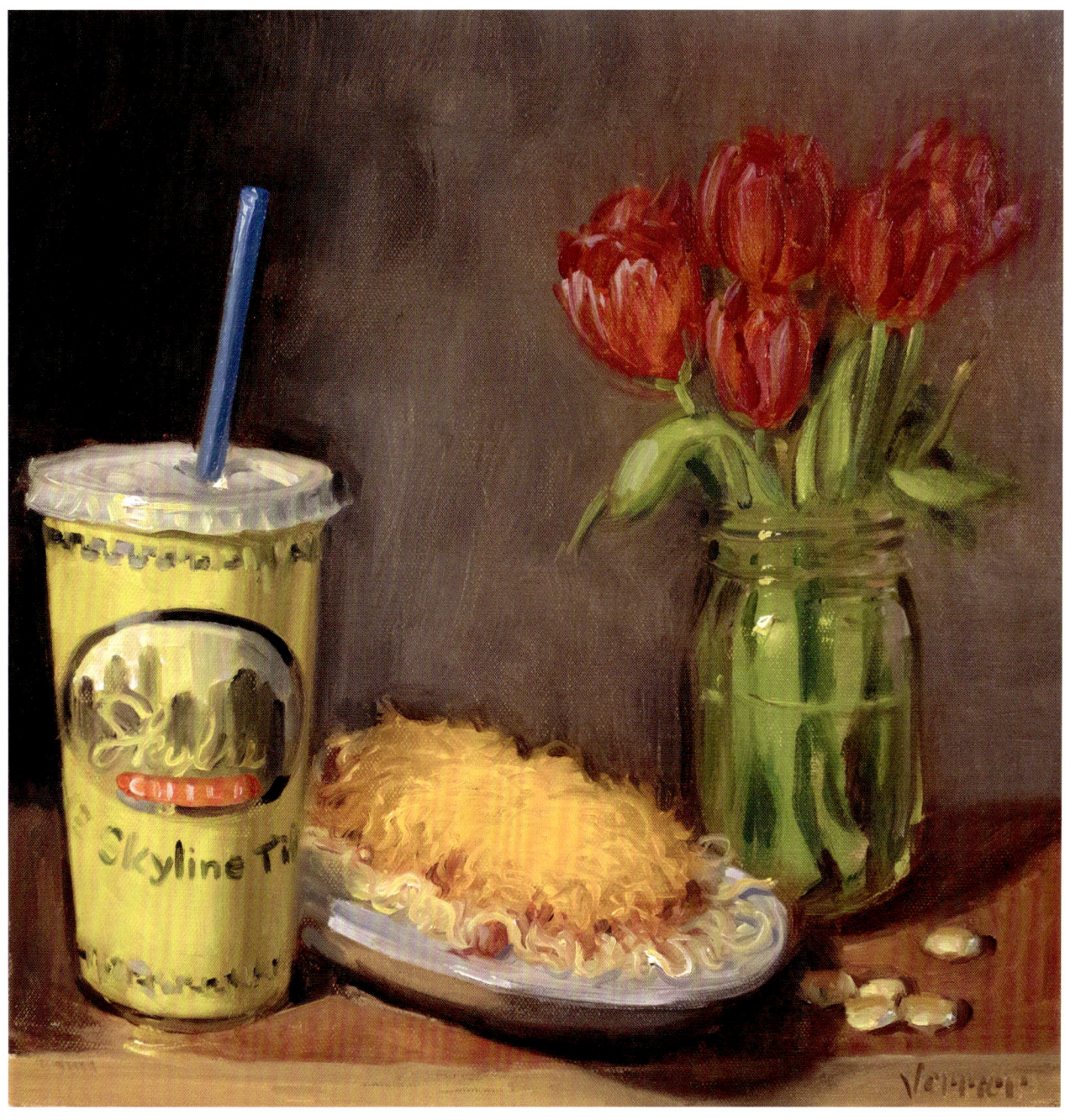

OPPOSITE PAGE:
Wendy's
18 x 24 in.

ABOVE:
Skyline Chili
20 x 20 in.

NOSTALGIA EATS

*I love when an image can harken back to a simpler, more innocent time in our lives. Oil paintings have an **amazing** power to portray those simple things, and I love that.*

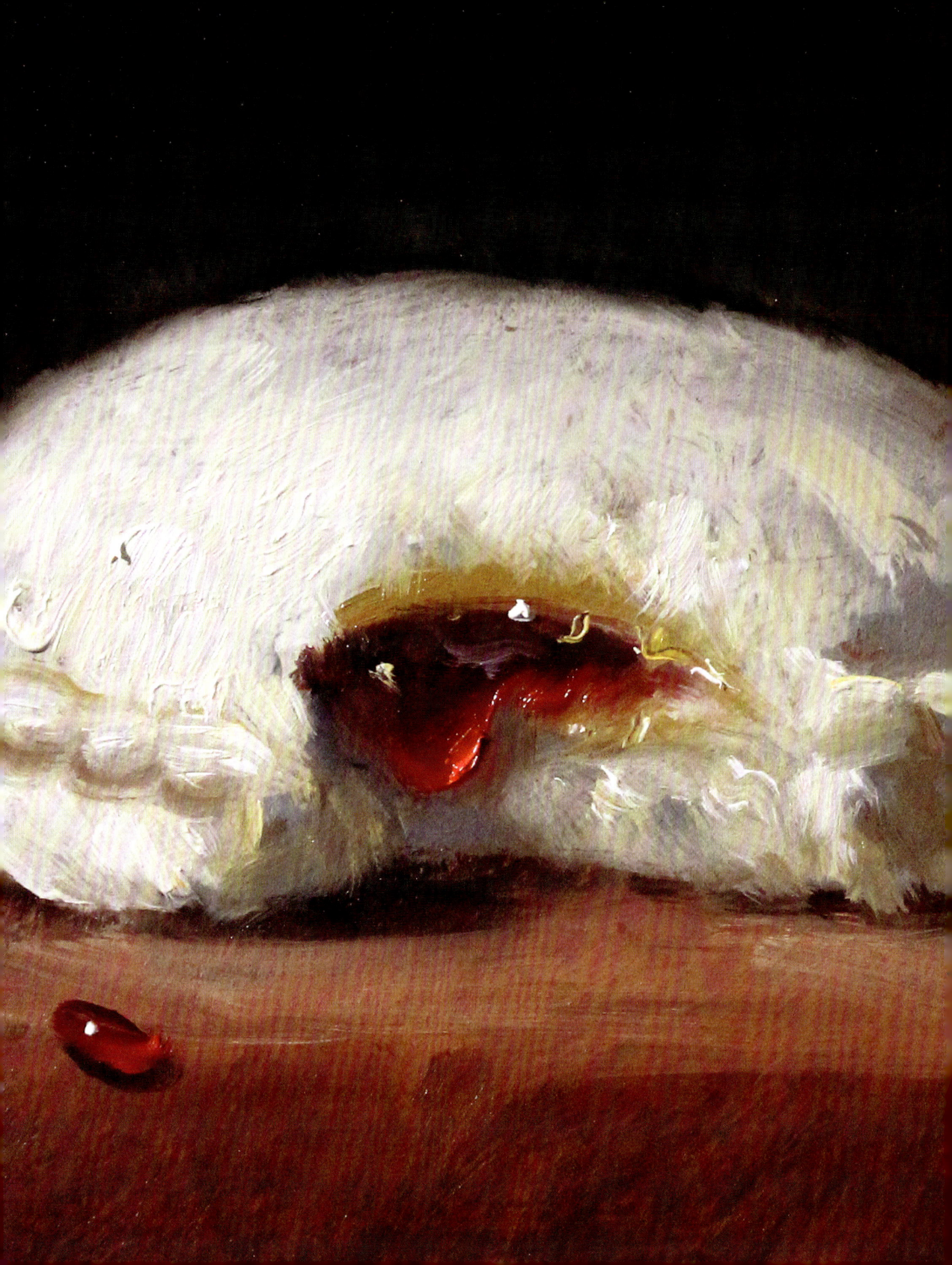

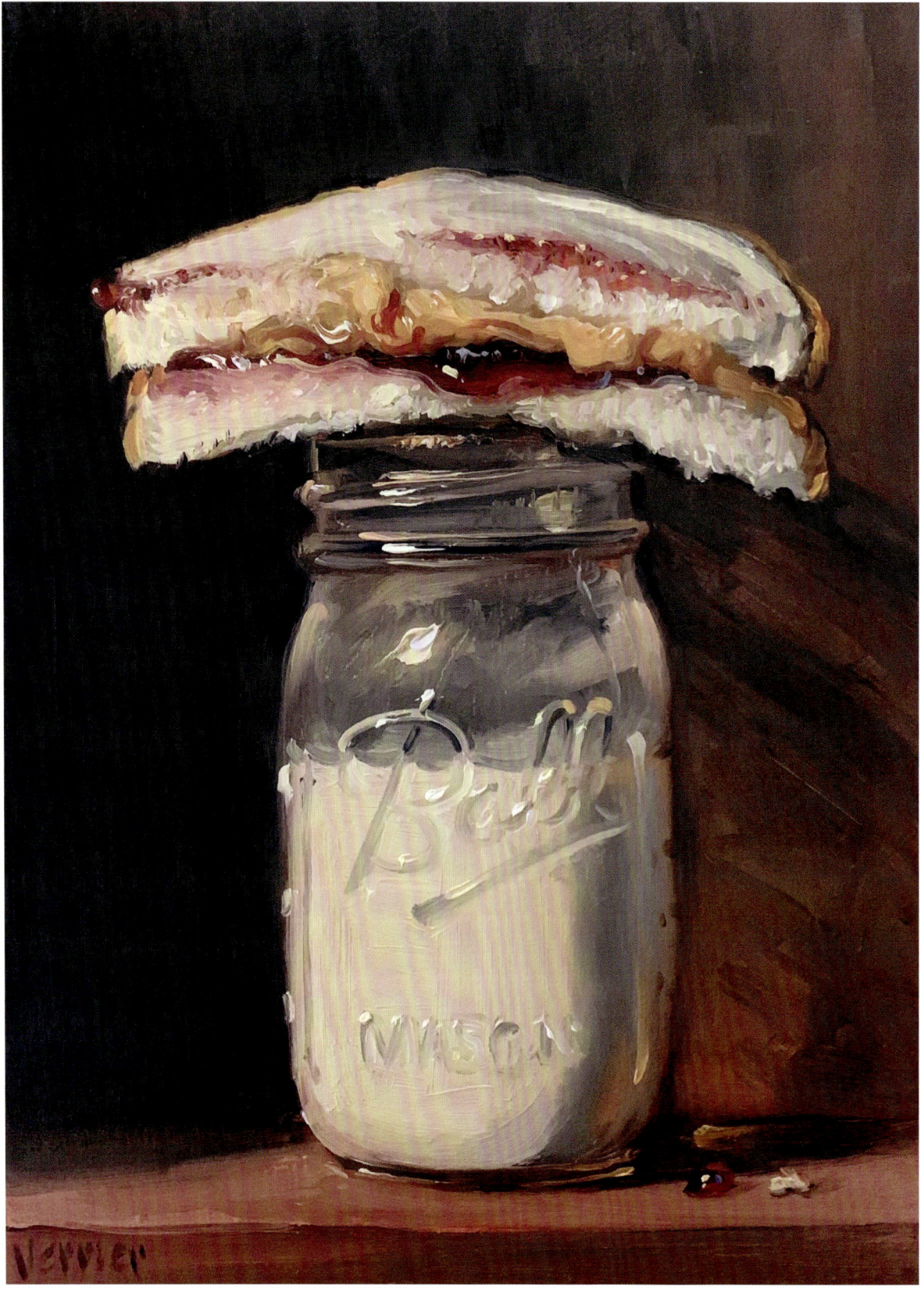

Vernier

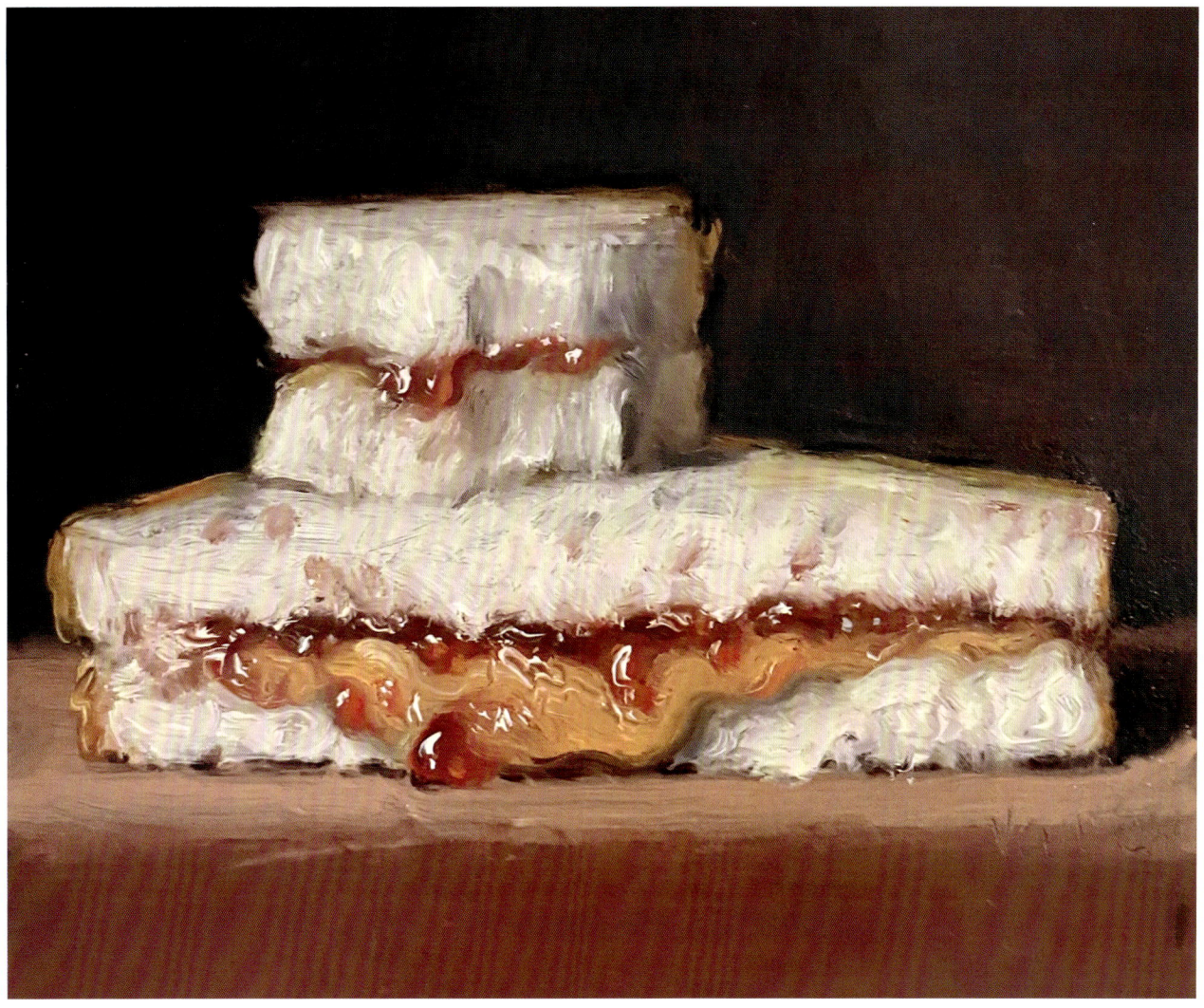

OPPOSITE PAGE:
PB&J & Jar of Milk No.2
8 x 10 in.

ABOVE:
PB&J Half Eaten
10 x 8 in.

PB&J & Jar of Milk No. 2 by Noah Verrier

I remember driving in the car, and the image popped into my head. I thought it was too cheesy and almost didn't paint it. I just wanted to paint a memory, make it beautiful, and somehow not overly commercial-looking. It ended up going viral with millions of views across all platforms and landed a place in Buzzfeed.

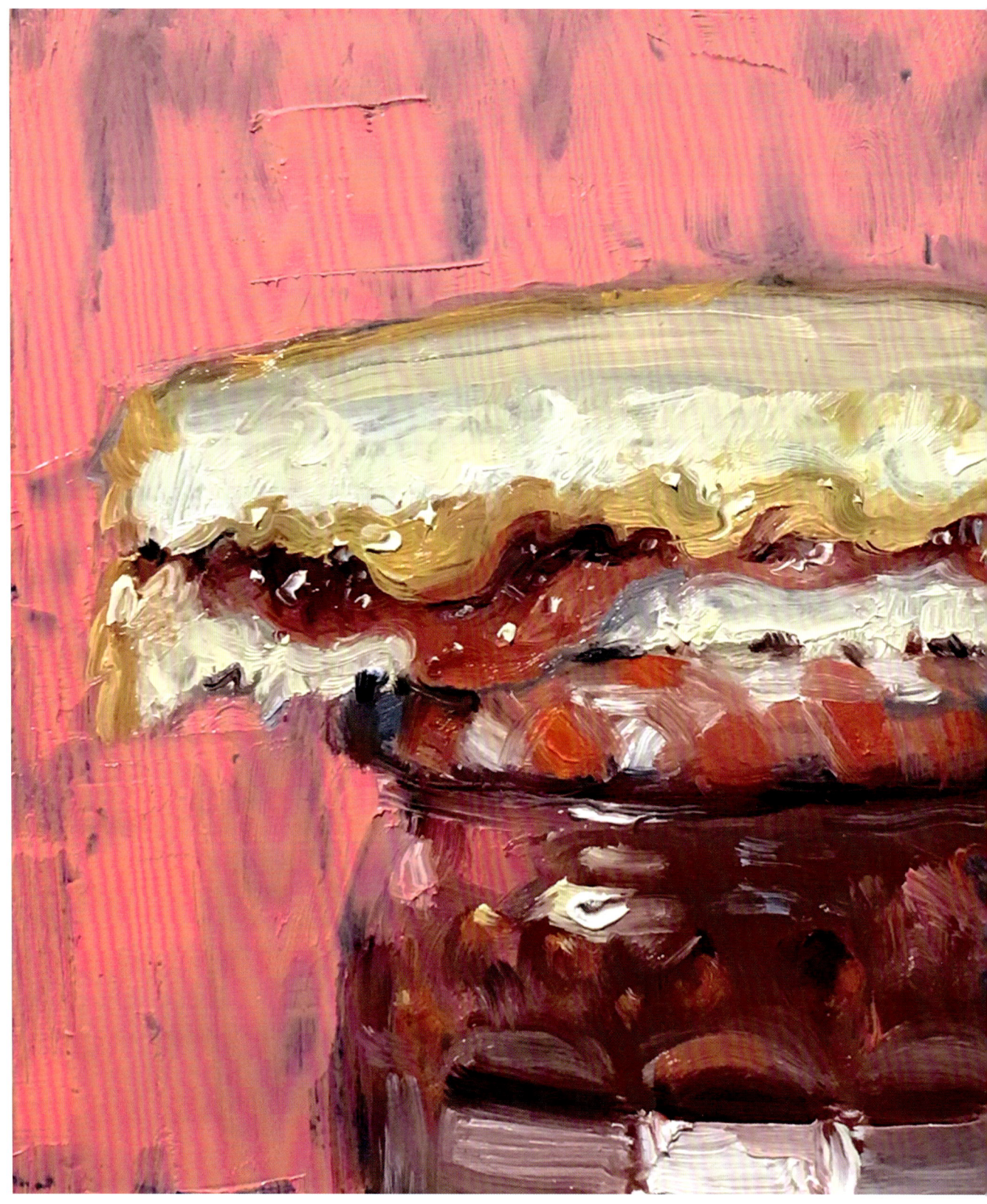

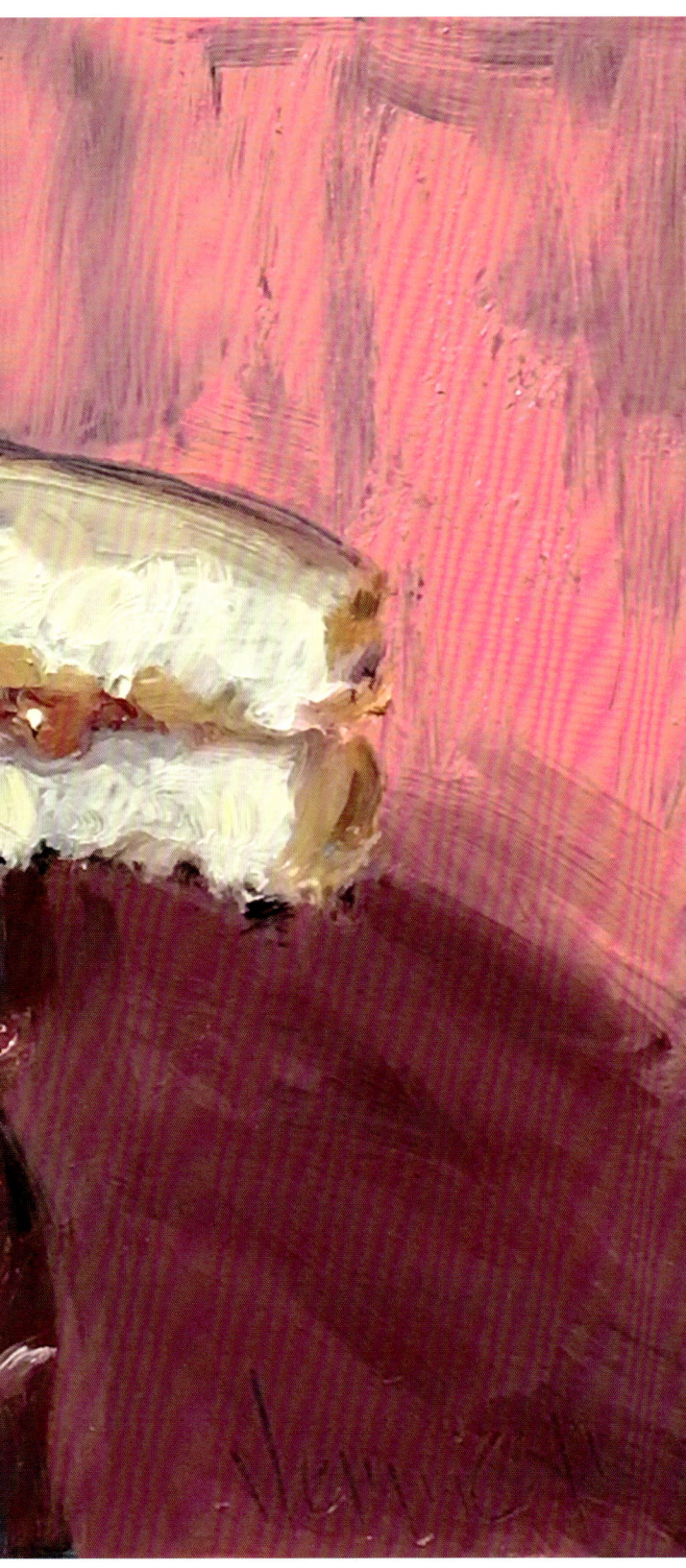

PB&J Bonne Maman
9 x 8 in.

NEXT PAGE:
PB&J & Jar of Milk
12 x 9 in.

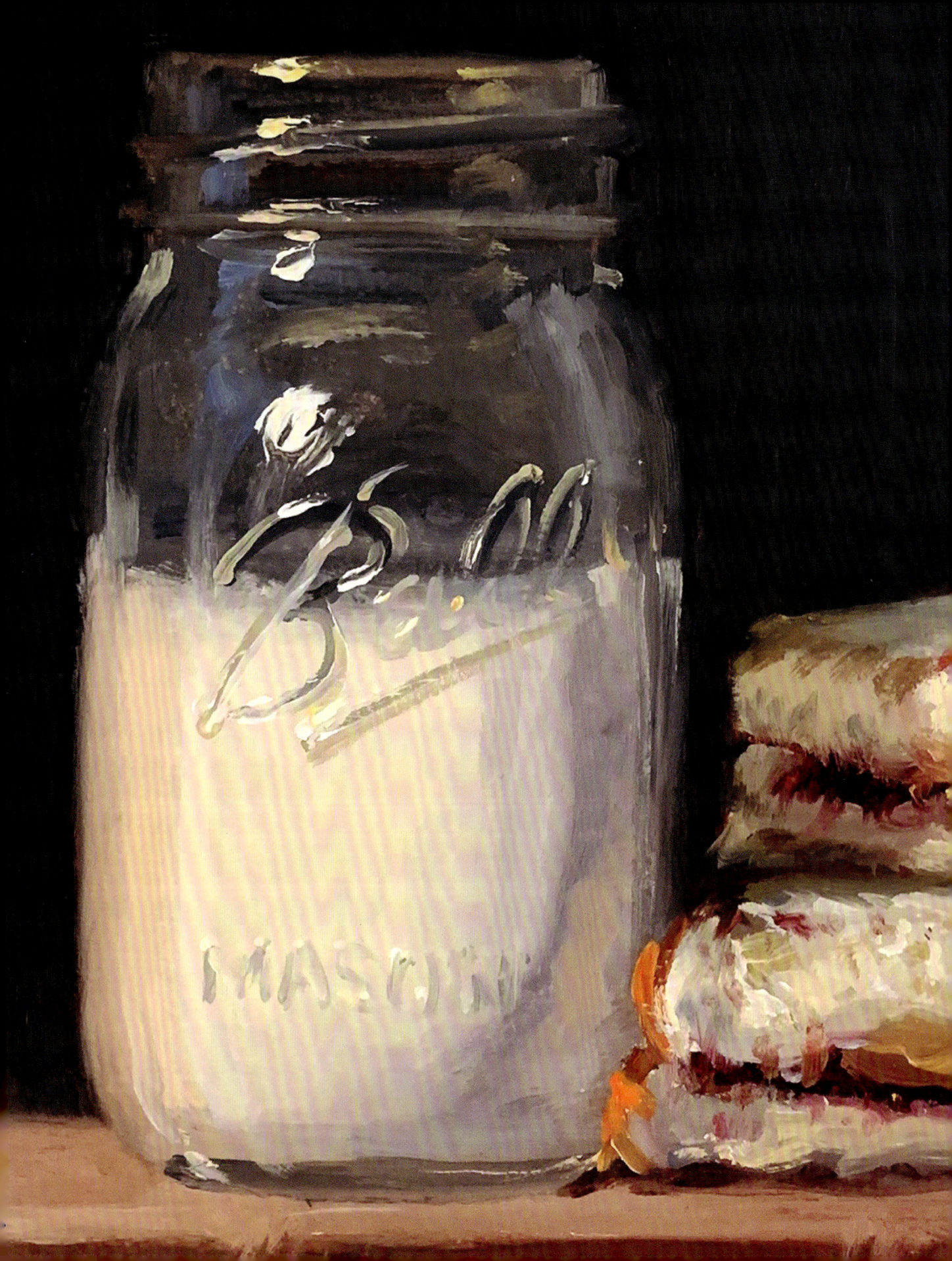

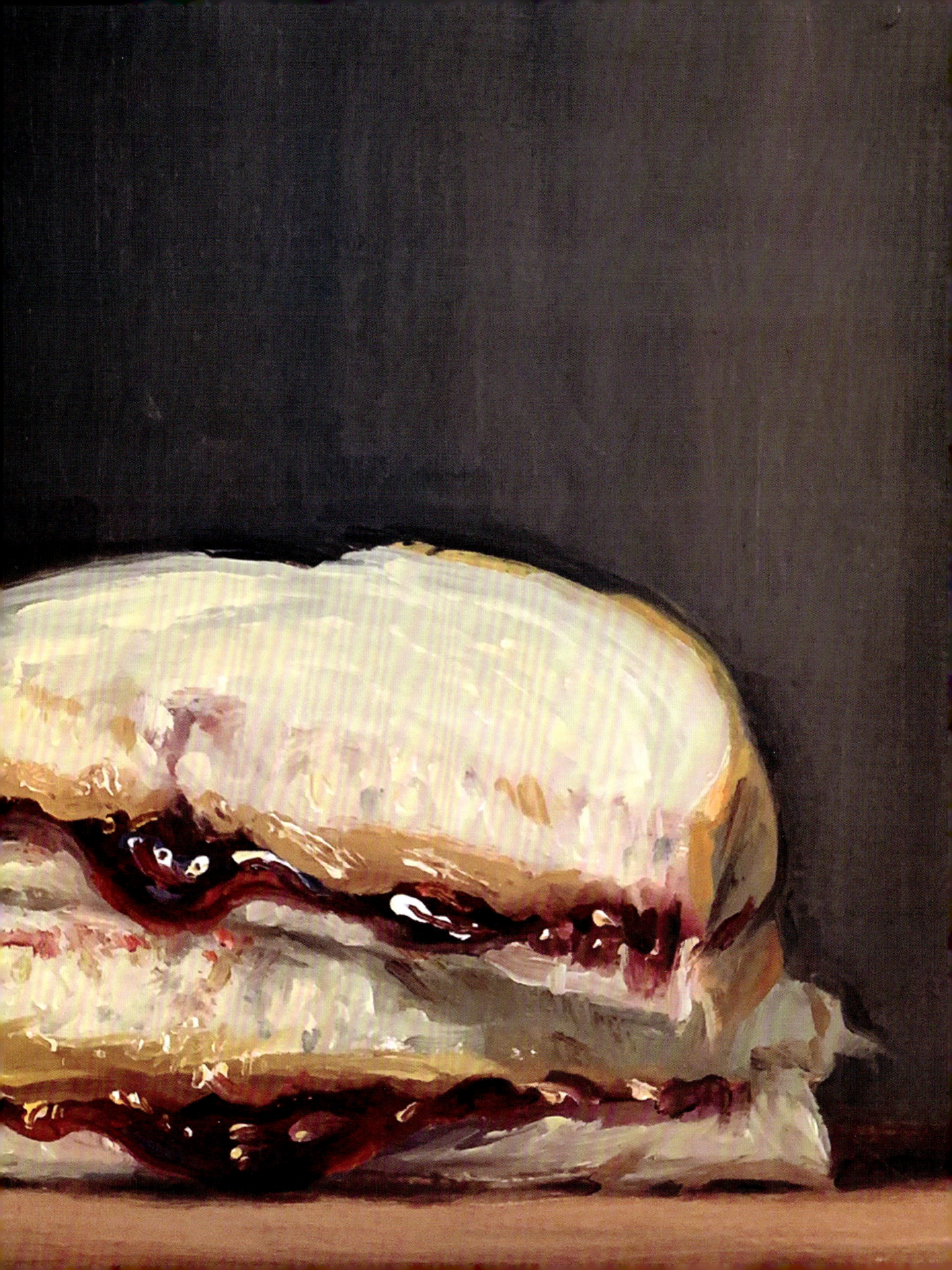

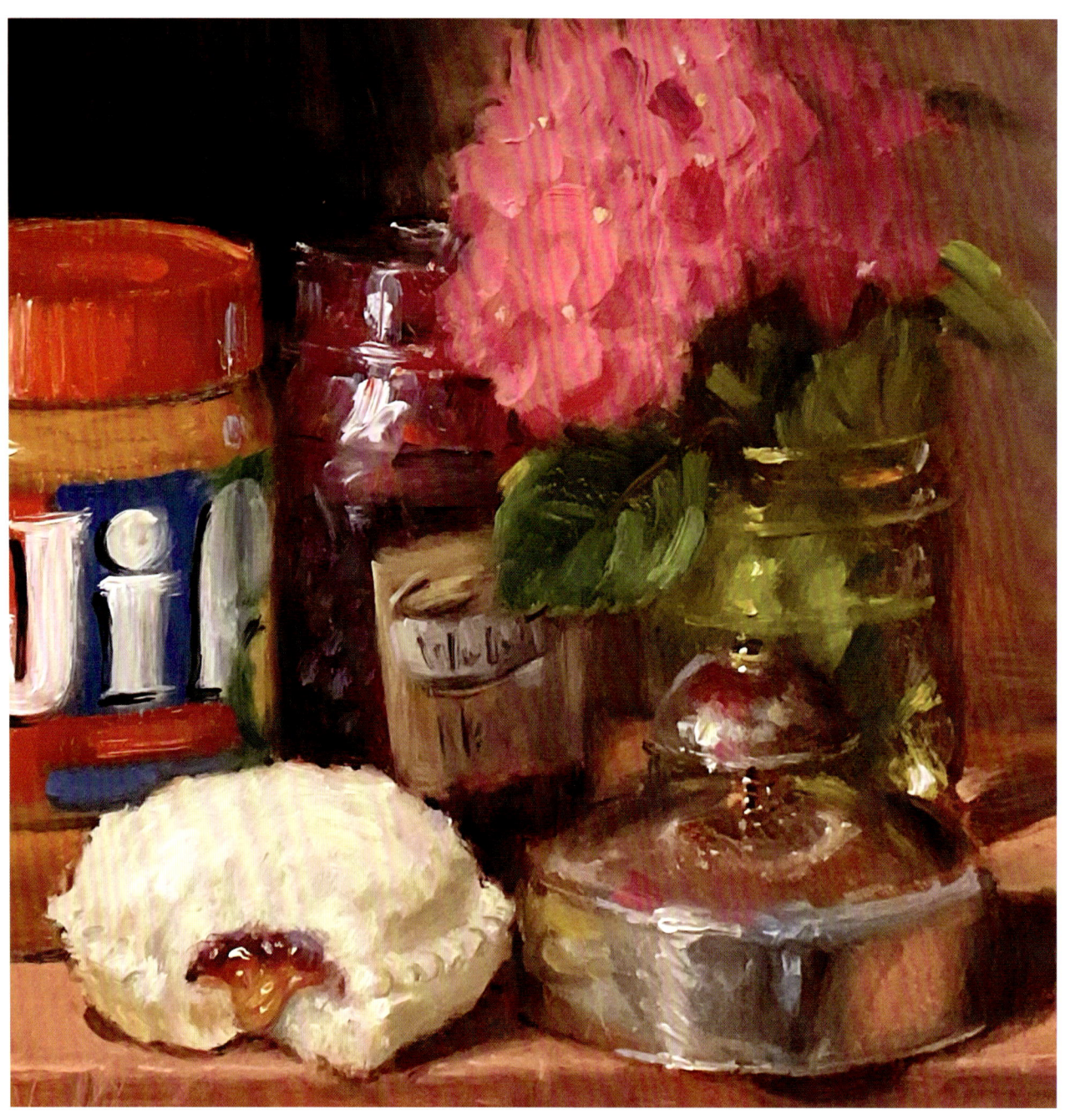

Homemade Uncrustable
20 x 20 in.

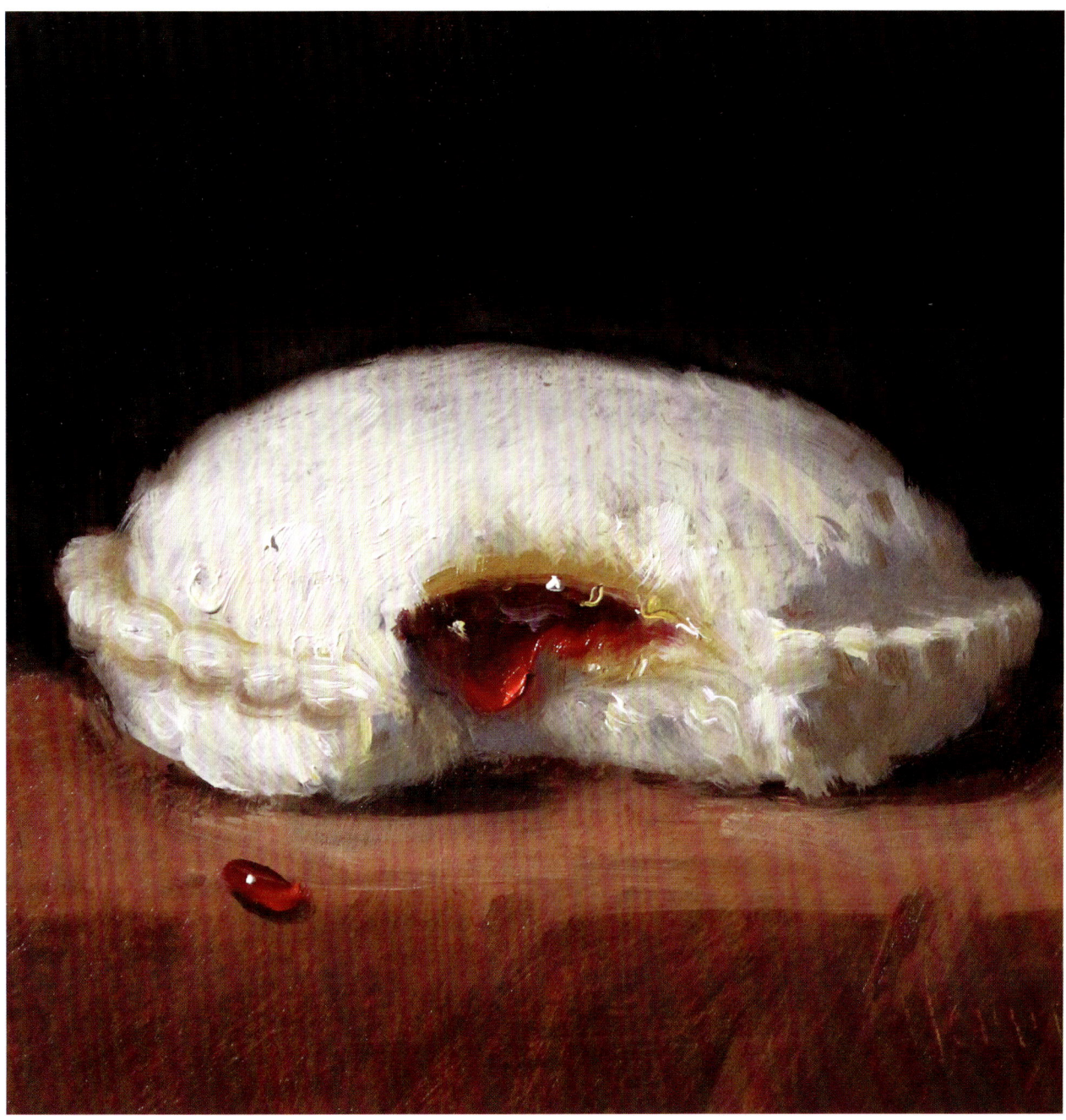

Uncrustable
10 x 8 in.

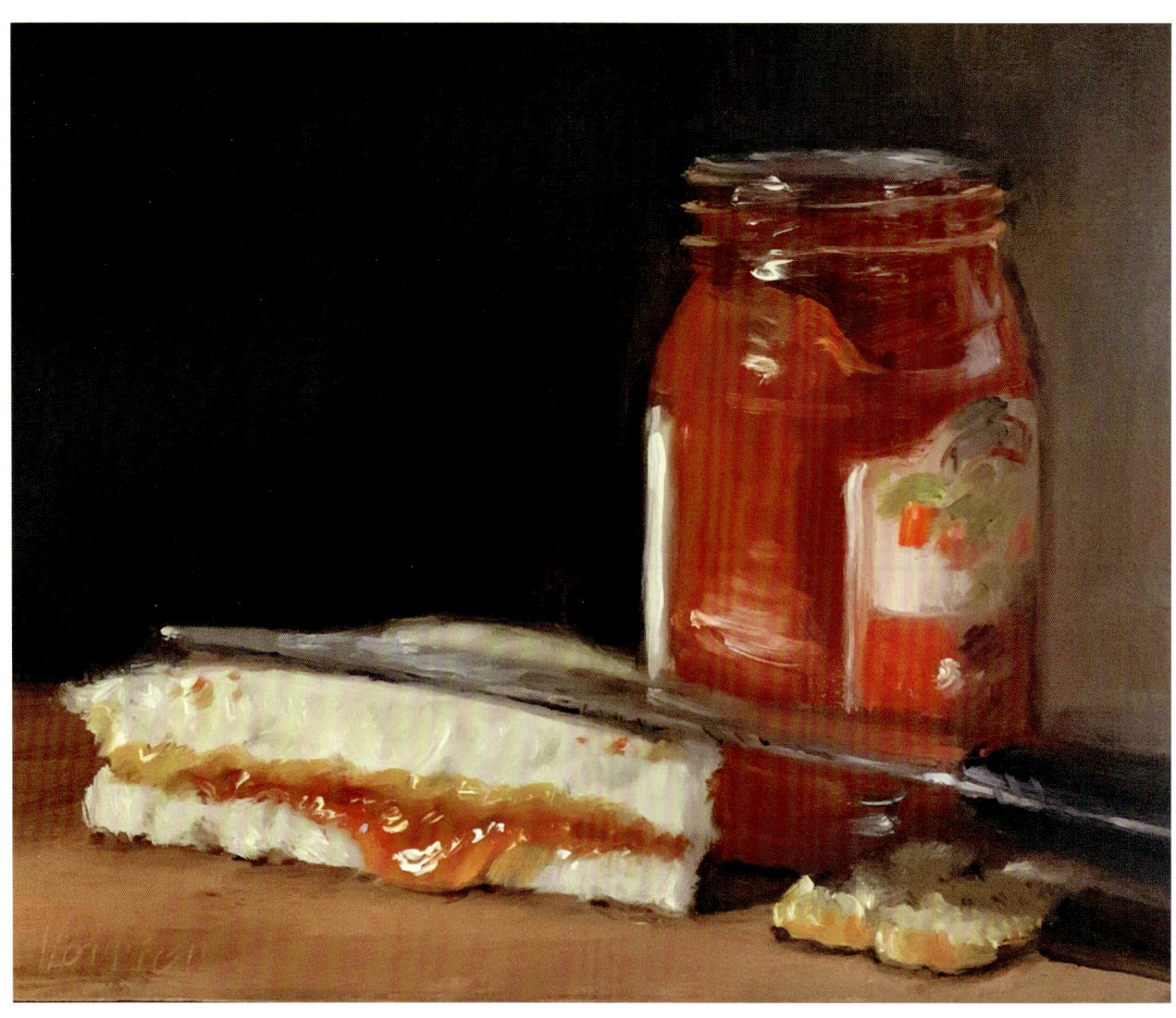

PB&J Crustless

12 x 9 in.

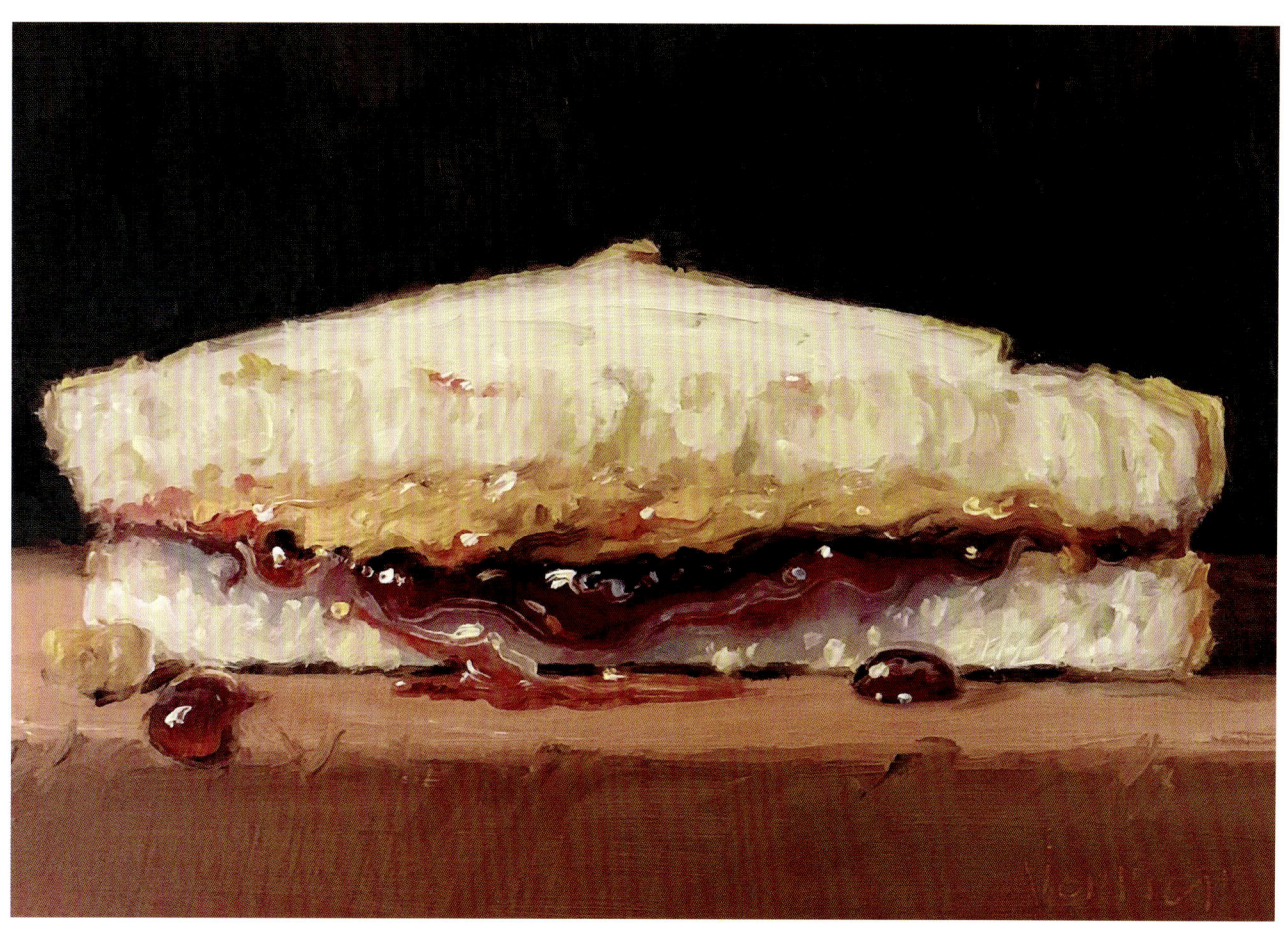

PB&J Half

9 x 6 in.

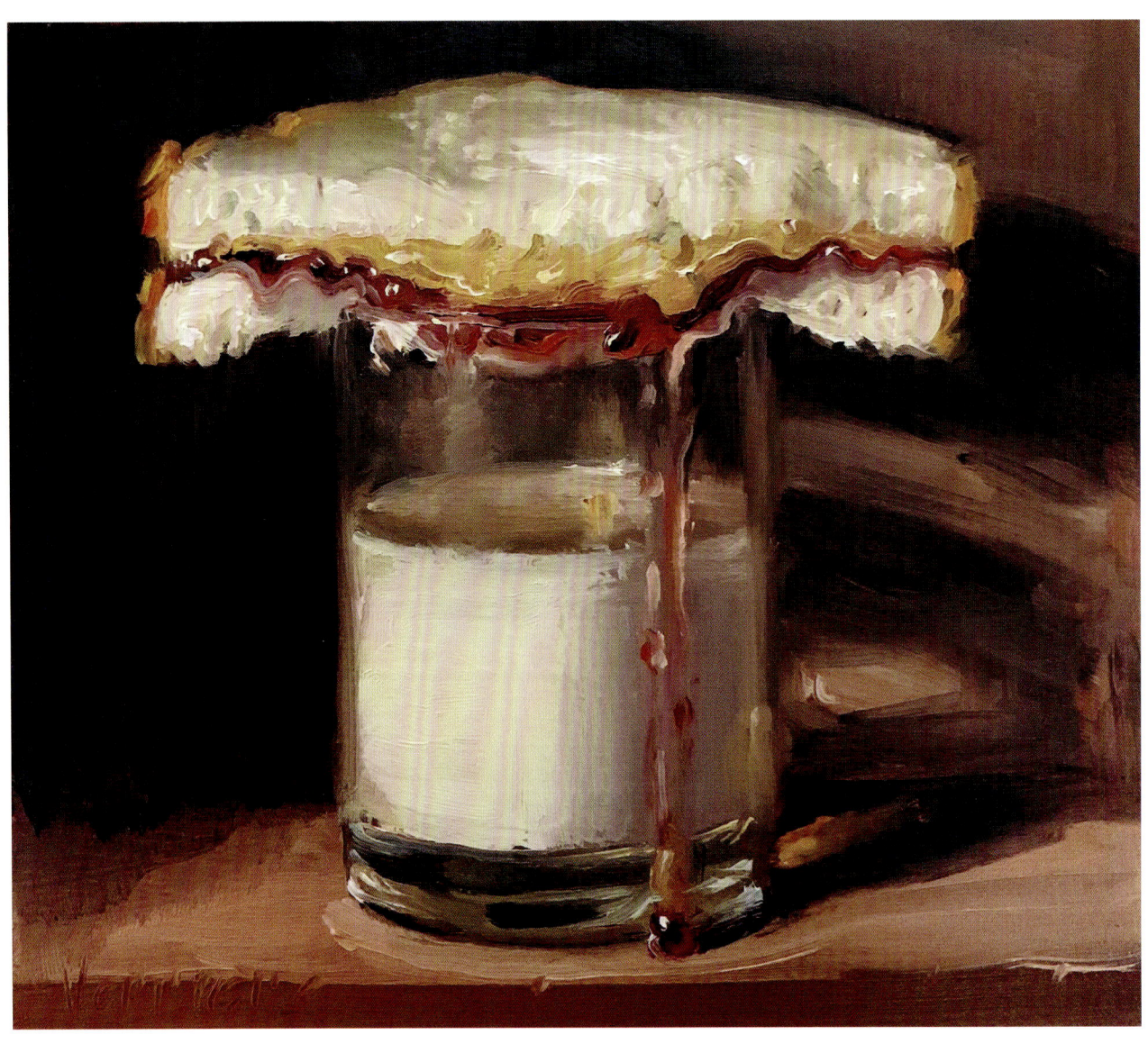

PB&J & Glass of Milk

9 x 8 in.

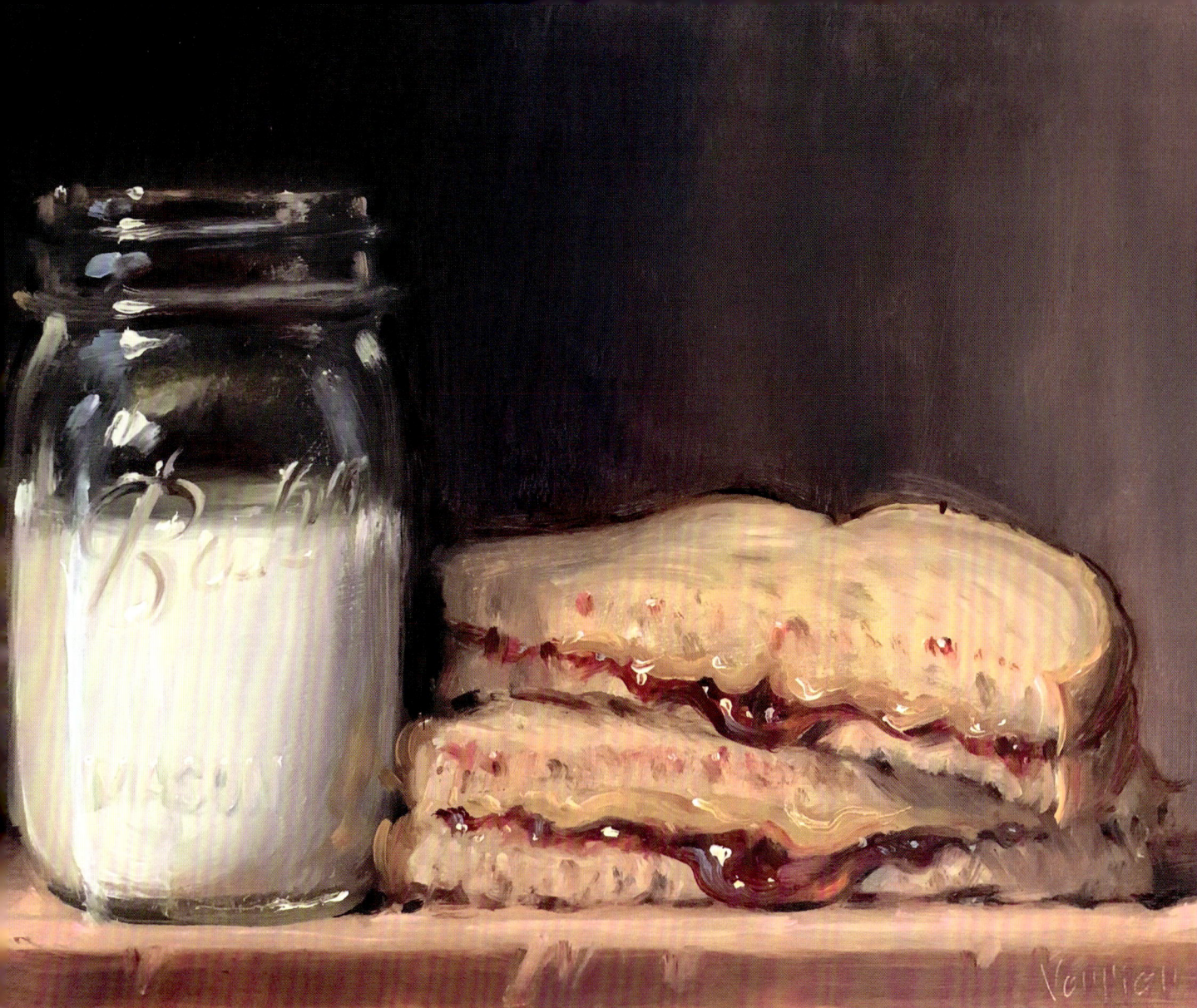

PB&J & Jar of Milk (Wheat)

12 x 9 in.

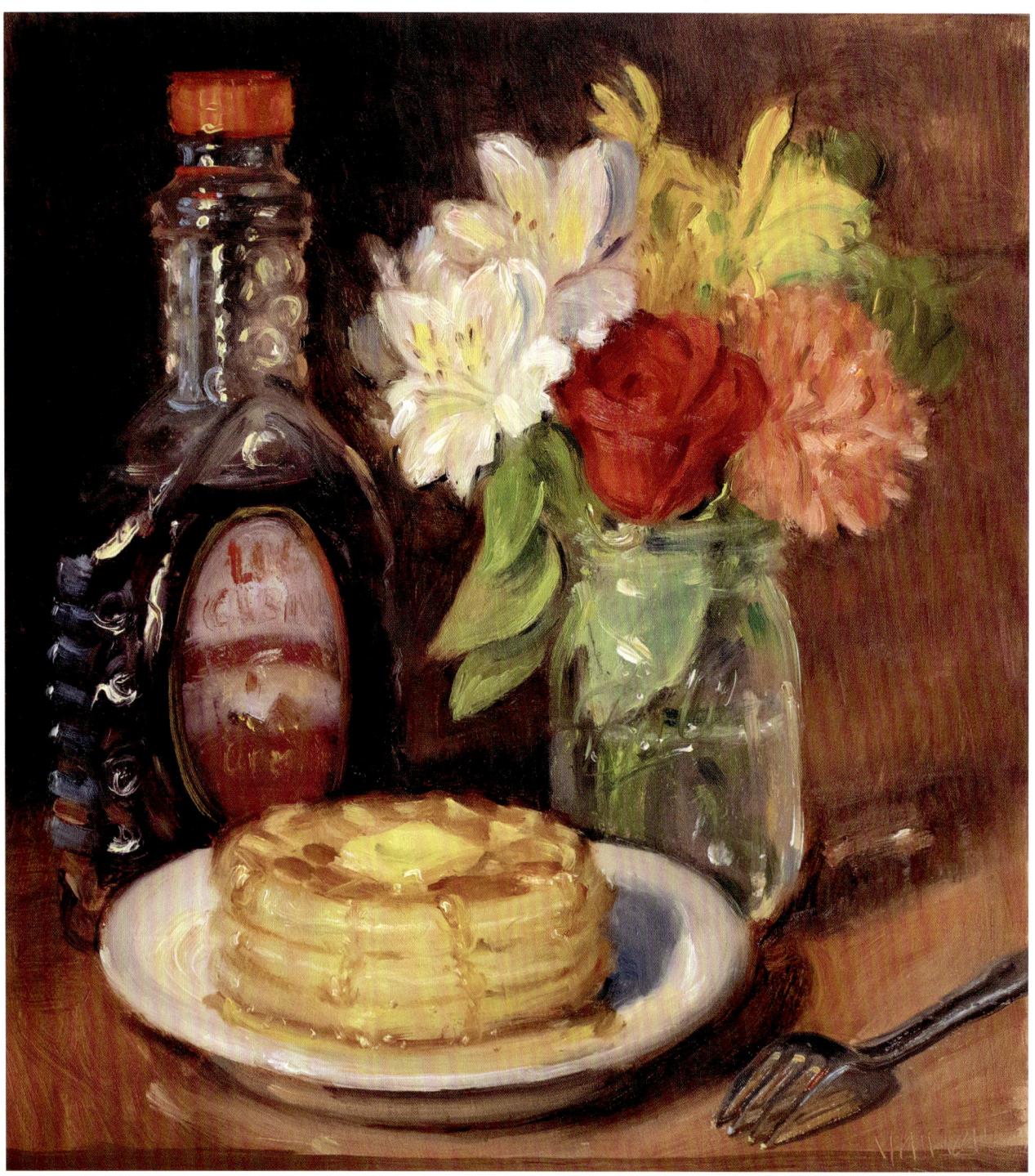

Waffles

8 x 9 in.

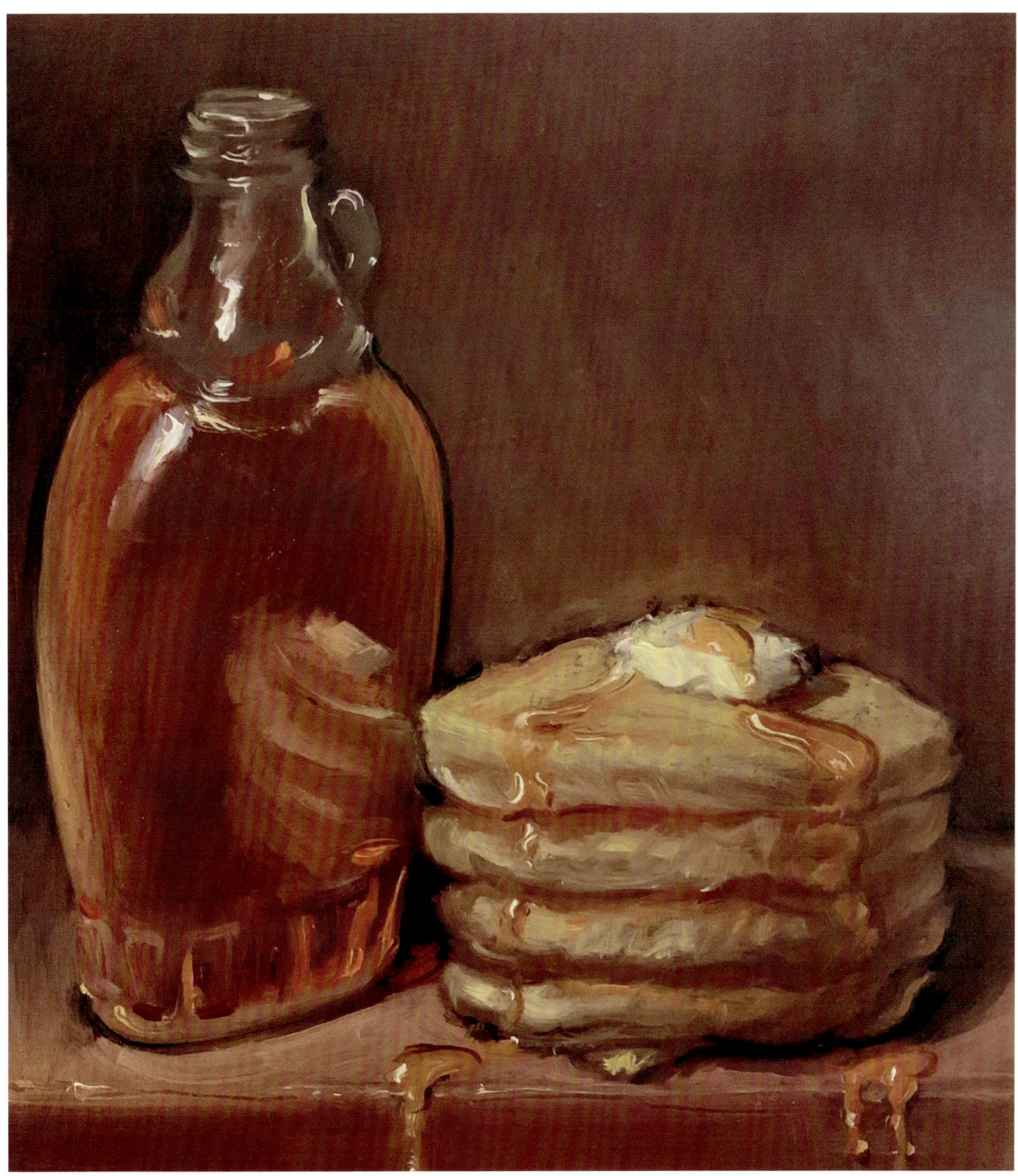

Pancakes

8 x 9 in.

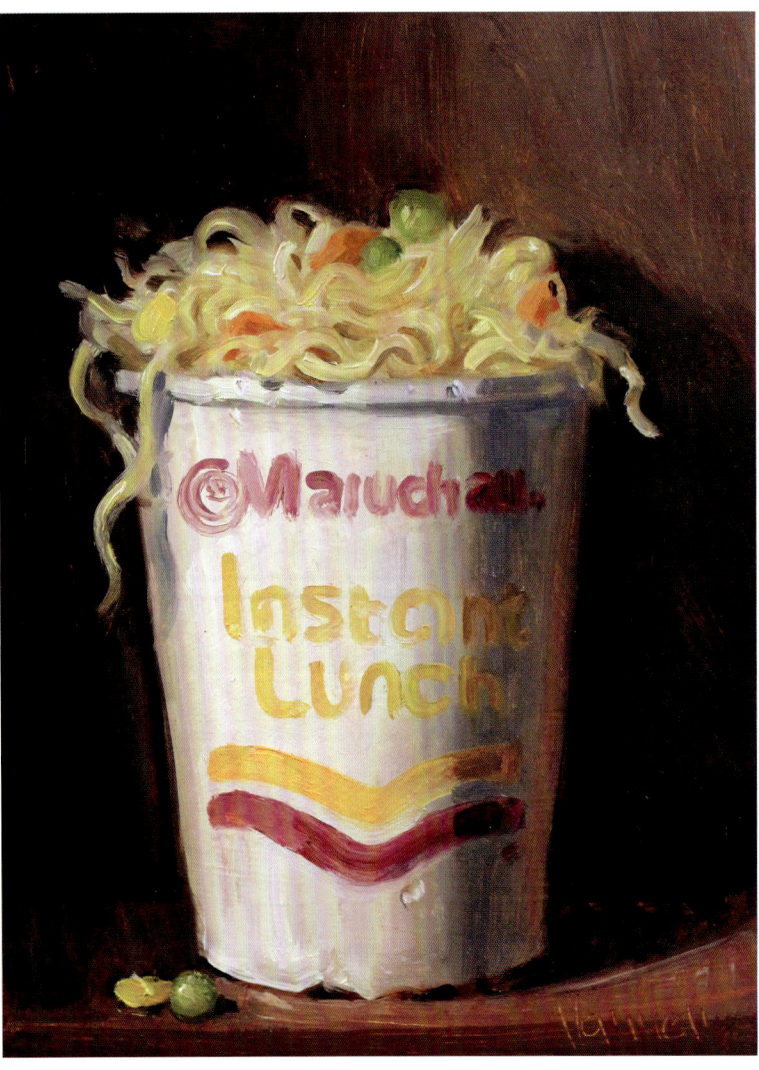

Ramen by Ashlyn Hall

When I see this painting, not only do I feel a quirky sense of joy in finding artistic beauty in something typically seen as "cheap" or "mundane", but also a sense of comfort and nostalgia. Growing up, sometimes a ramen noodle cup was the best thing we had to eat at the time. And I'm sure I speak for many when it comes to cheap and convenient foods from childhood. But getting to see it interpreted in a new light of artistic expression and praise, it almost makes me feel proud to have a positive association with the ramen noodle cup. I love Noah's work and am happy that someone has a unique vision to highlight comfort foods and items of our time, in the same way old masters would paint a vase of flowers, or a bowl of fruit. Simple but effective, to say the least.

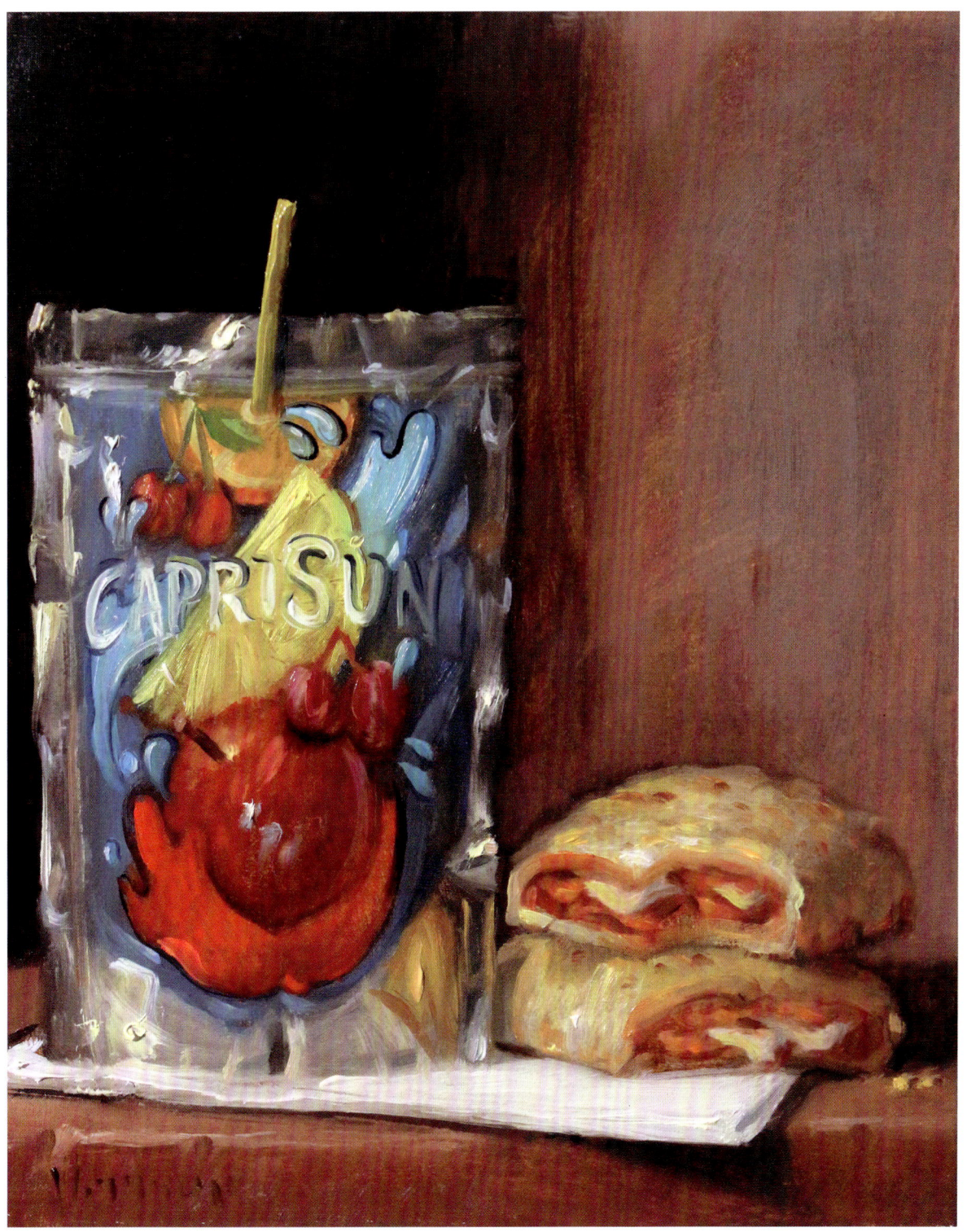

Capri Sun & Hot Pocket

9 x 12 in.

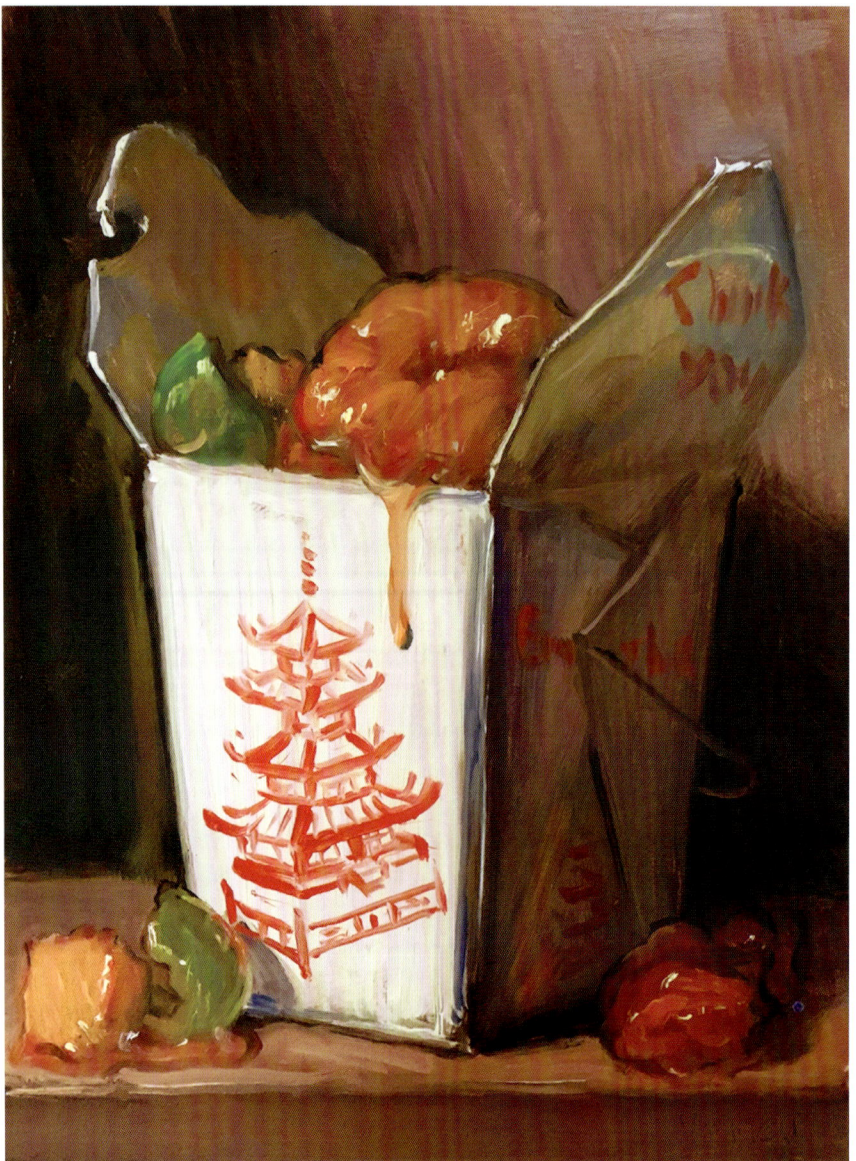

Sweet & Shrimp in Takeout Box by Naomi Lee

The sweet and sour shrimp in the painting knows it's the main character. It recalls those late-night DoorDash orders, seeing the steam rise from the carton when you open it, and devouring it cross-legged on the couch in front of the TV. The lights from the show you've binged thousands of times make the sauce glisten like it's under stage lights. The sweet, sticky bite of something deep-fried always hit the spot. There's comfort in how it's painted — messy, glowing, real.

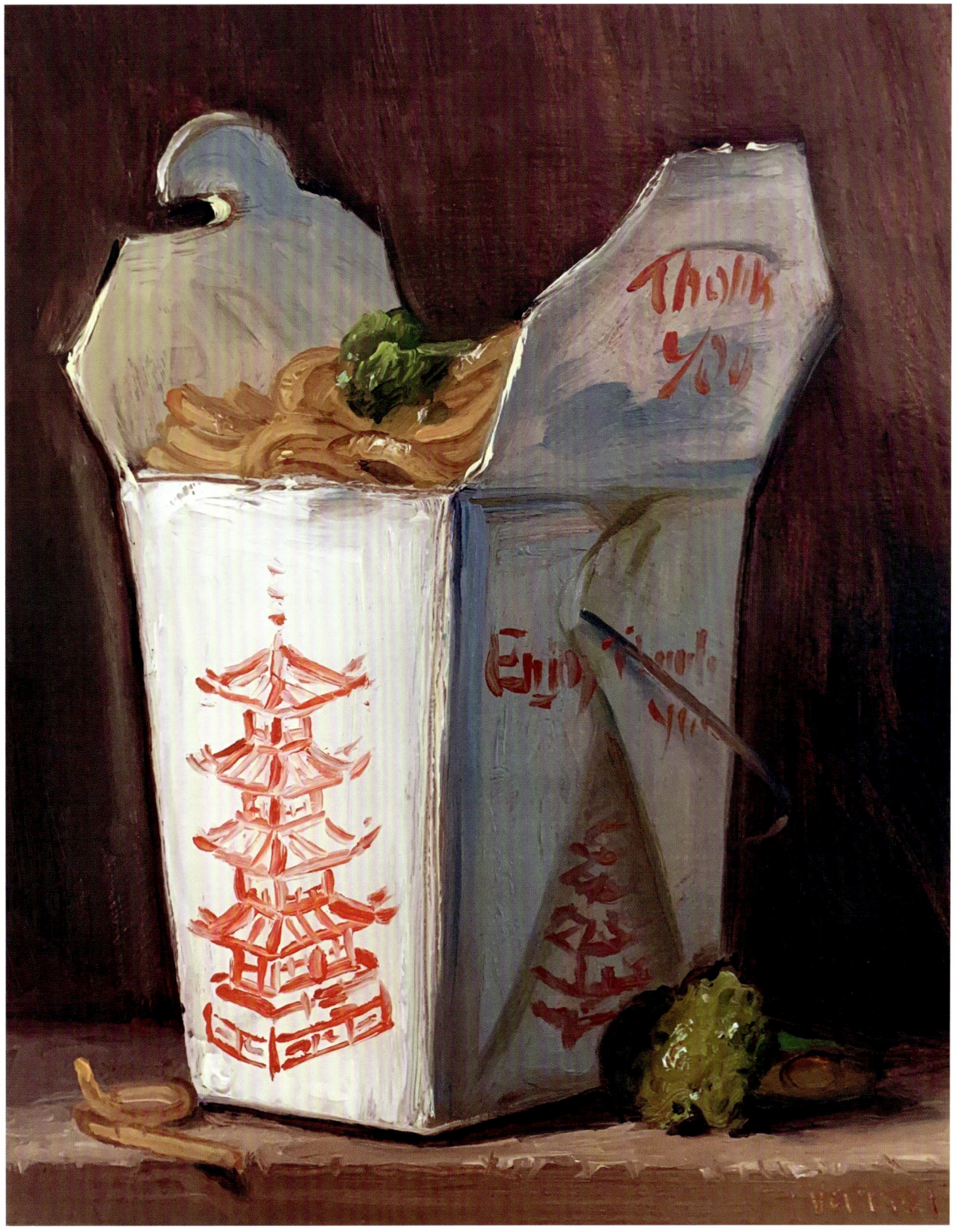

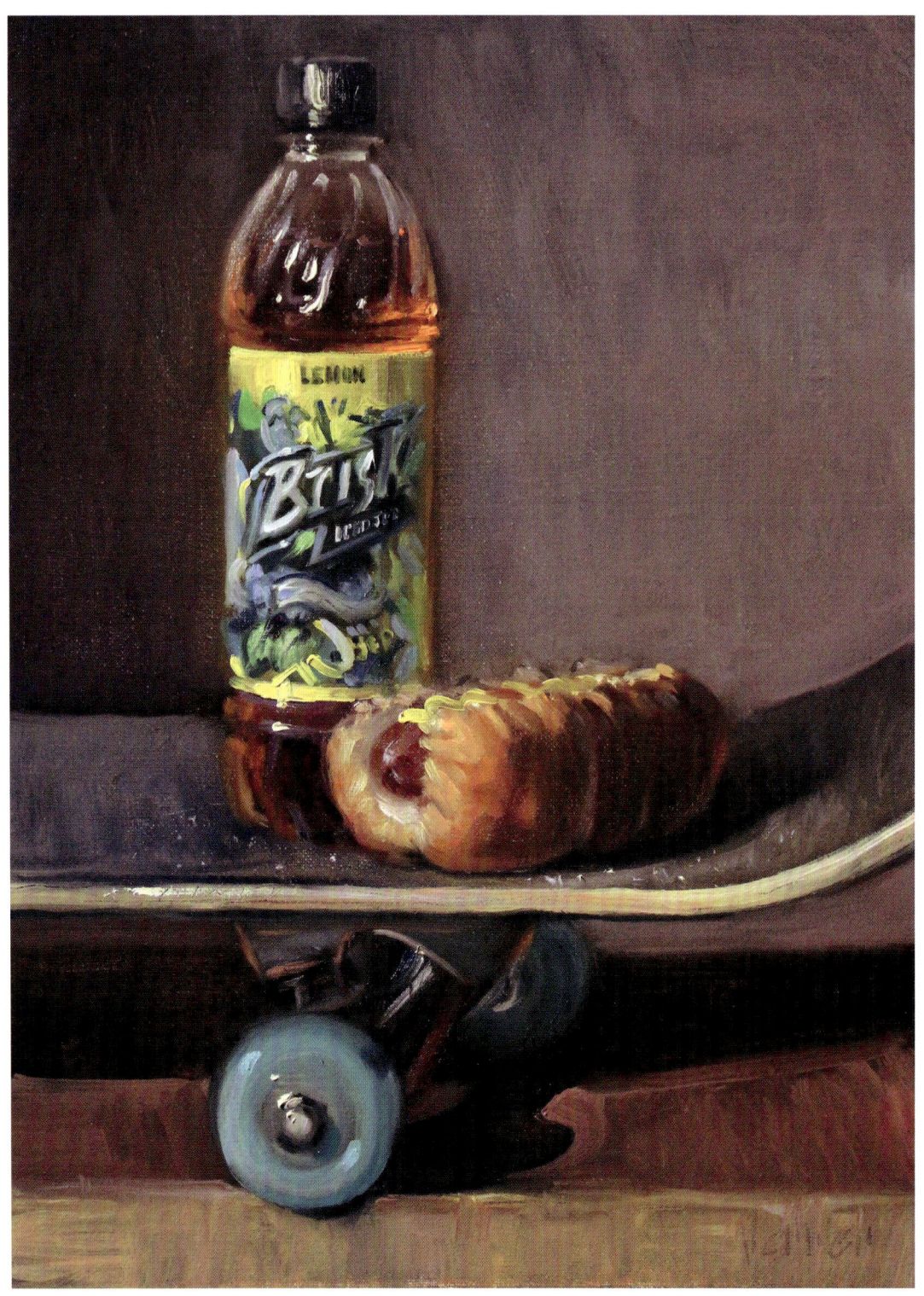

Brisk Tea & Hot Dog

11 x 14 in.

OPPOSITE PAGE:

Wonder Bread

9 x 12 in.

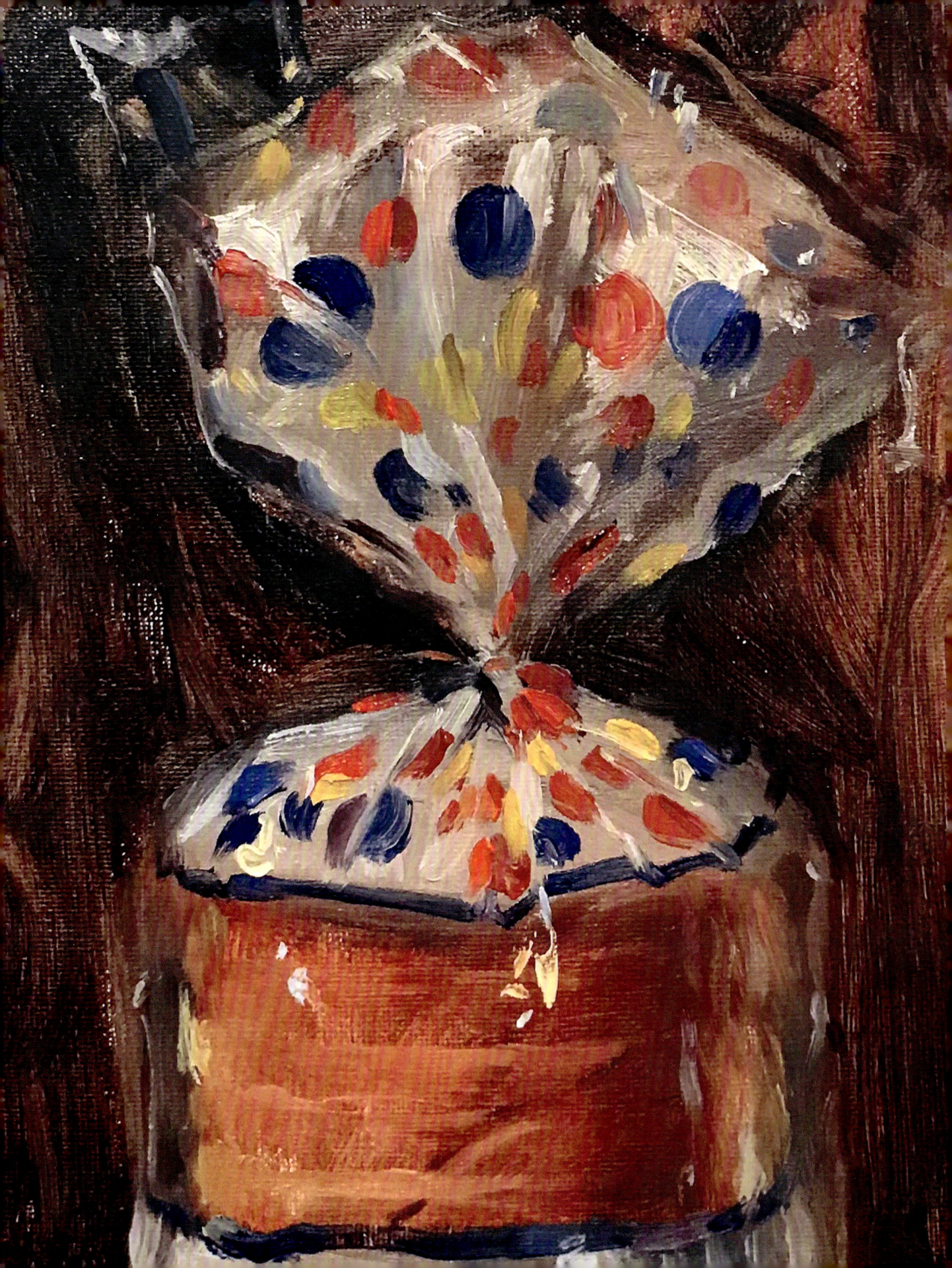

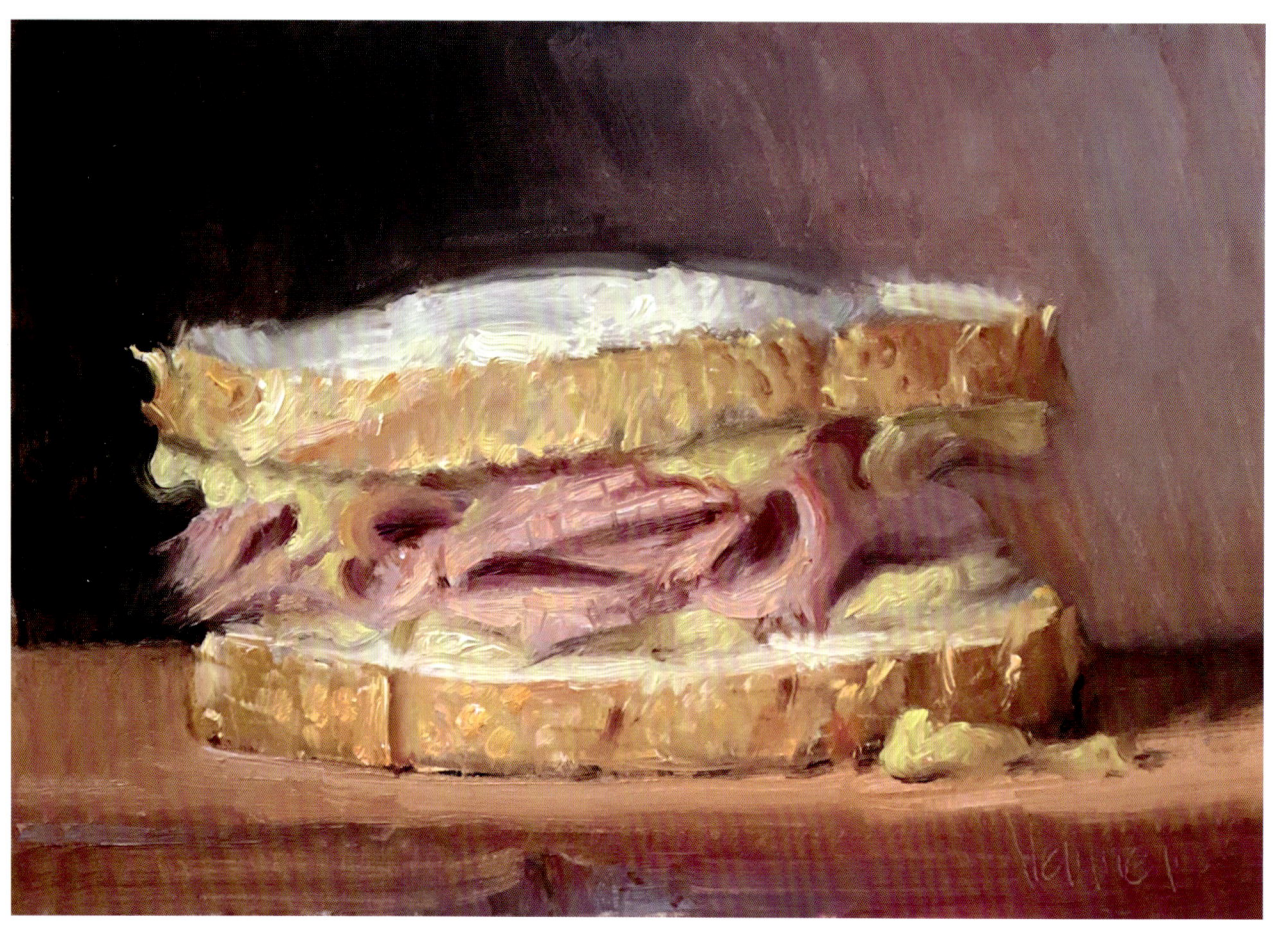

Corned Beef Sandwich

10 x 8 in.

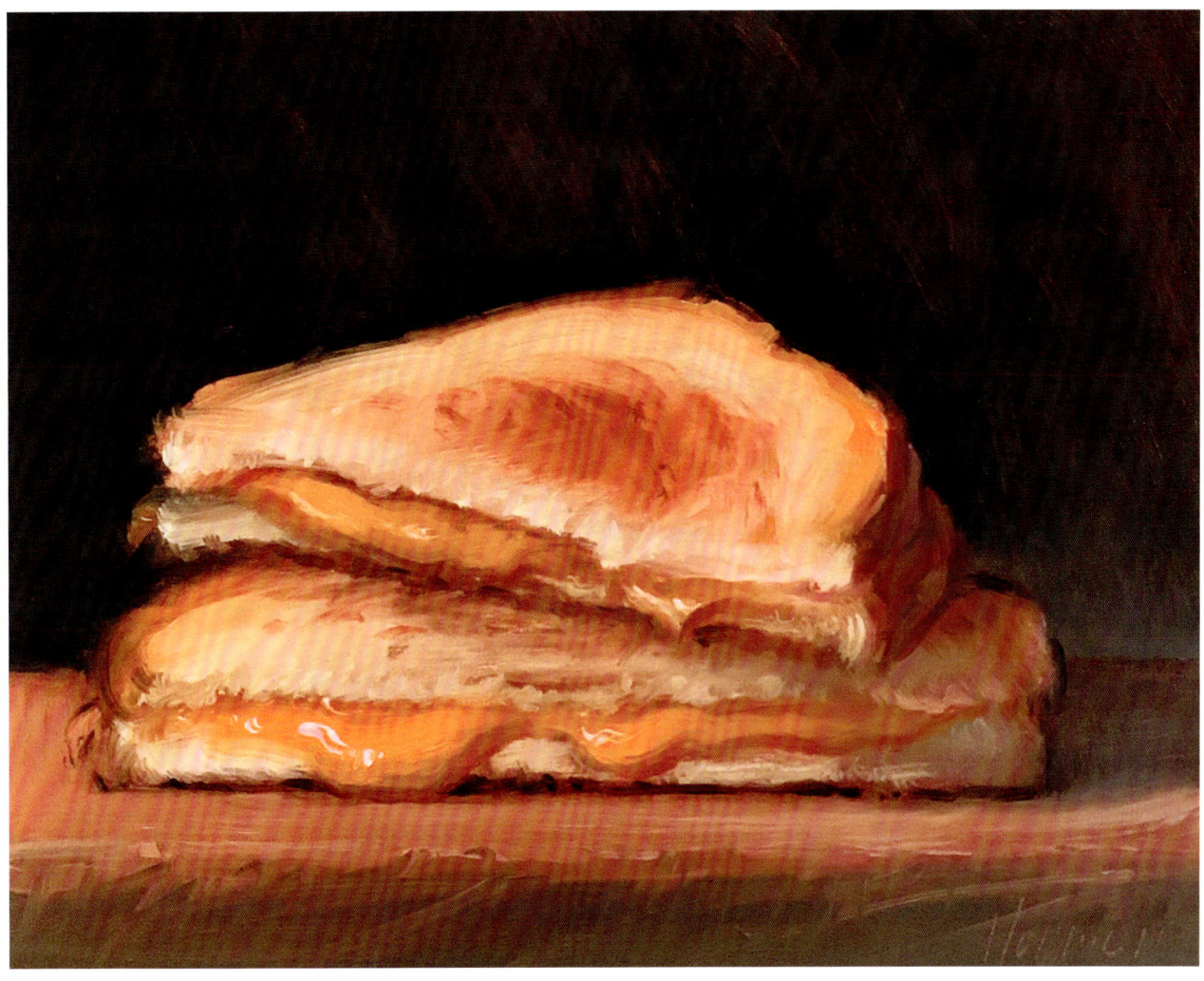

Grilled Cheese
10 x 8 inches

Grilled Cheese by Cole Bleu

This grilled cheese painting is a love letter to post-party diner culture. Nothing hits harder after a night of dancing (and maybe one too many tequila shots) than a slutty little grilled cheese—golden, gooey, and totally unbothered. And the cheese drip? It makes me relive that moment of relief. That exact moment when you slide into a vinyl booth in West LA at 2 AM, eyeliner smudged, heart pounding, and order the one thing that never lets you down. It's my favorite feeling. This painting IS my favorite feeling.

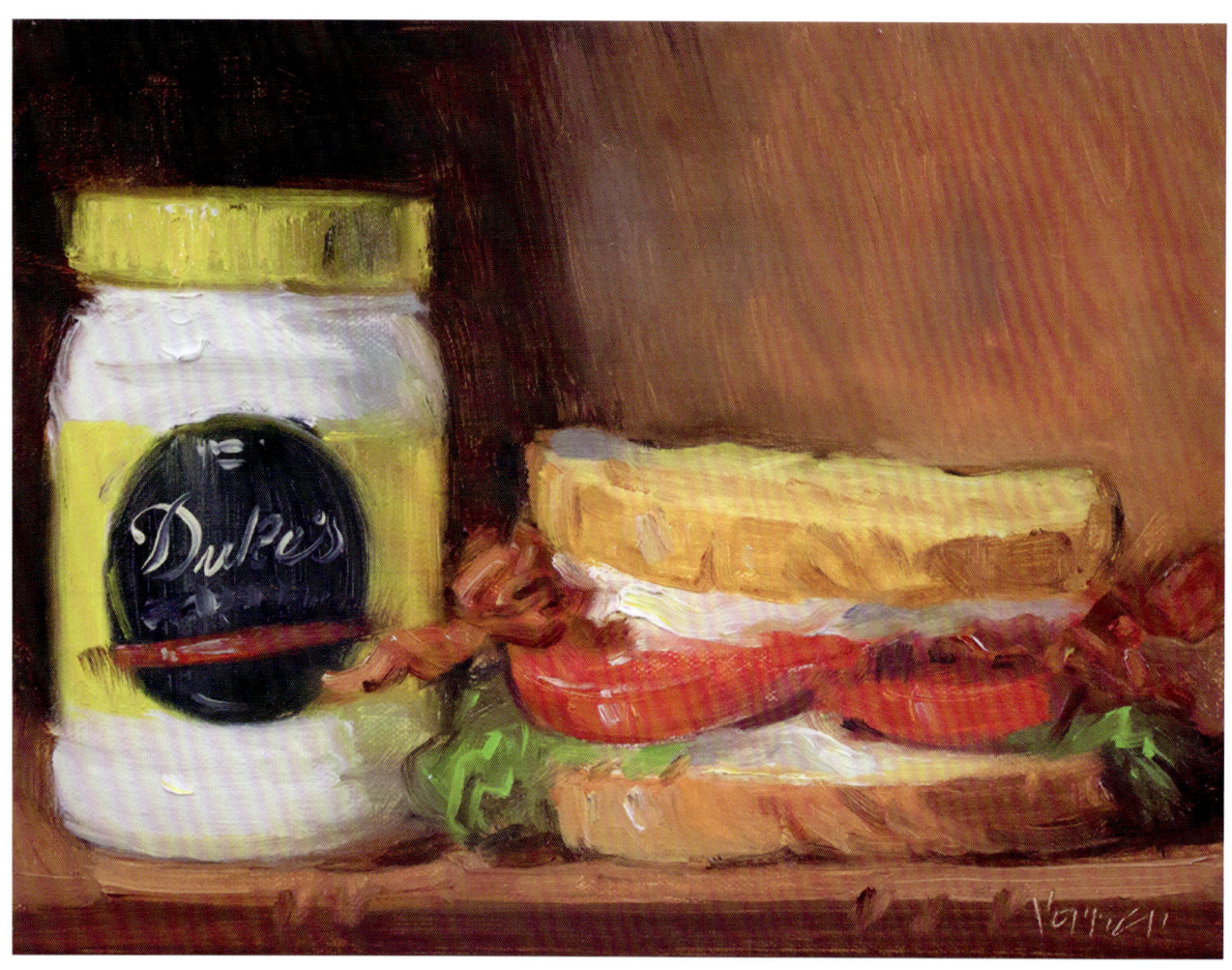

Duke's BLT

12 x 9 in.

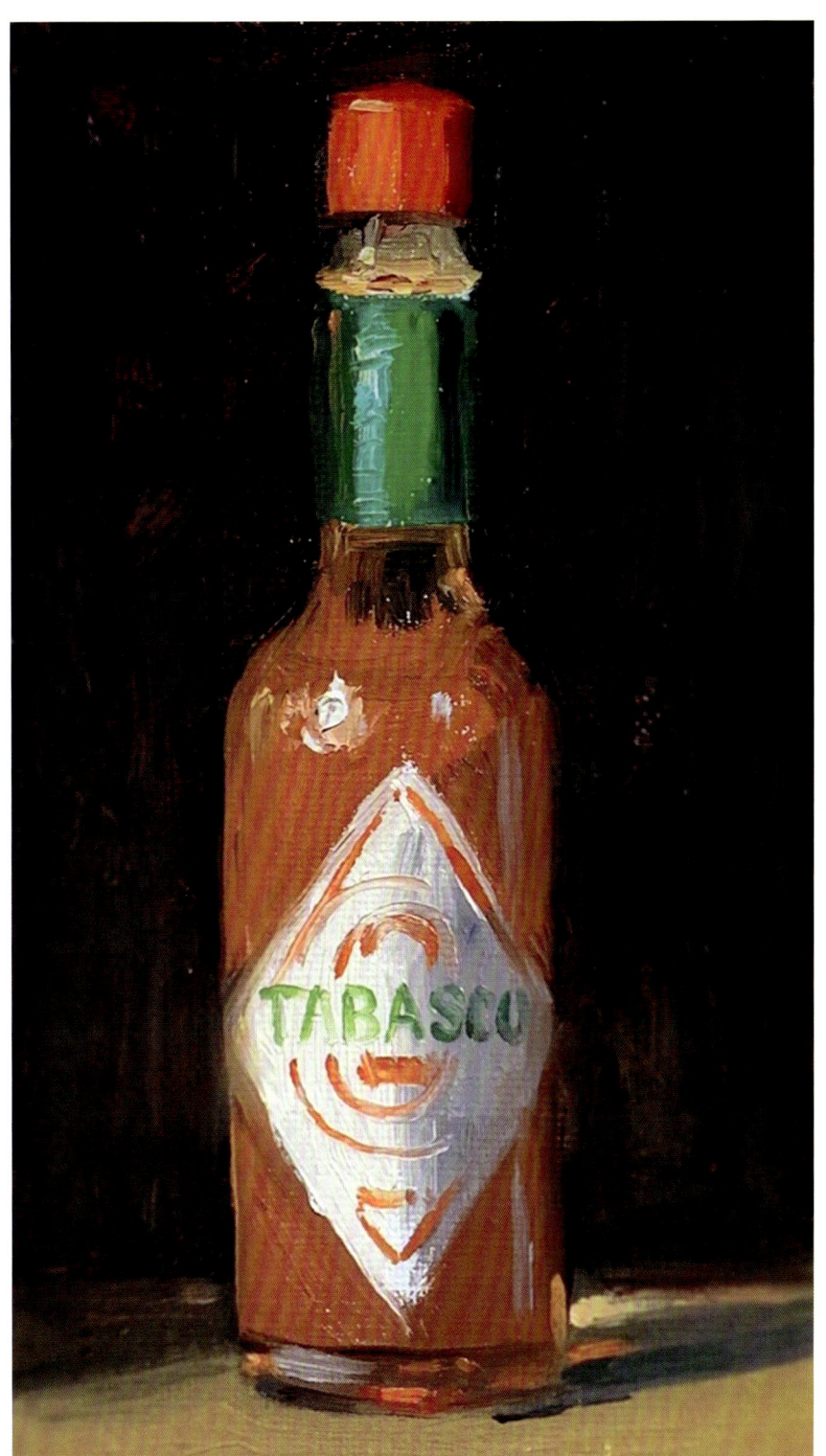

Tabasco
7 x 9 in.

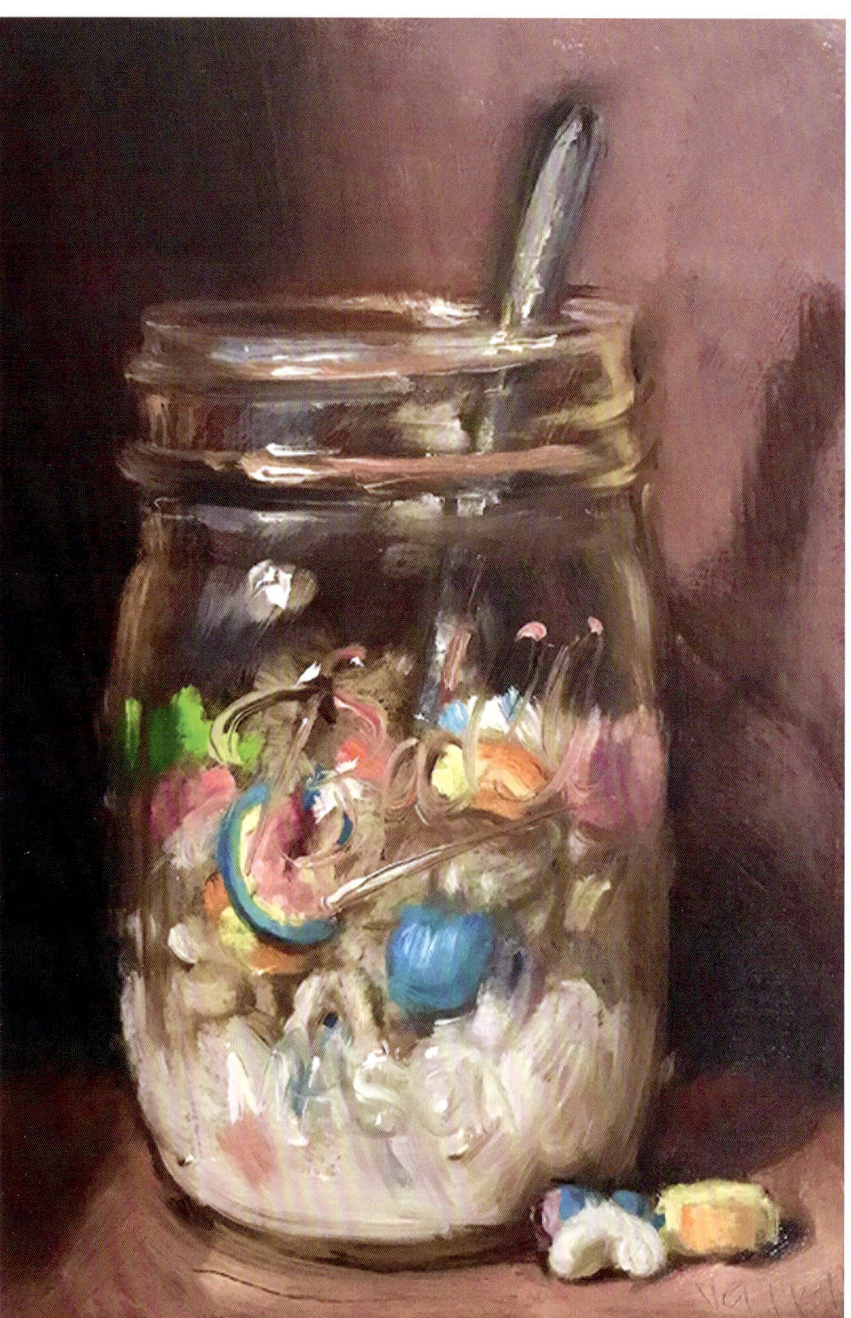

Lucky Charms by Mel Thompson

*My breakfast, lunch, and dinner when I'm over it. It's been a **week**, and joy matters more than fiber. The milk makes it a balanced meal, right? The painting bottled up my childhood nostalgia with grown-up apathy, and somehow, that combo feels like self-care.*

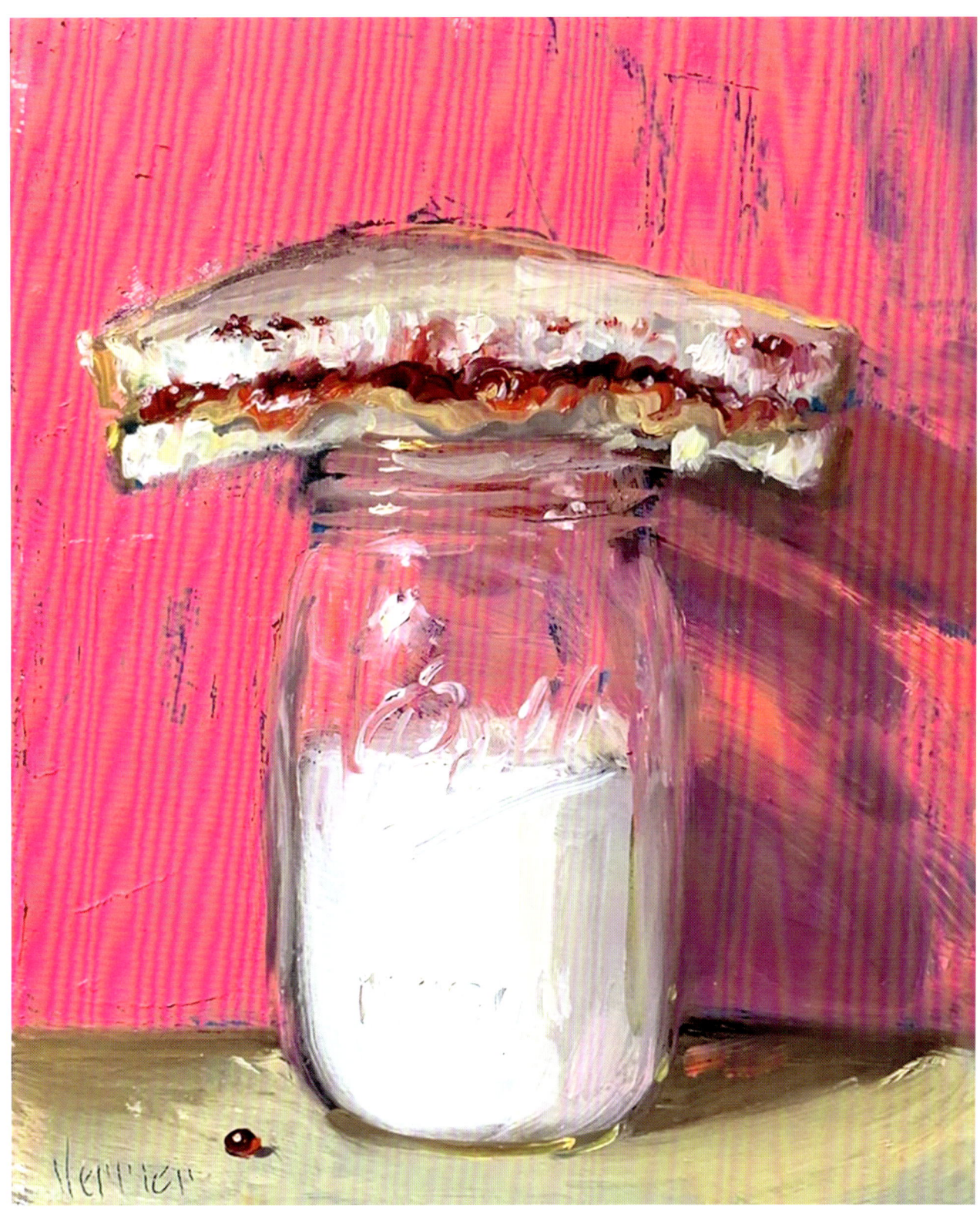

PB&J & Jar of Milk (Pink & Gold)
18 x 24 in.

BOOZE AND BEVVIES

*One of my **favorite** things about painting drinks is the unique can designs and the shiny glassware involved. I also like the fact that I can partake in a little drink before or after.*

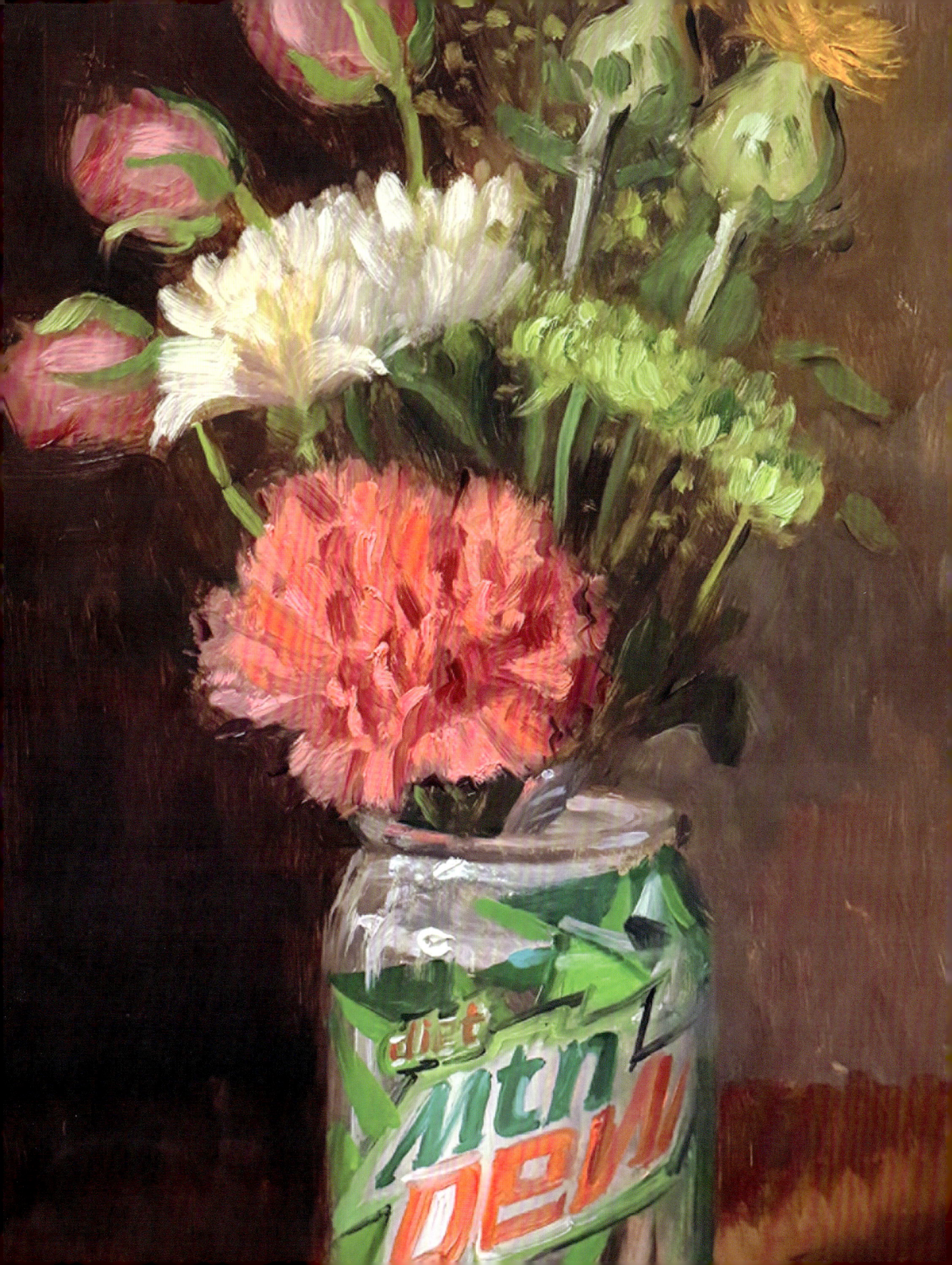

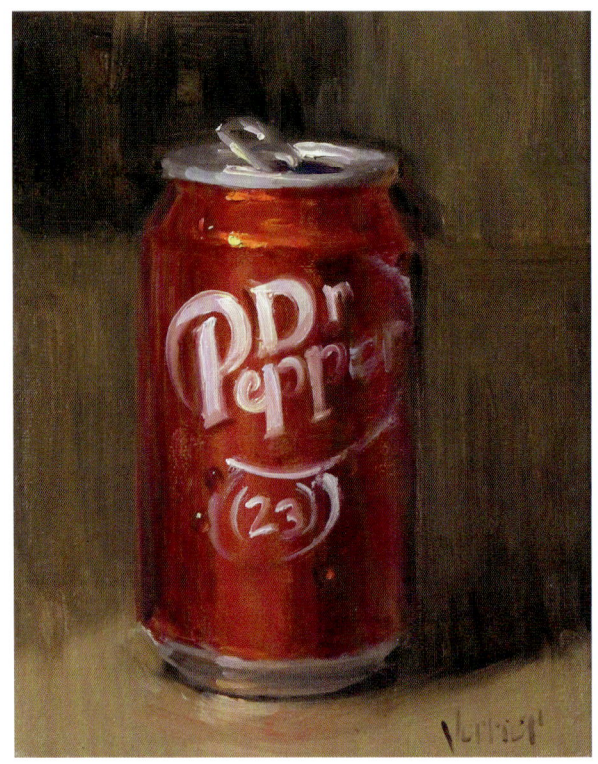

Dr. Pepper 8 x 10 in.

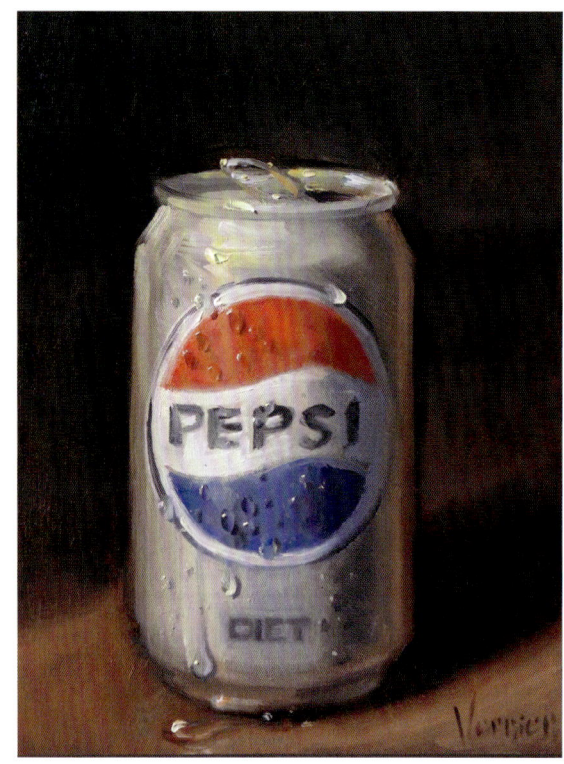

Diet Pepsi 8 x 10 in.

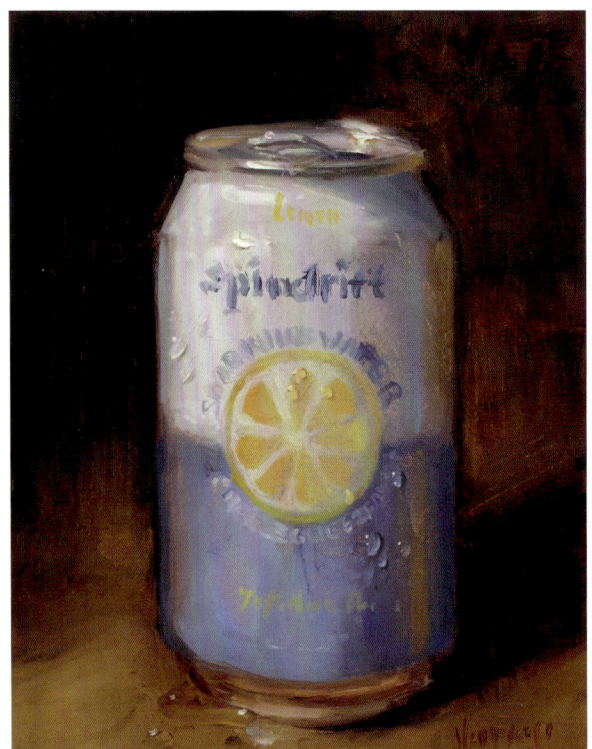

Spindrift 8 x 10 in.

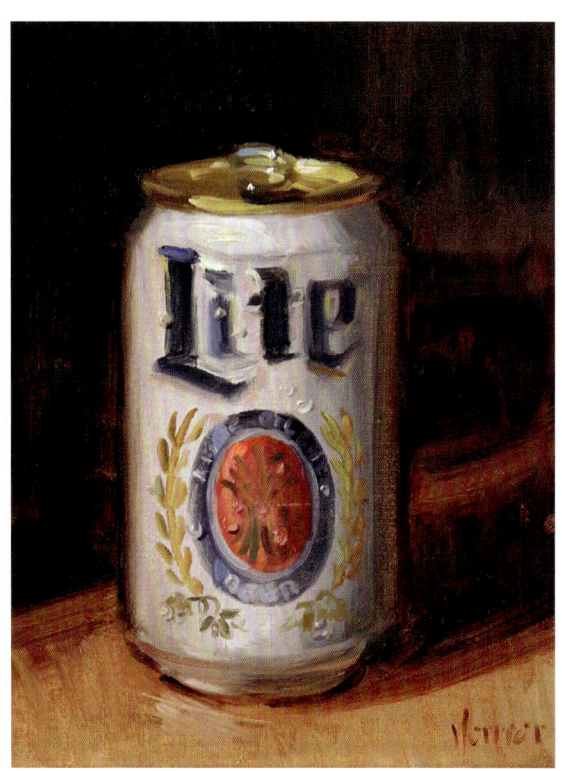

Miller Lite 8 x 10 in.

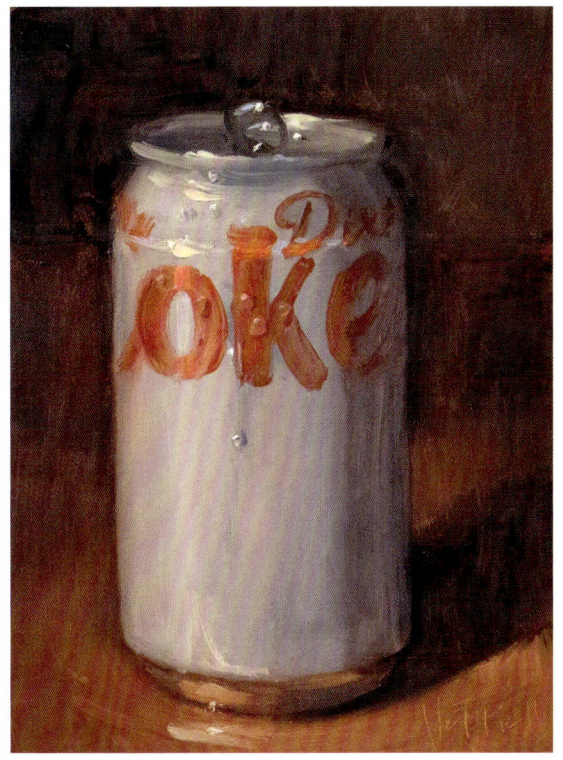

Diet Coke 8 x 10 in.

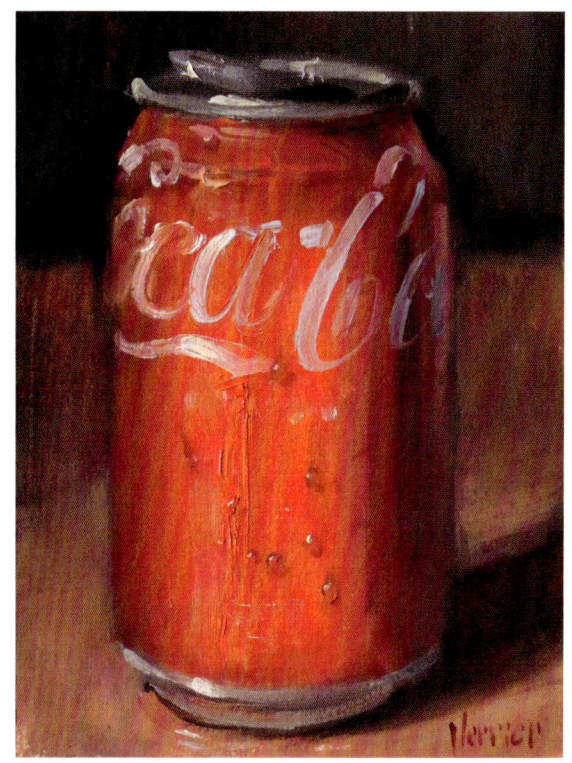

Coke 5 x 7 in.

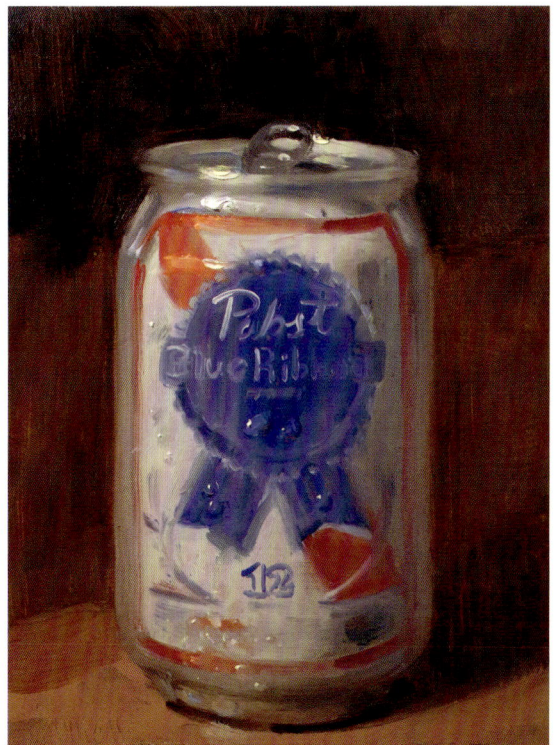

Pabst Blue Ribbon 8 x 10 in.

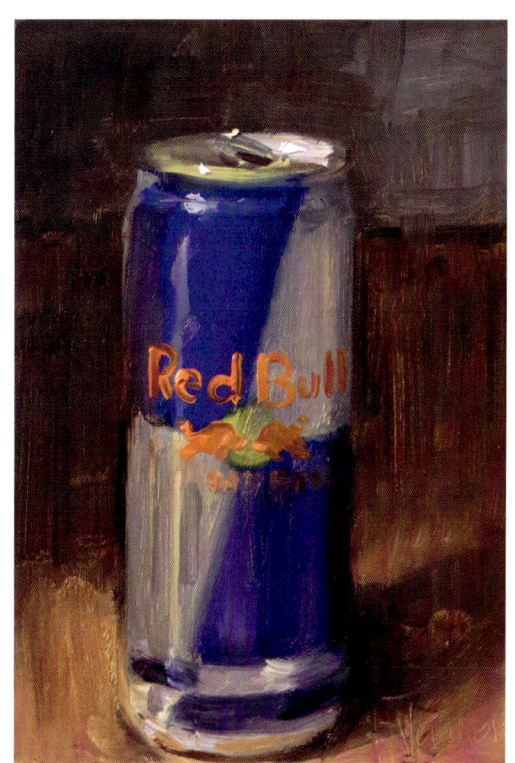

Red Bull 6 x 9 in.

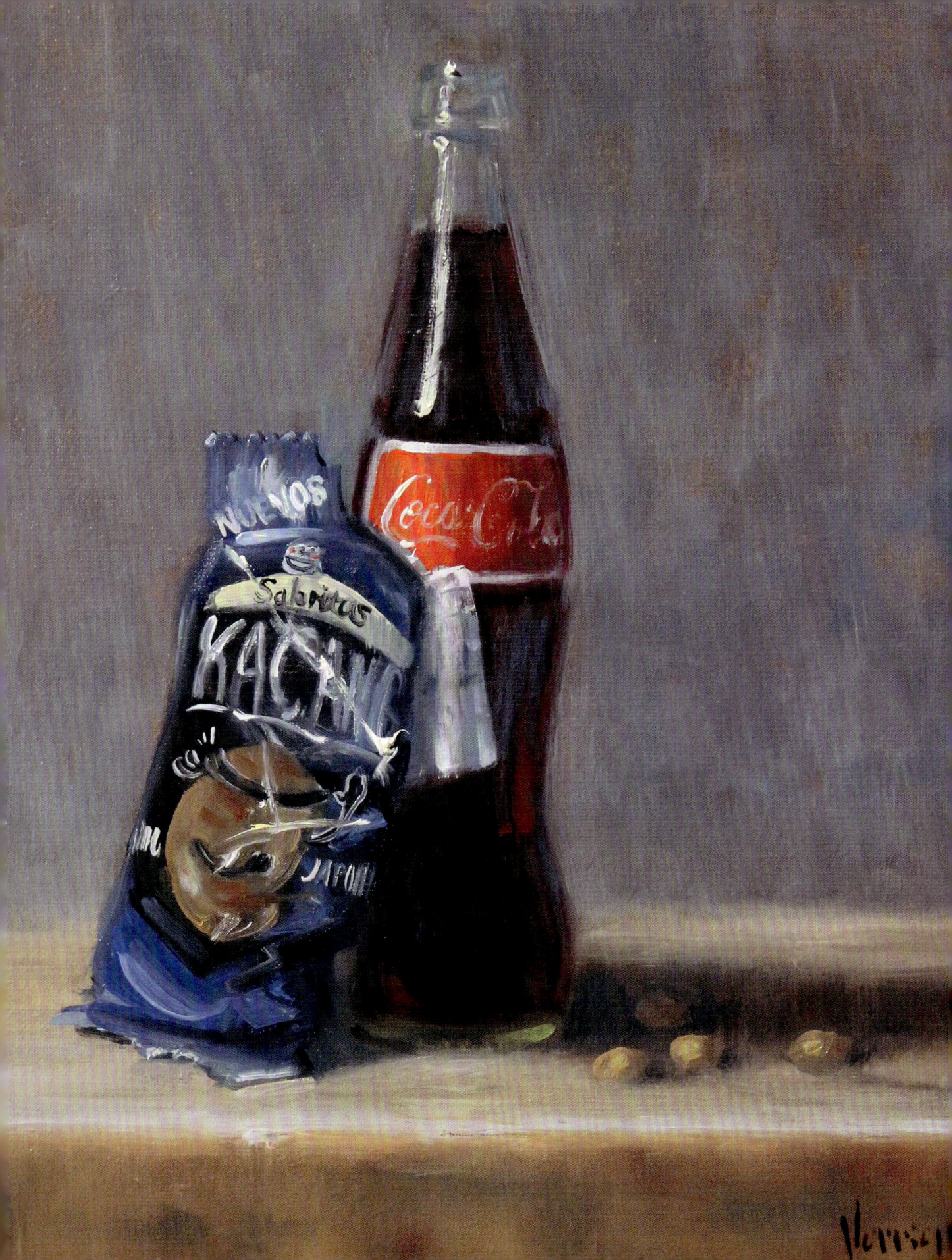

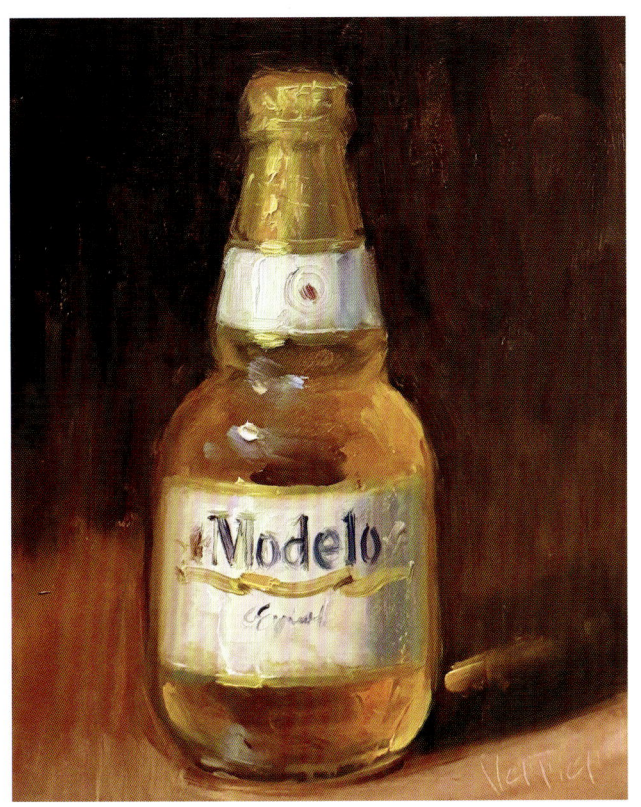

Modelo
8 x 10 in.

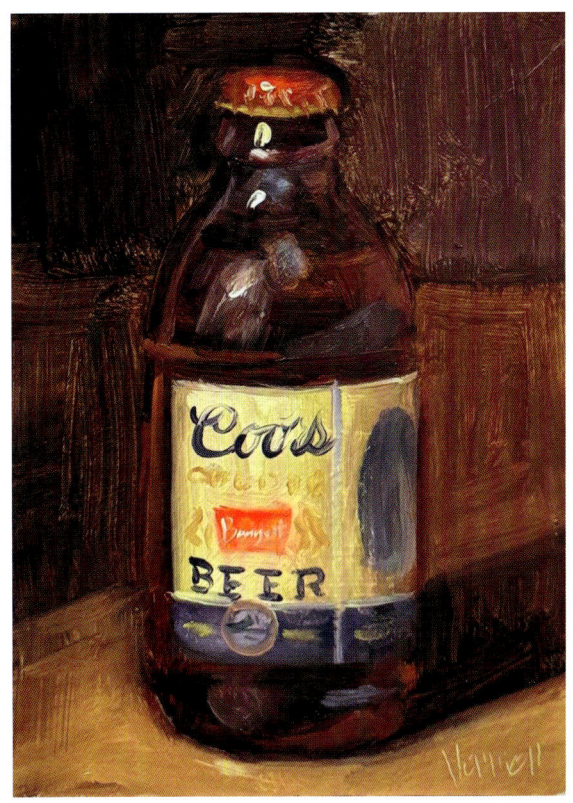

Coors Banquet
8 x 10 in.

OPPOSITE PAGE:
Coke & Nuts
11 x 14 in.

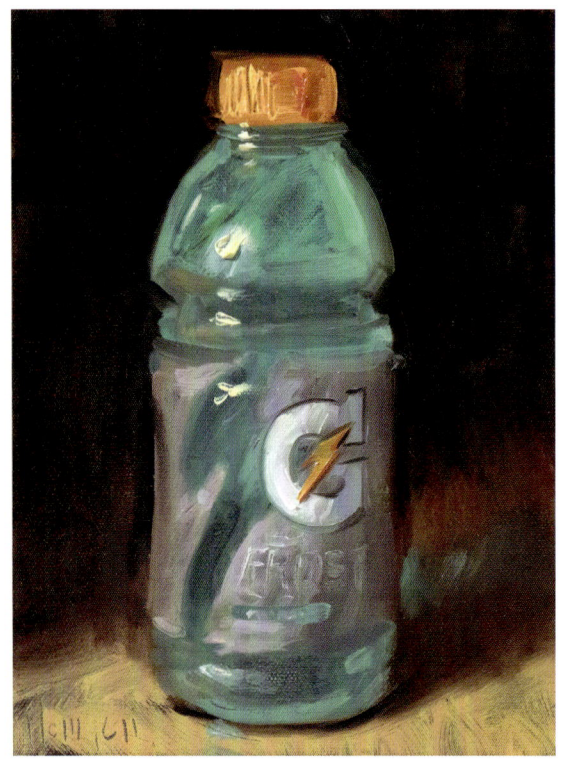

Arctic Blitz Gatorade 8 x 10 in.

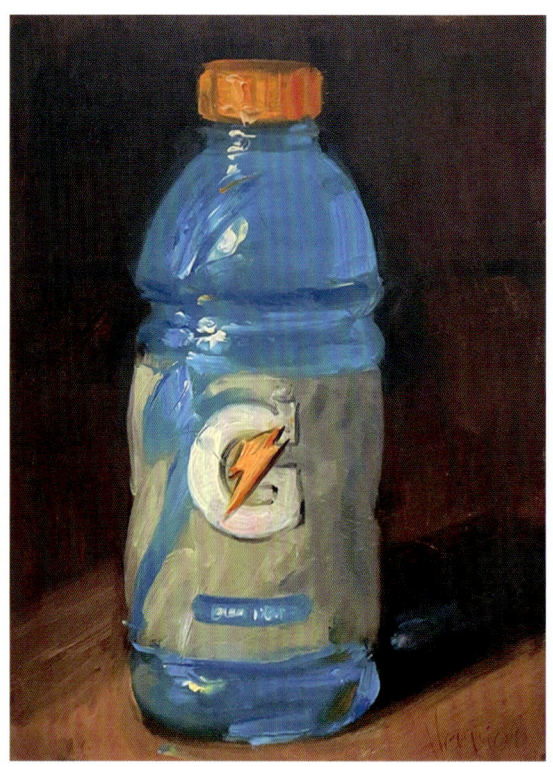

Blue Gatorade 8 x 10 in.

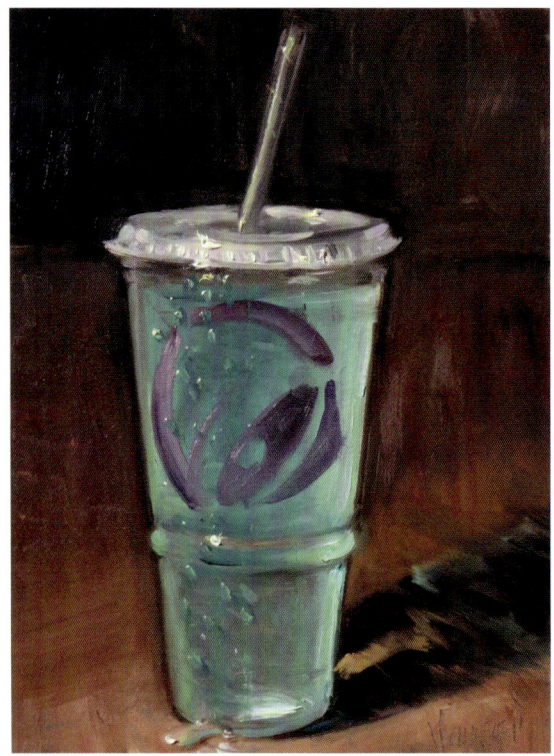

Baja Blast 9 x 10 in.

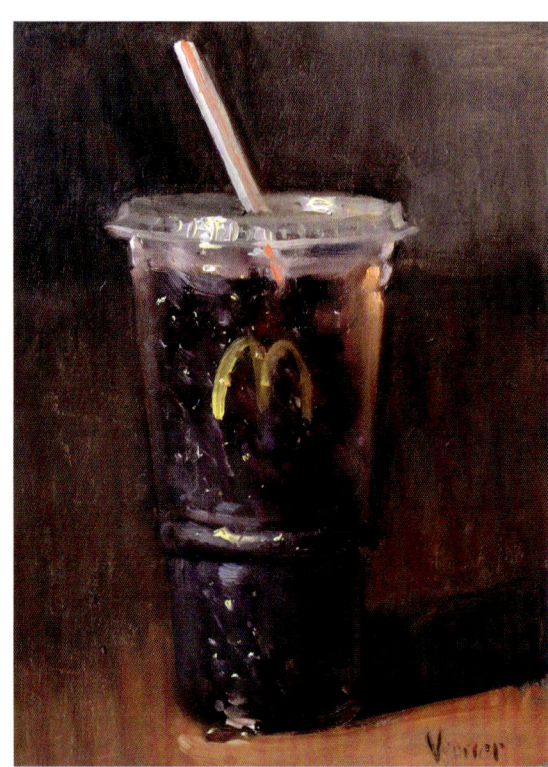

McDonald's Diet Coke 9 x 12 in.

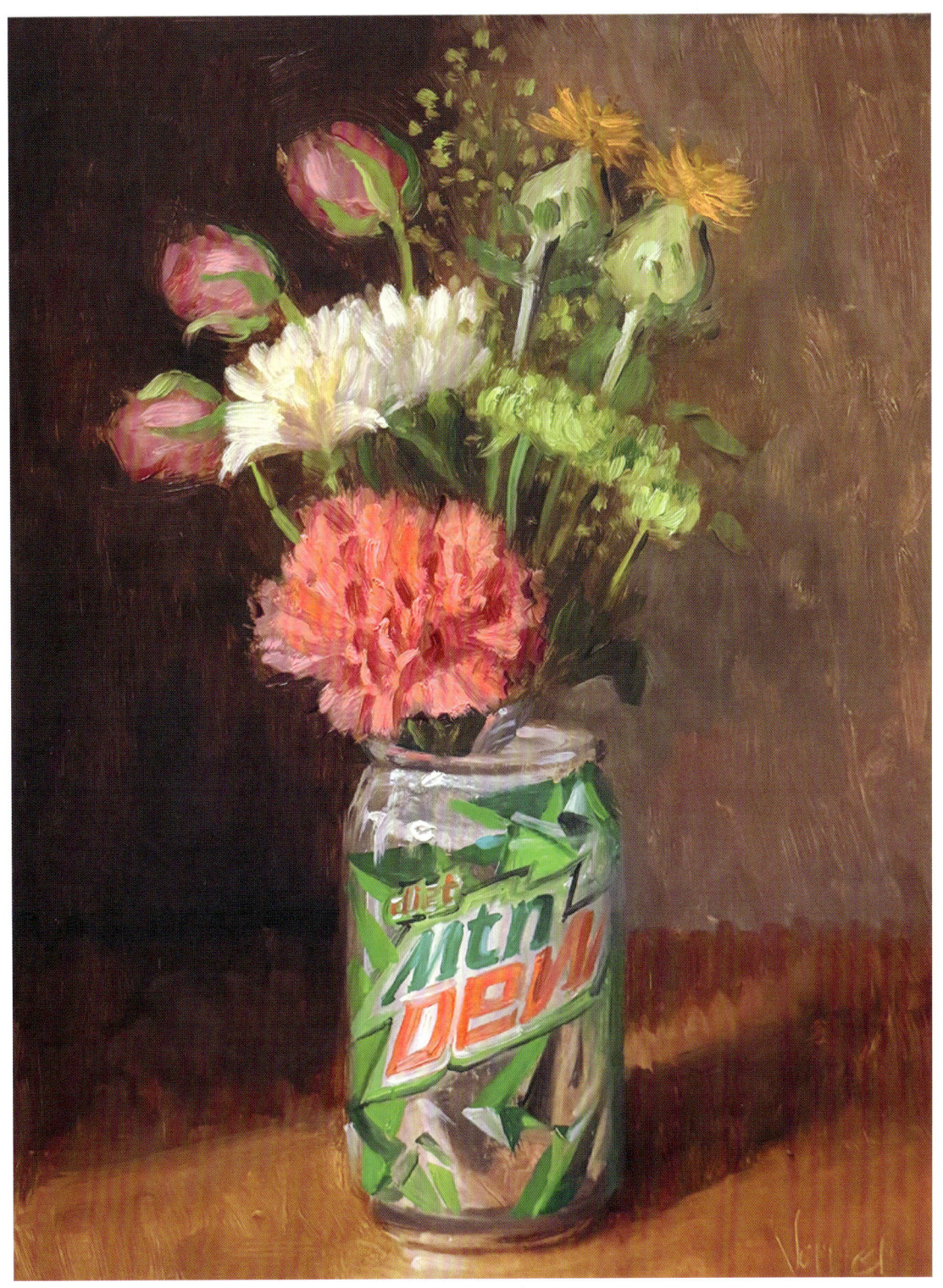

Diet Mountain Dew
8 x 10 in.

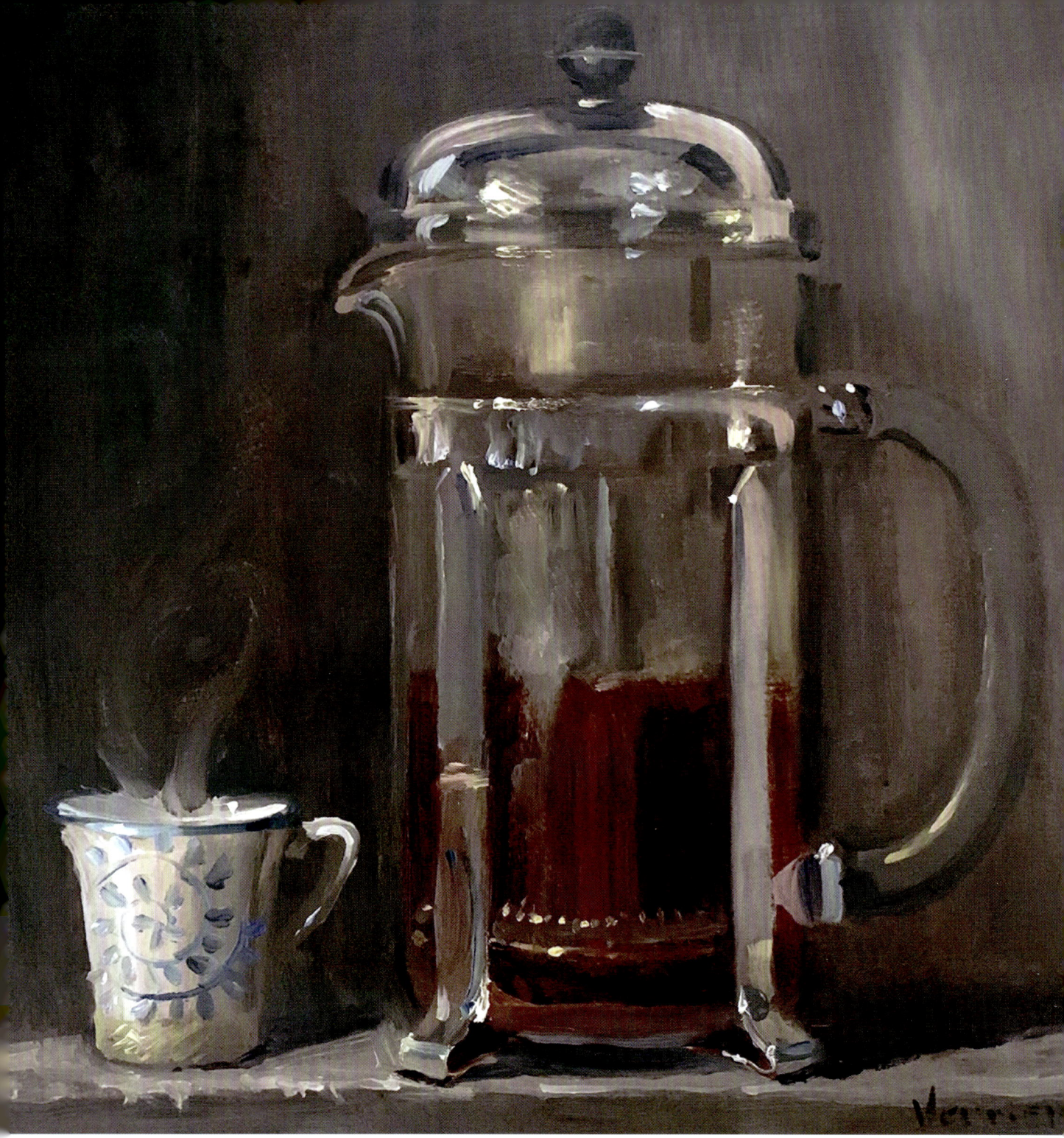

French Press
12 x 12 in.

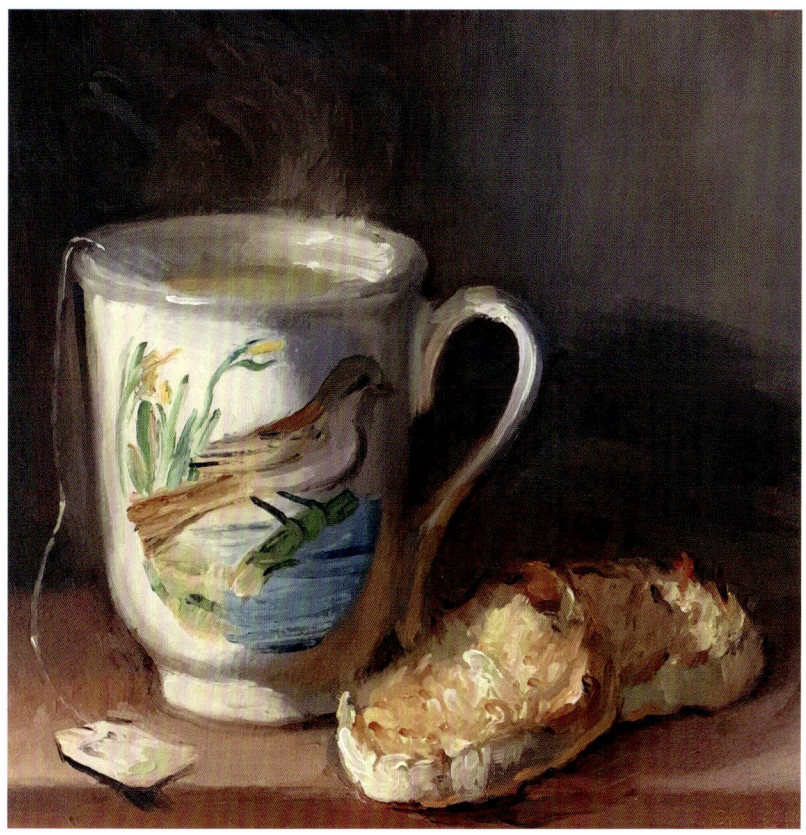

Tea & Crumpets
9 x 9 in.

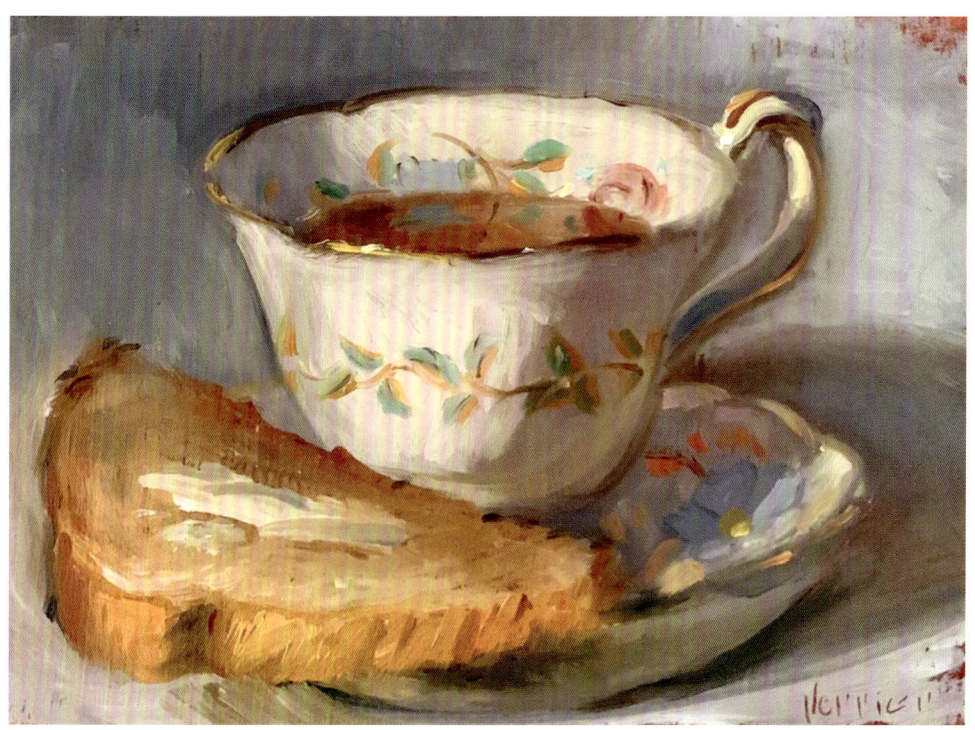

Tea & Toast
9 x 8 in.

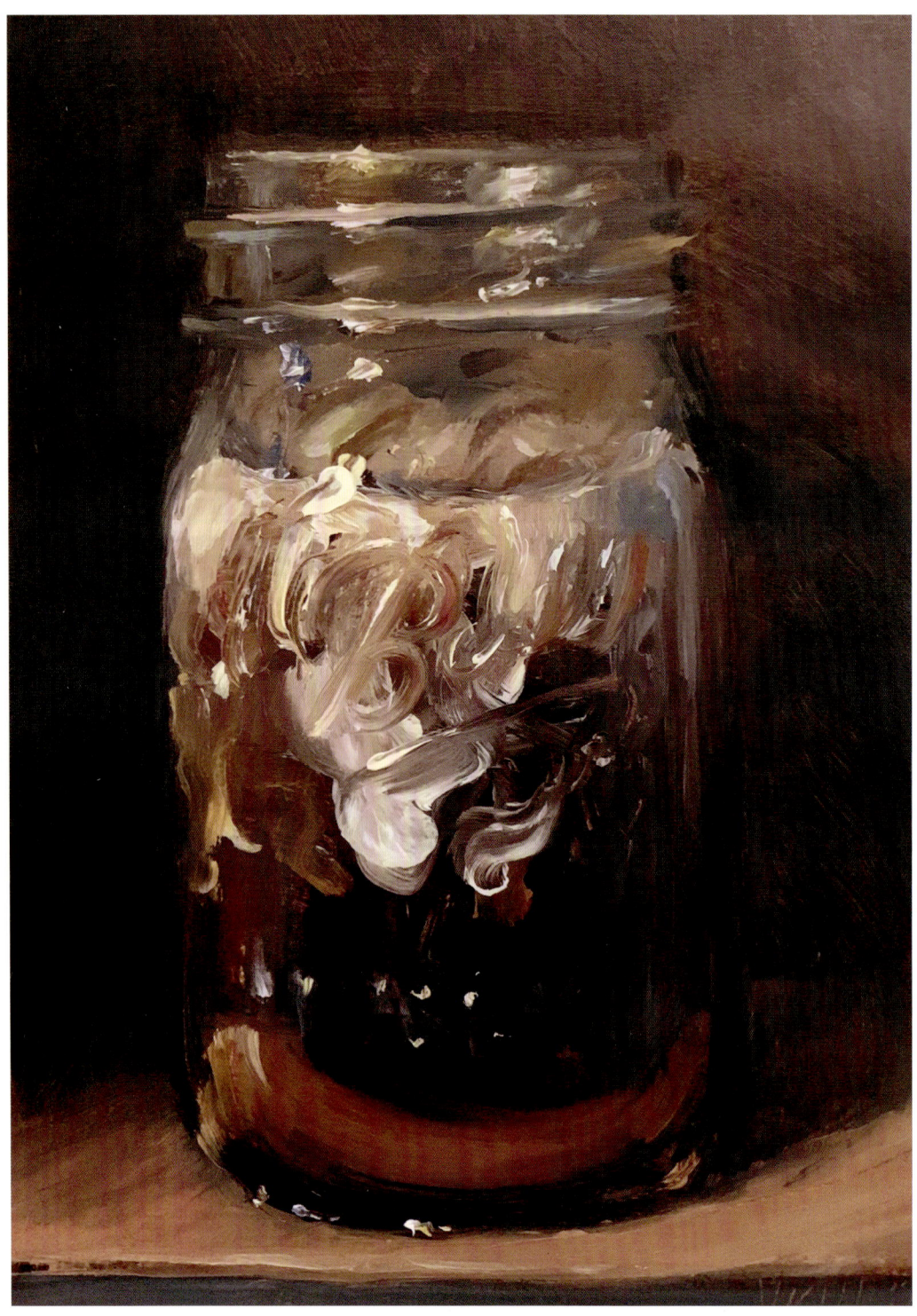

Iced Coffee
8 x 10 in.

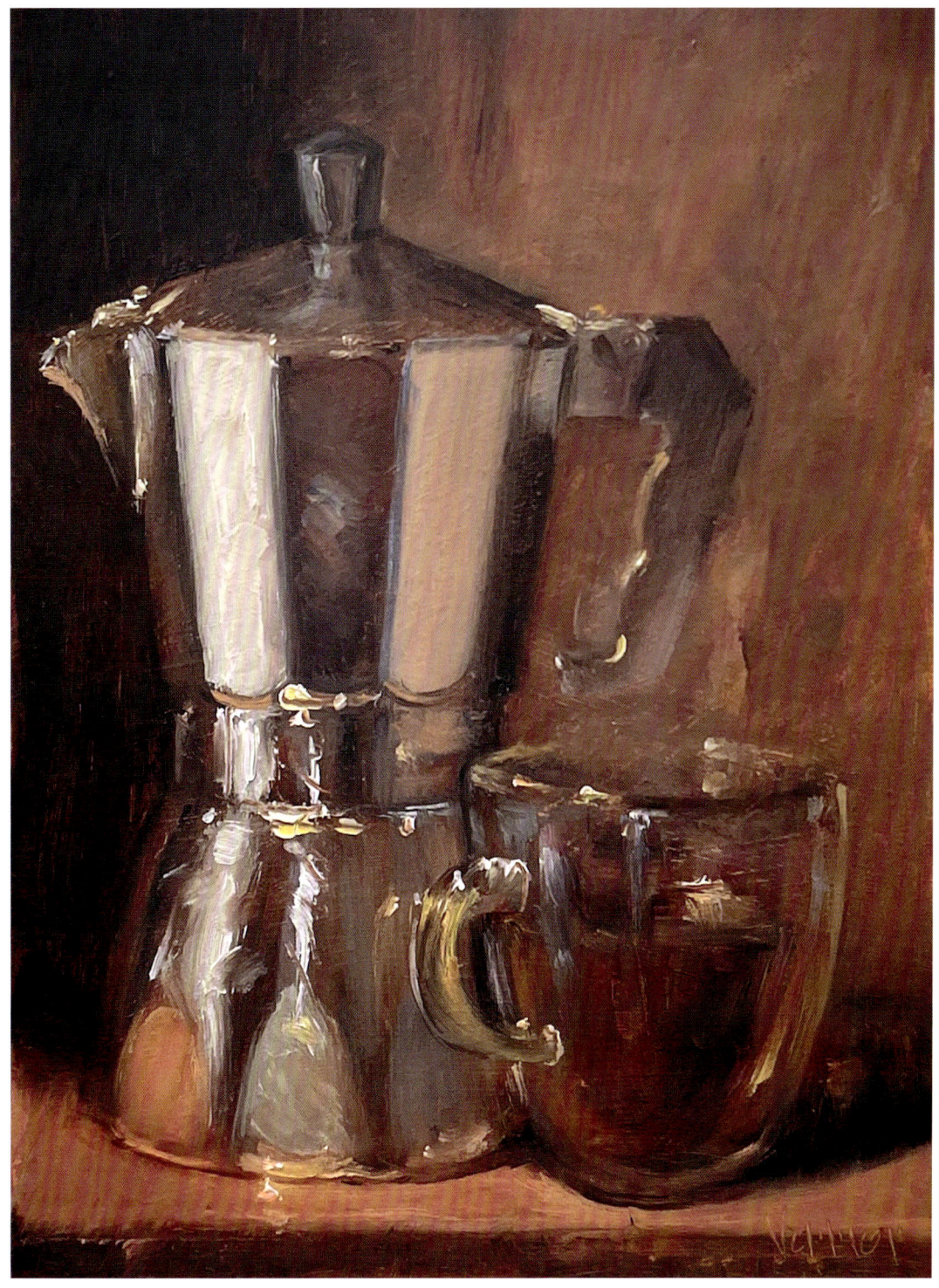

Moka Pot
10 x 12 in.

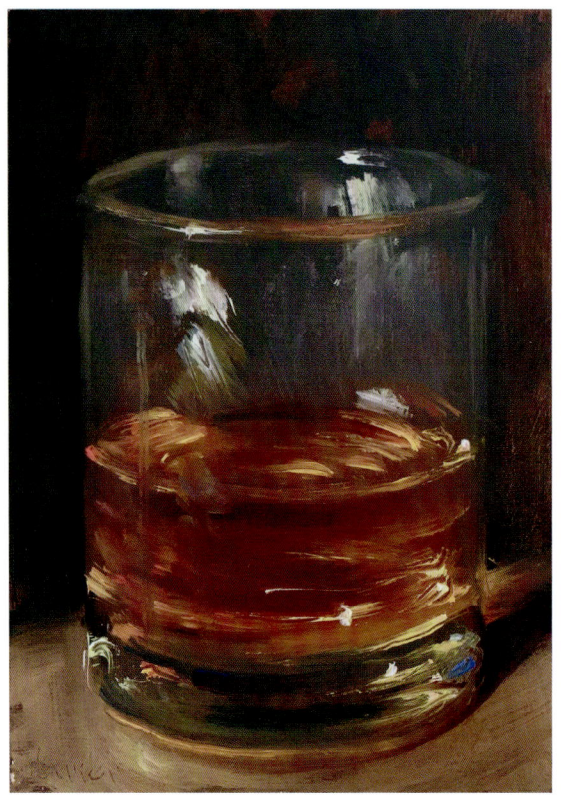

Whiskey
10 x 12 in.

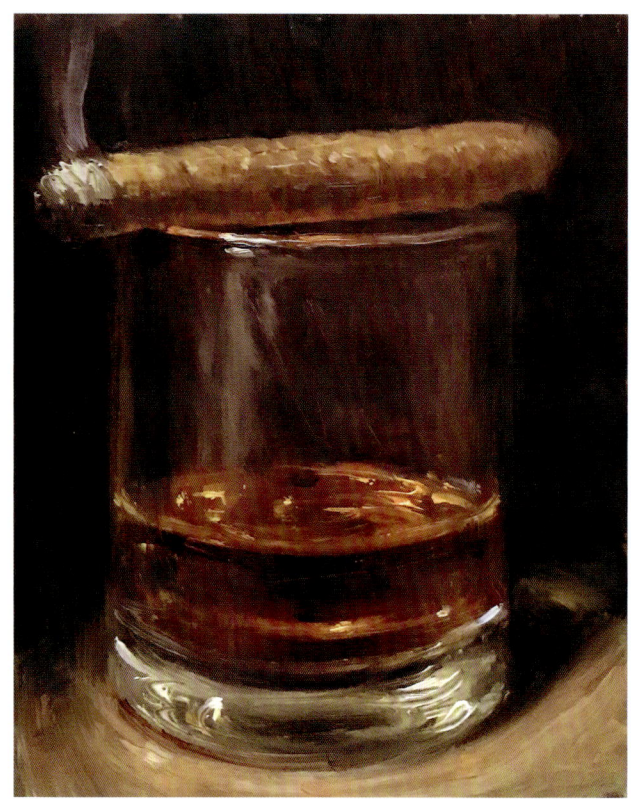

Whiskey with Cigar
10 x 12 in.

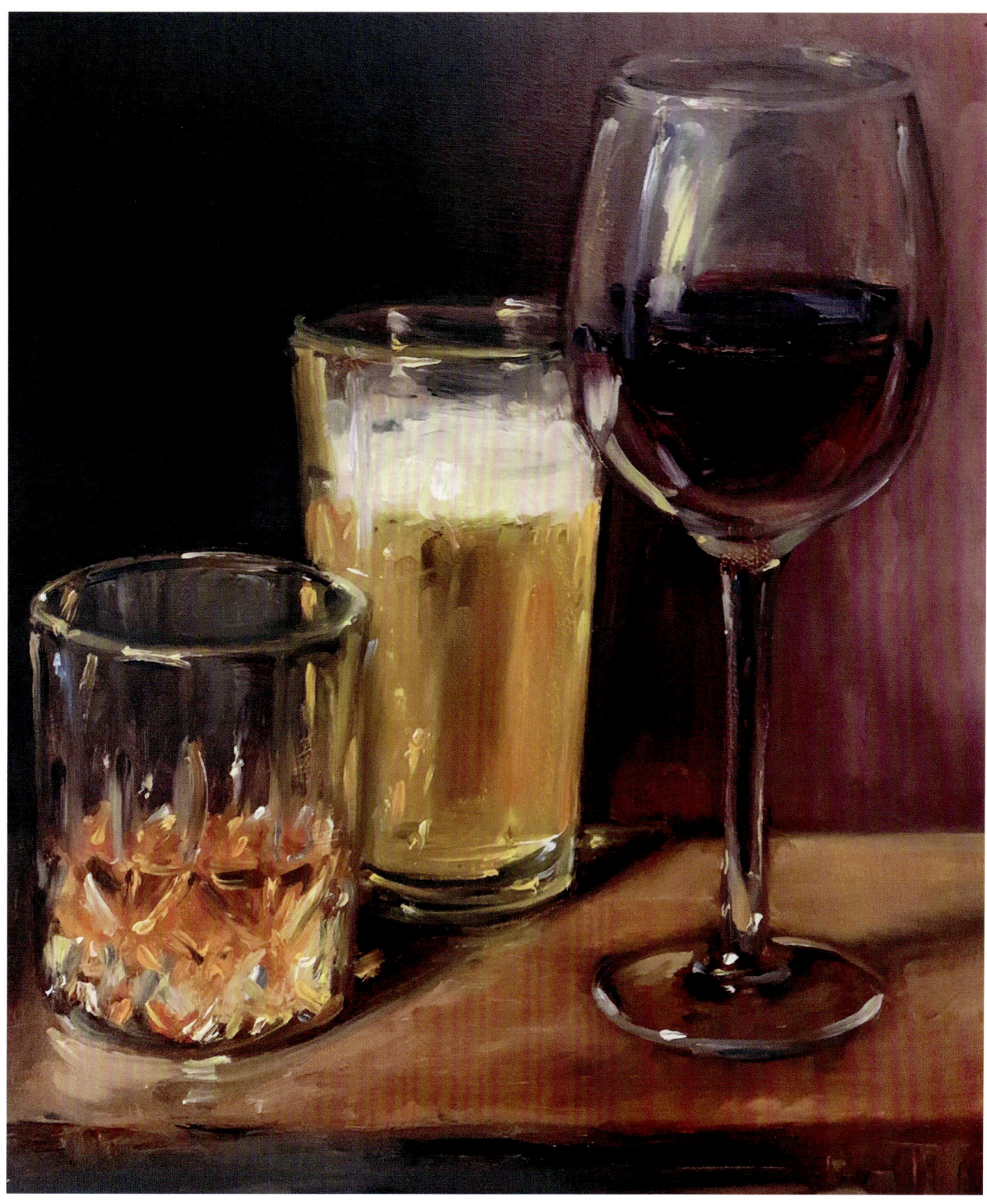

Whiskey, Beer, & Wine
10 x 12 in.

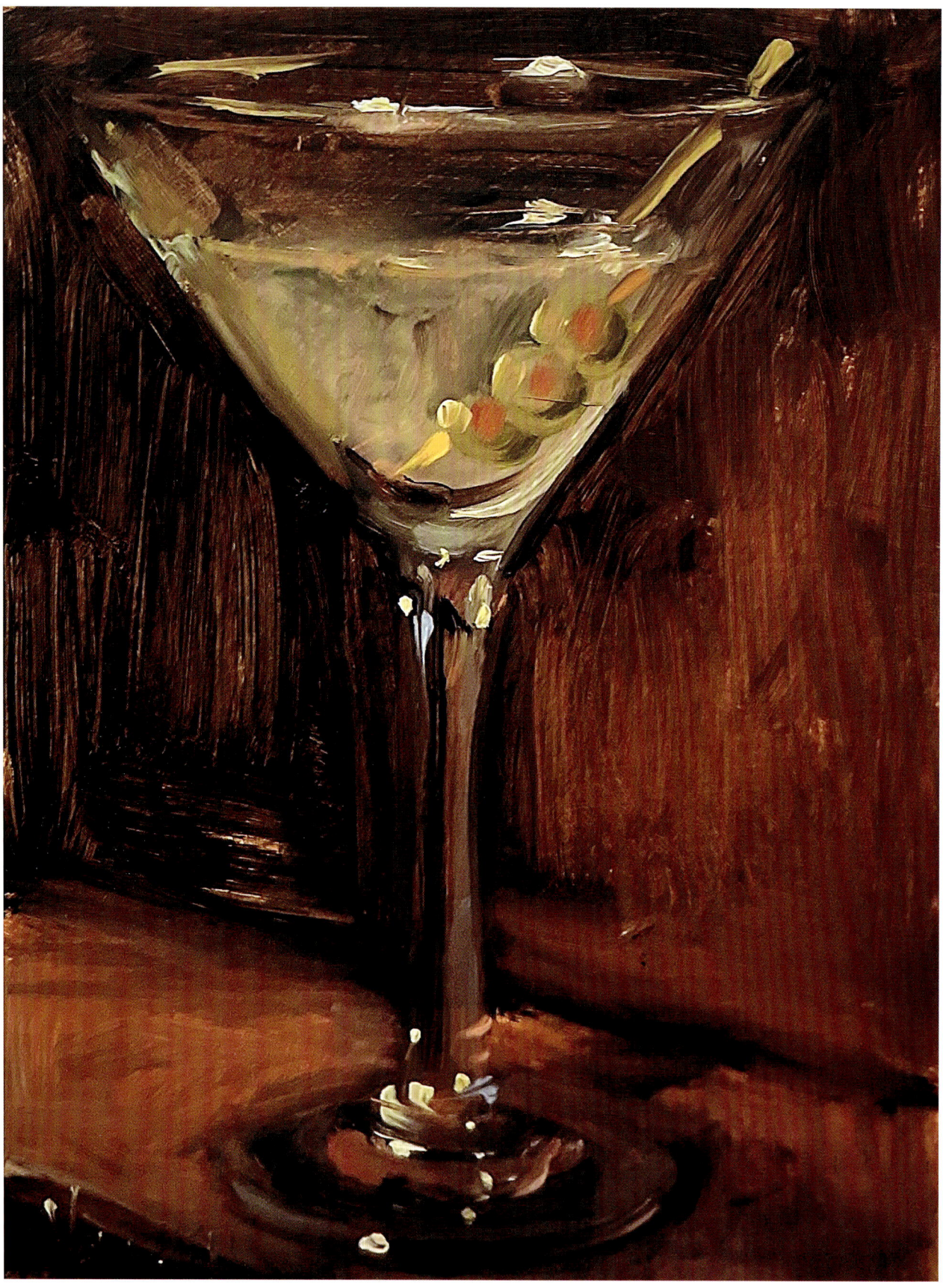

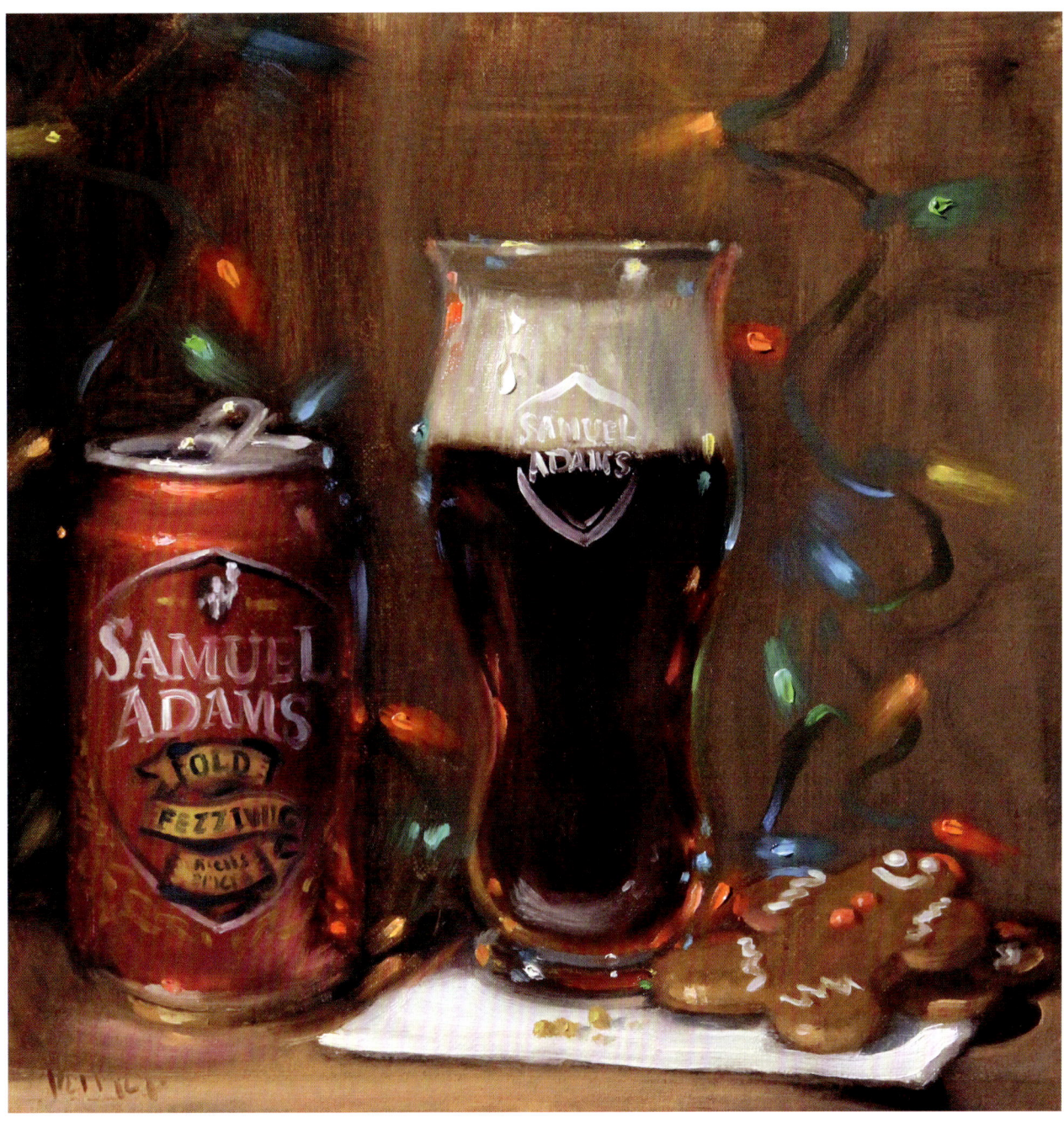

OPPOSITE PAGE:
Martini
10 x 12 in.

Samuel Adams
10 x 12 in.

Samuel Adams Beer   by Elizabeth Verrier

A man-cave must have!

SWEETS AND TREATS

*Desserts are just **waiting** to be painted. They invoke such happiness and are beautiful to look at, often the most colorful of subjects.*

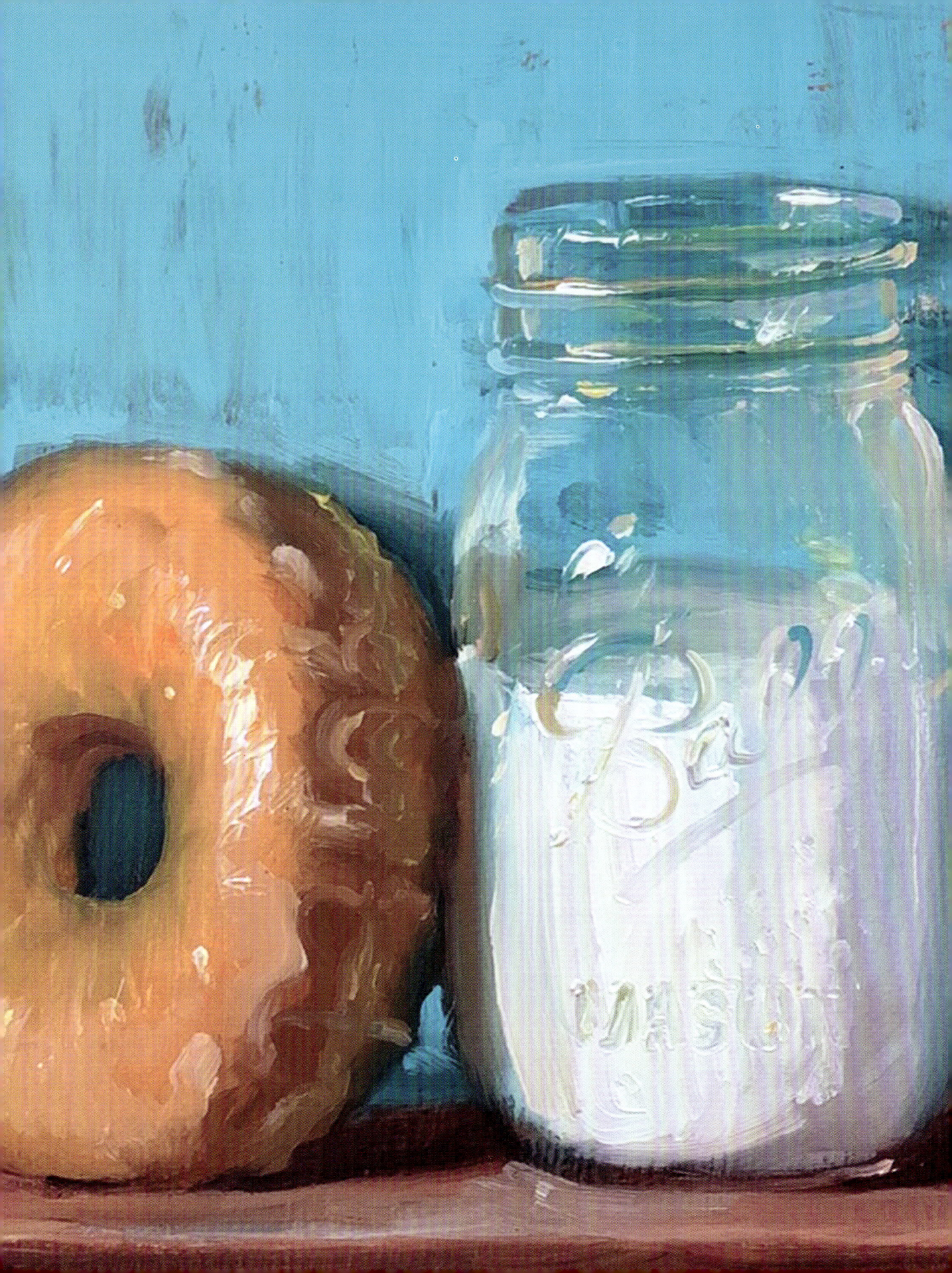

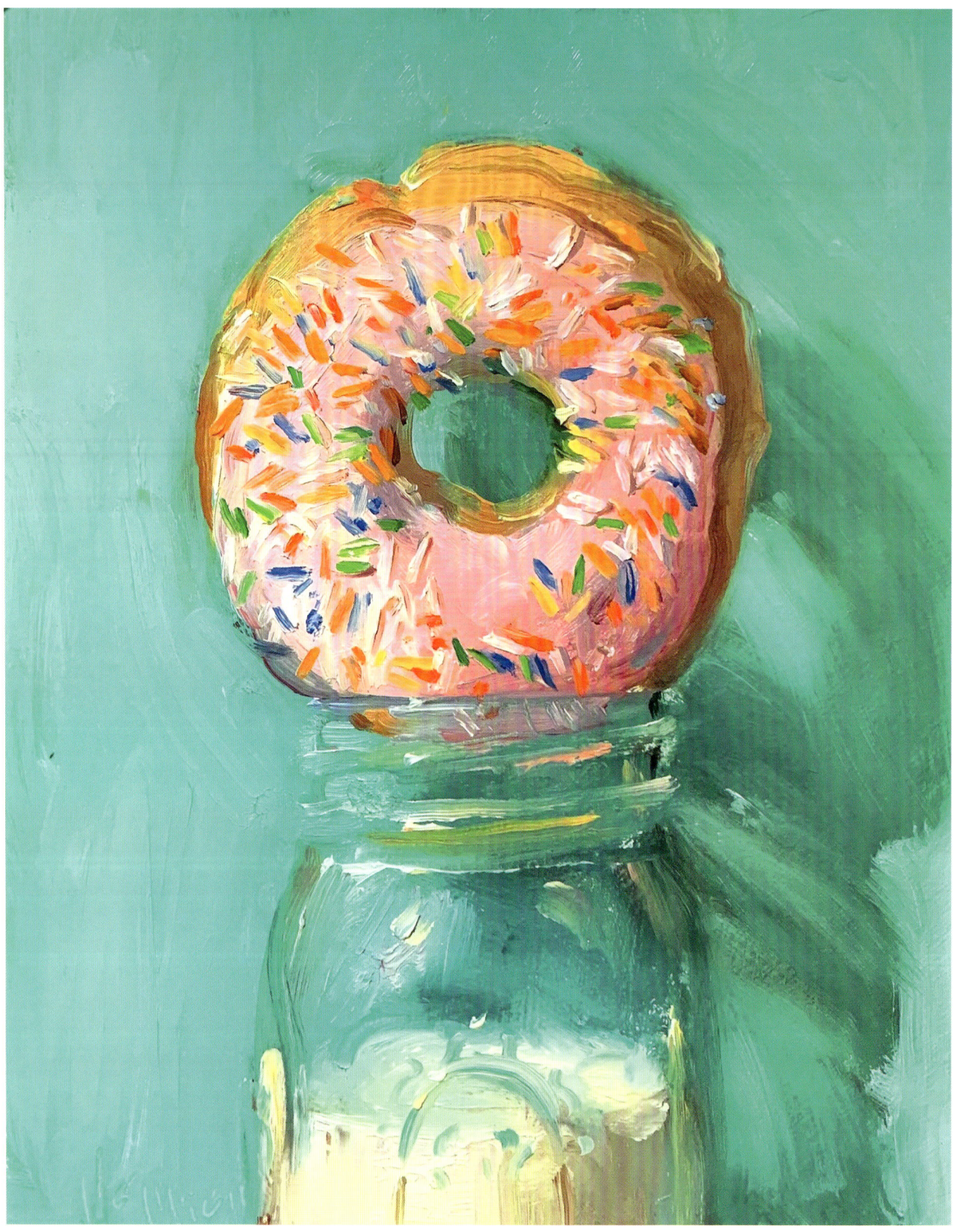

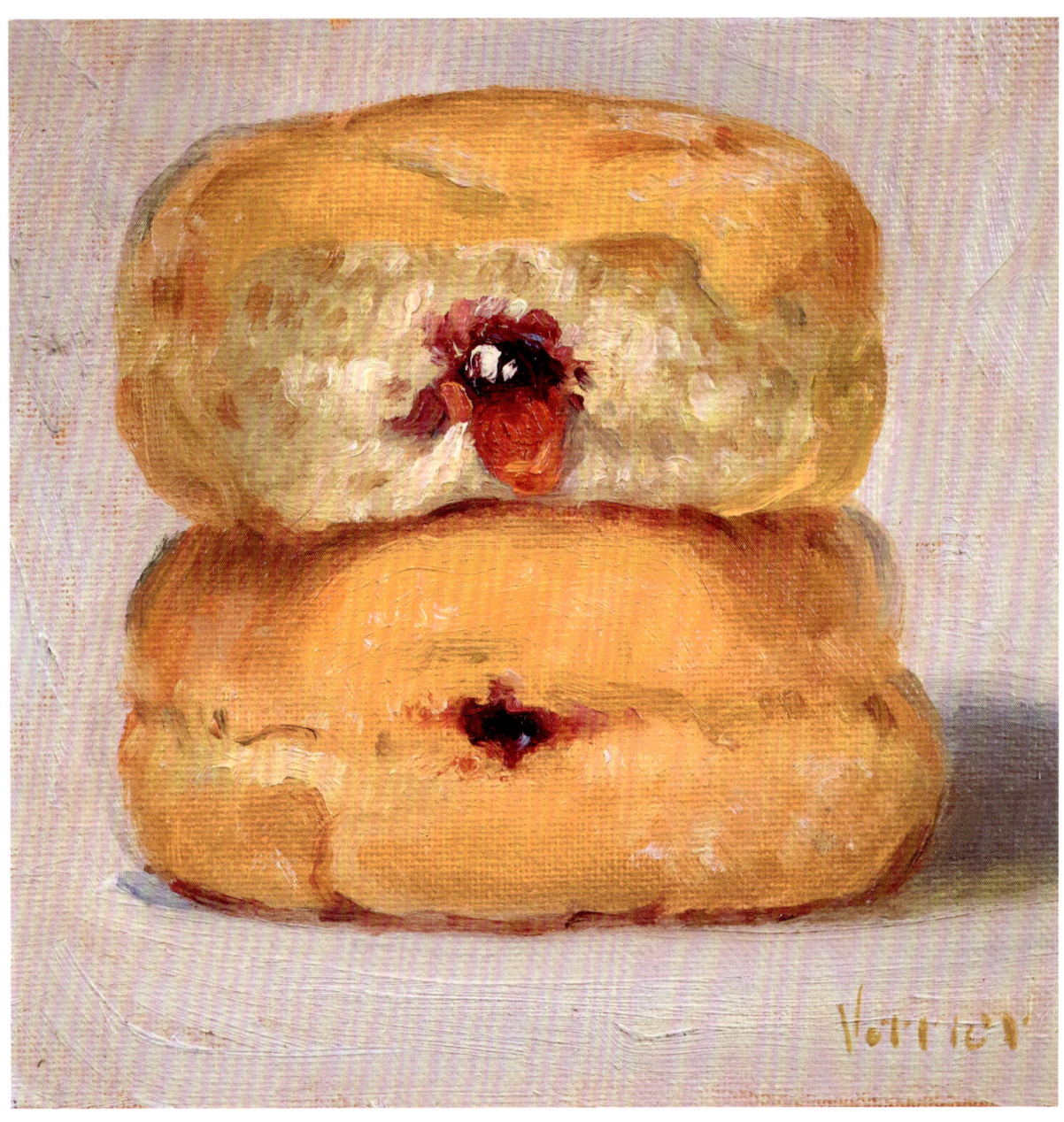

OPPOSITE PAGE:
Pink Iced Donut & Jar of Milk

11 x 14 in.

Jelly Donuts

6 x 7 in.

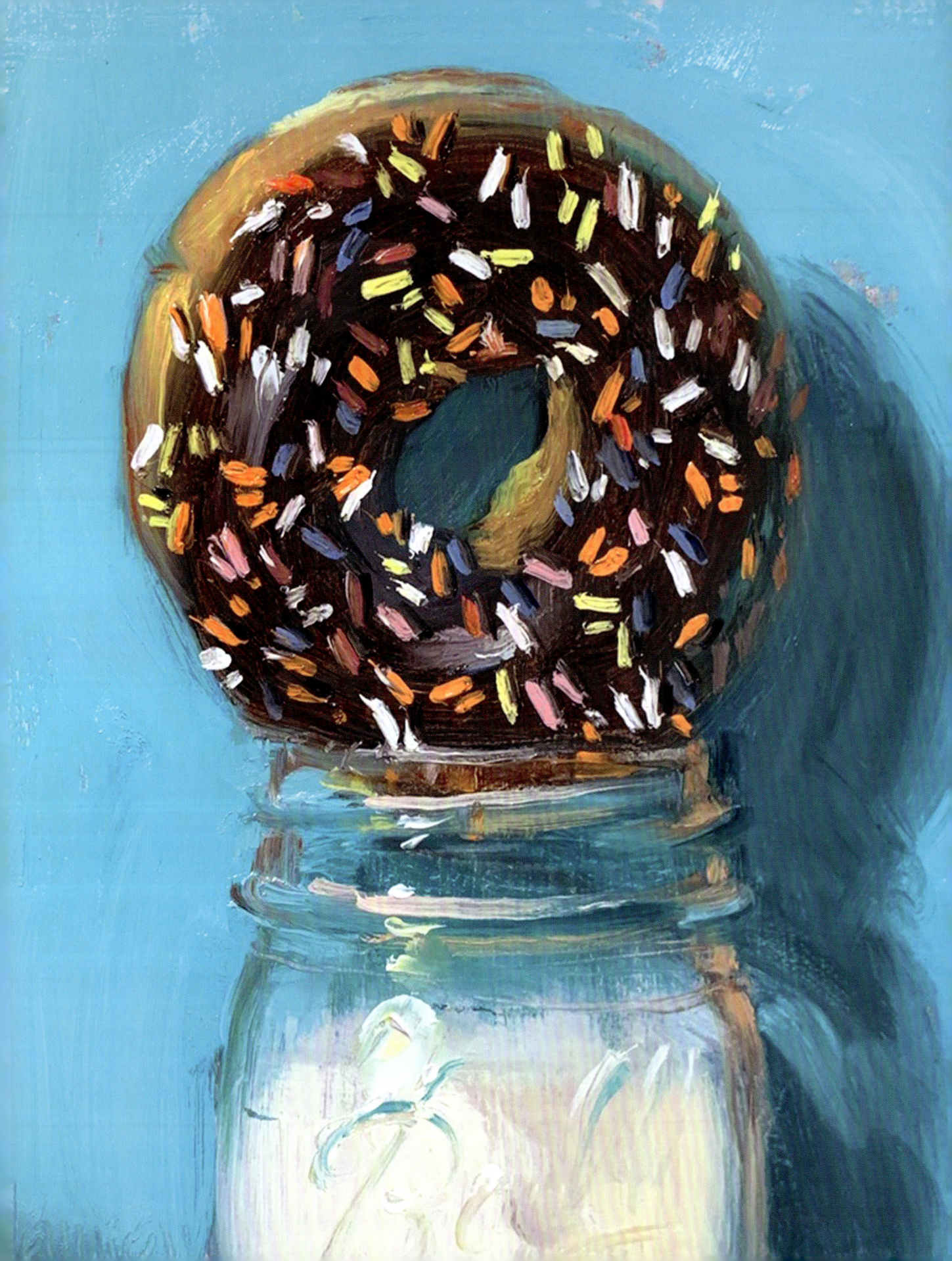

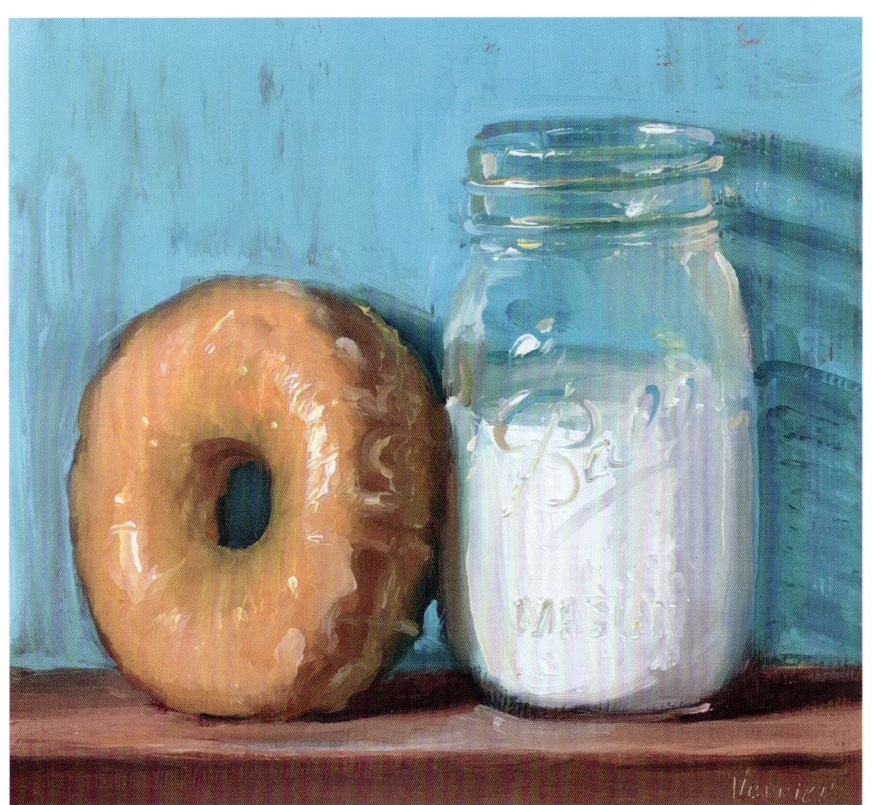

OPPOSITE PAGE:

**Chocolate Iced Donut
& Milk**

9 x 8 in.

Donut Milk

8 x 9 in.

Donut with Latte

8 x 9 in.

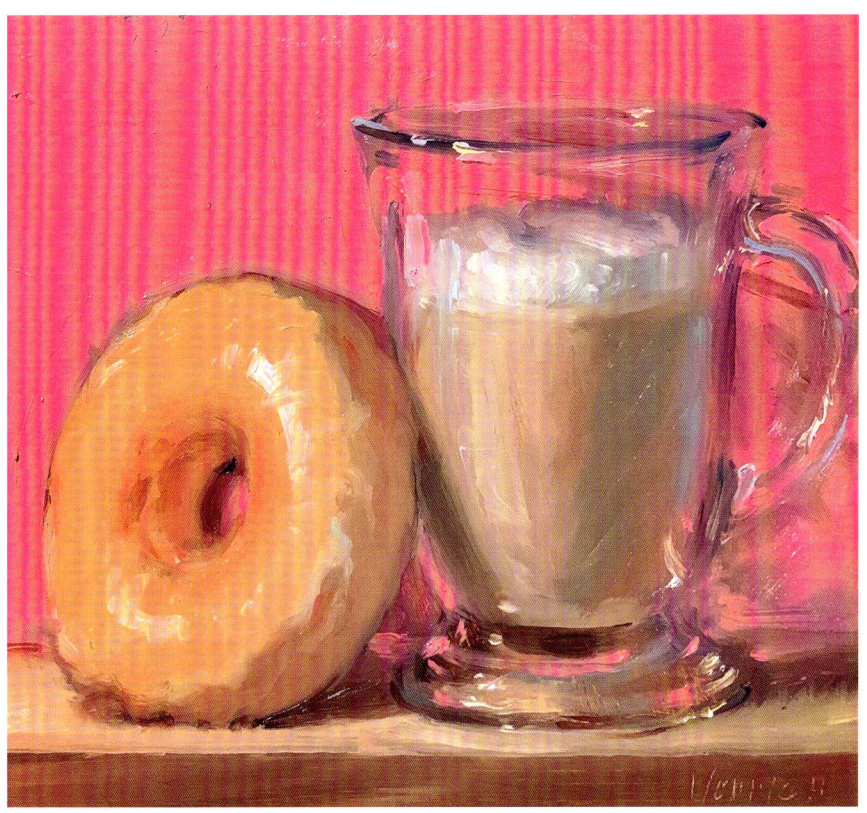

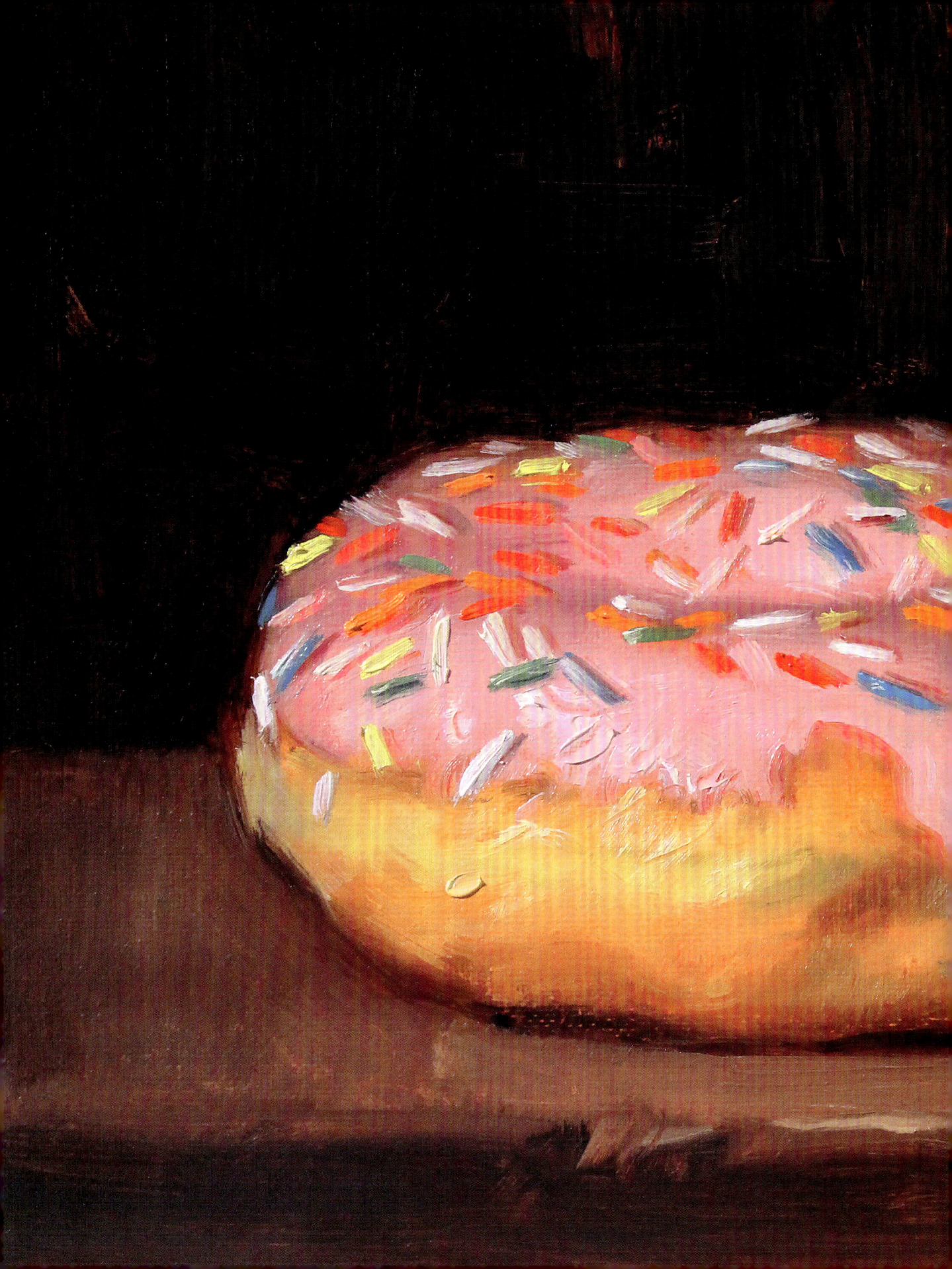

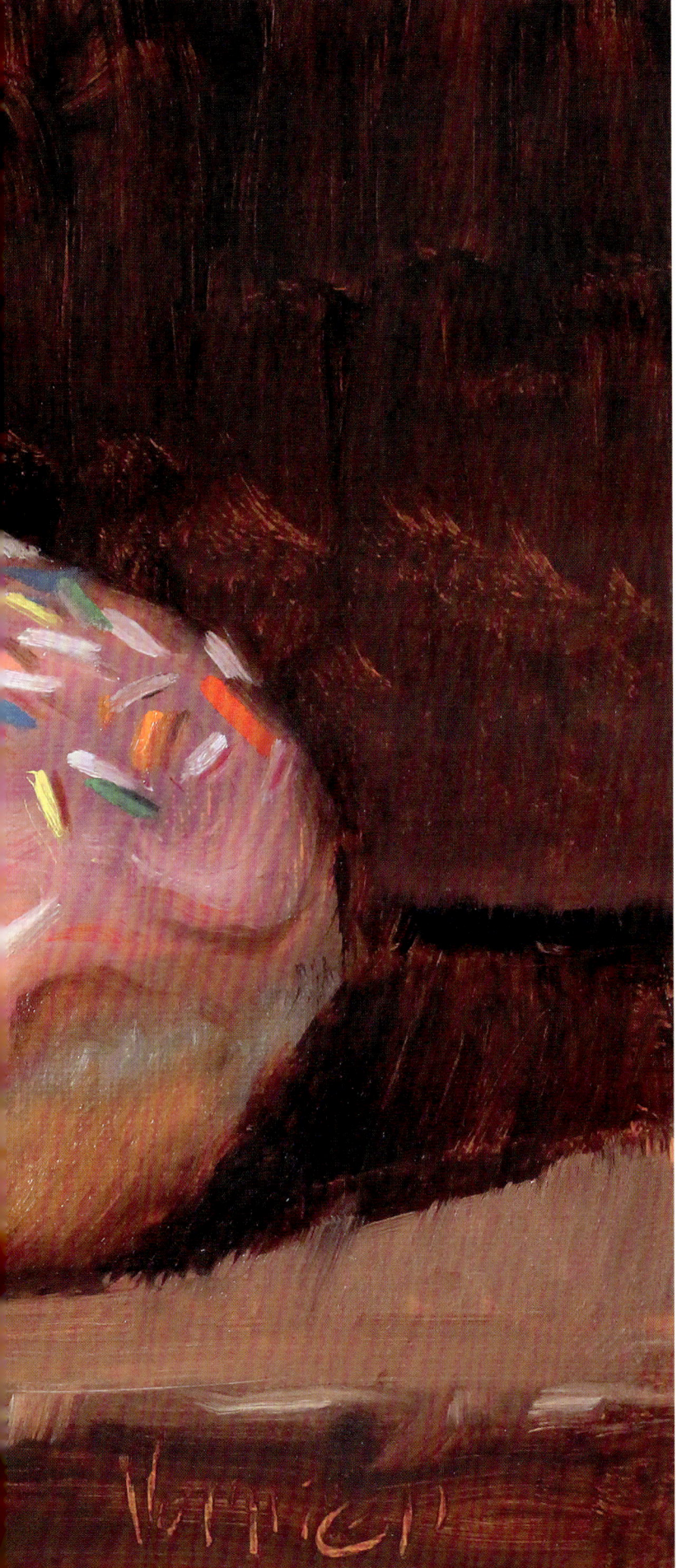

Pink Donut
8 x 10 in.

Pink Donut by Brooke Farlow

Never have I ever had a pink frosted donut with sprinkles; I just went to a donut shop a week ago, and they did not have that specific donut. It's not fair that Homer Simpson gets to have one and I don't. This painting reminds me of the time I went to Universal Studios with my family, where I saw a giant The Simpsons *Lard Lad Donut in a box. Just a giant pink frosted donut, probably four times the size of a regular donut. I think it was meant to be eaten as a cake. This painting brings me joy and desire. The donut looks good, and I want to try it.*

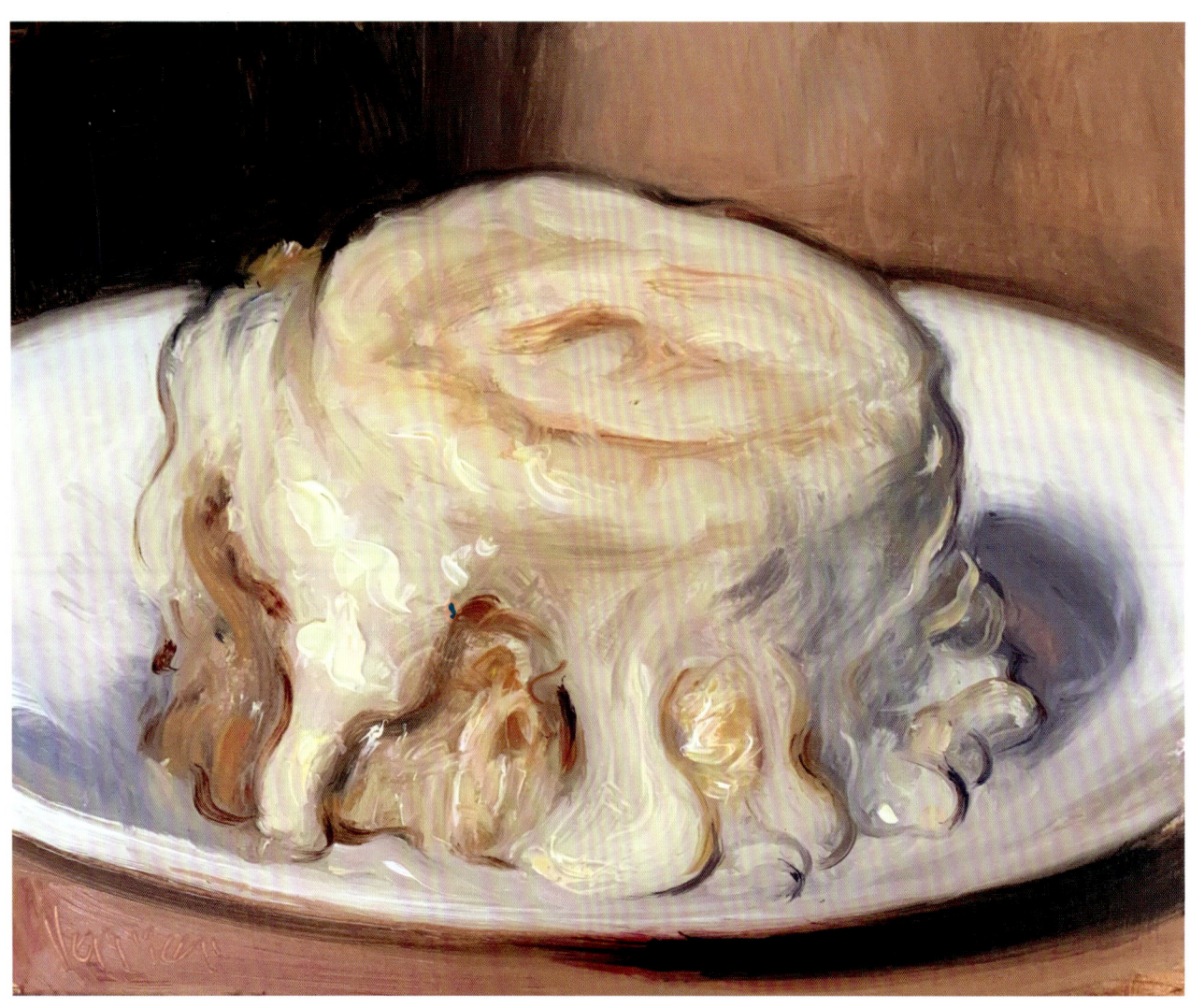

Cinnabon

8 x 9 in.

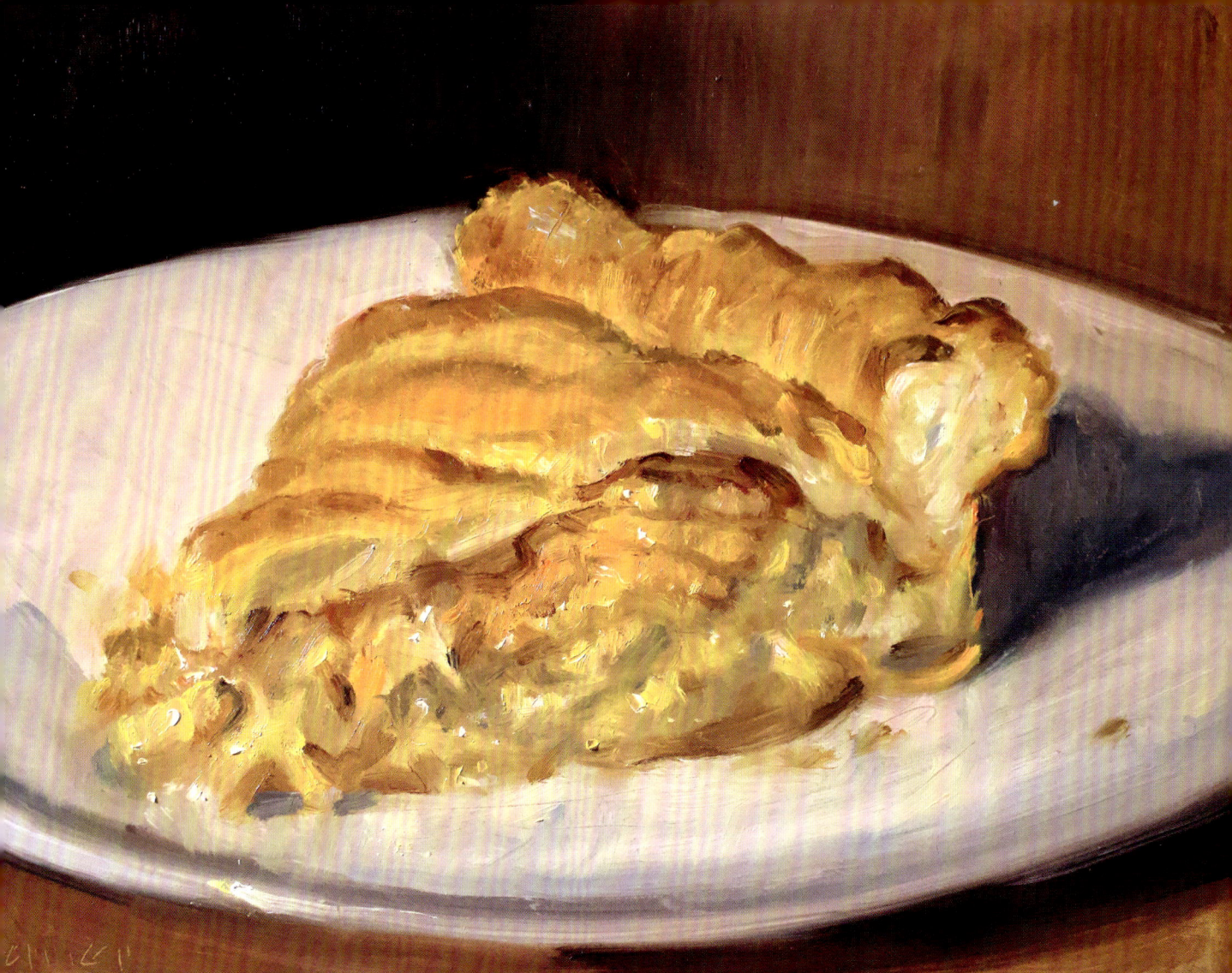

Apple Pie
18 x 18 in.

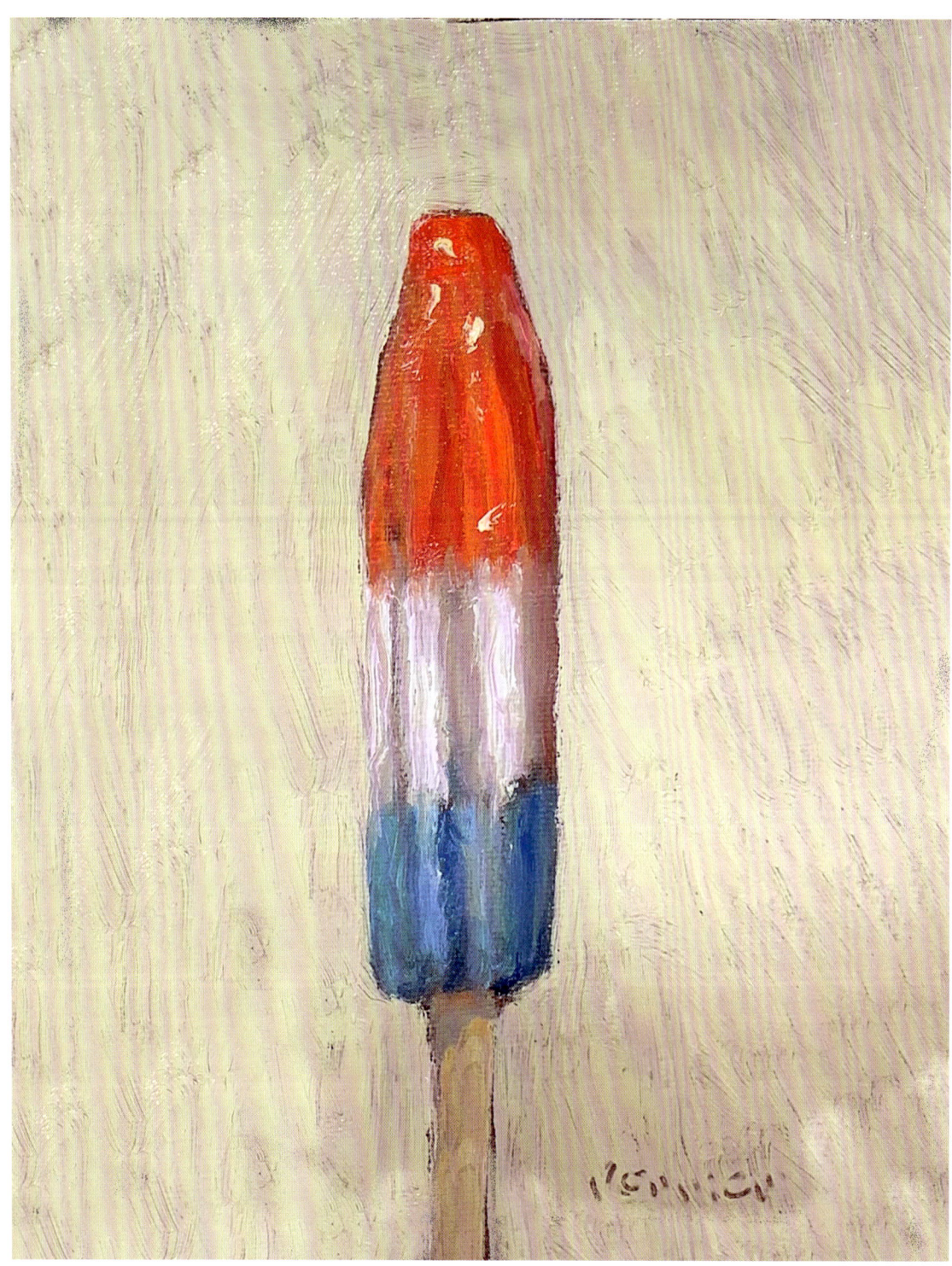

Bomb Pop
5 x 7 in.

OPPOSITE PAGE:
Jelly Beans
8 x 10 in.

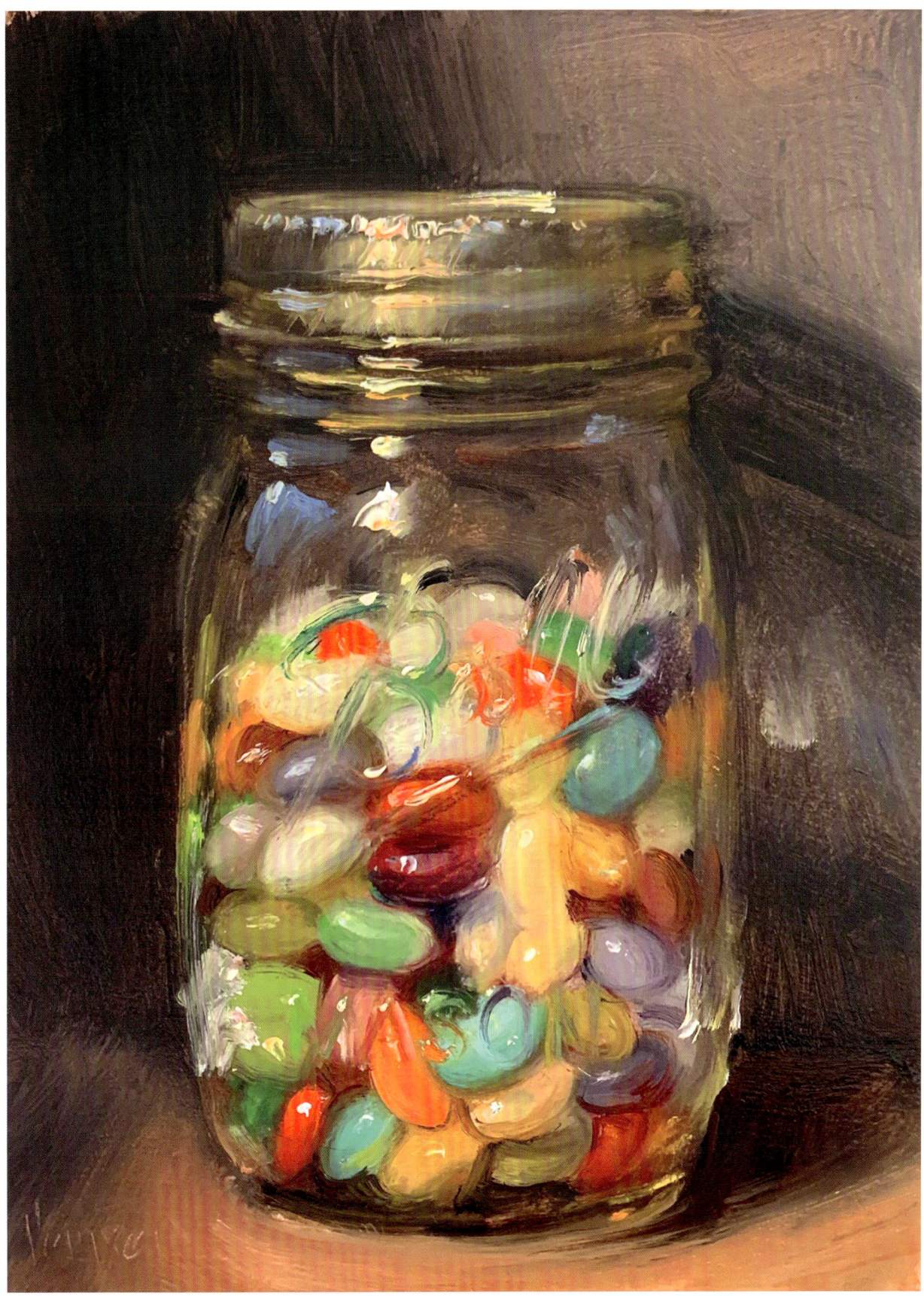

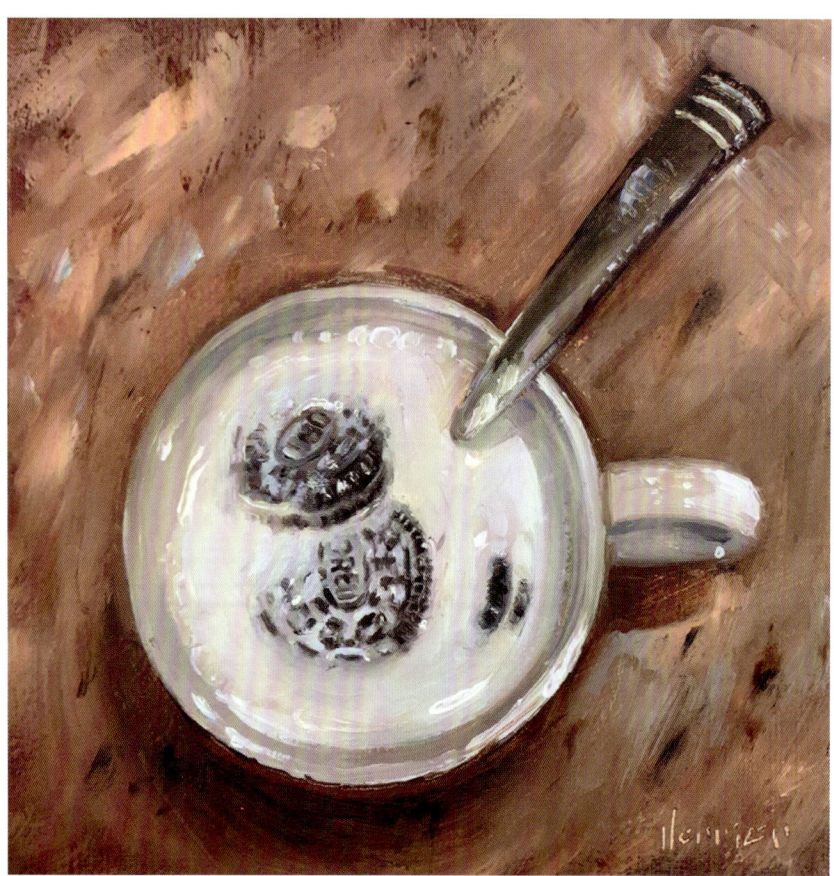

Oreos in Milk
8 x 8 in.

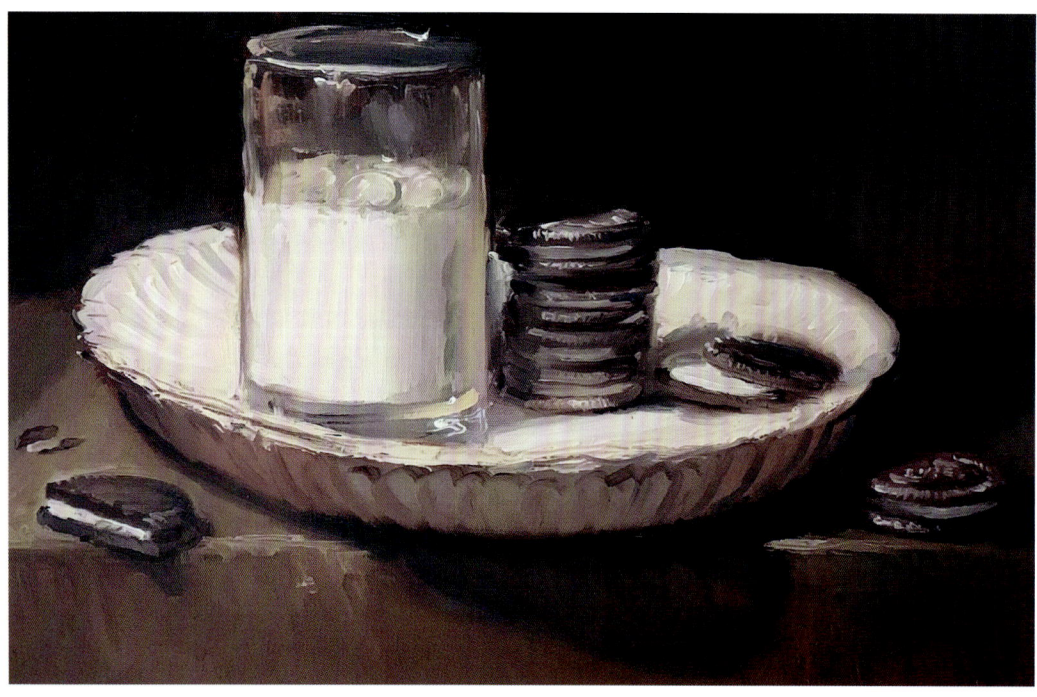

Oreos & Milk
9 x 12 in.

OPPOSITE PAGE:
**Coffee &
Macarons**
9 x 8 in.

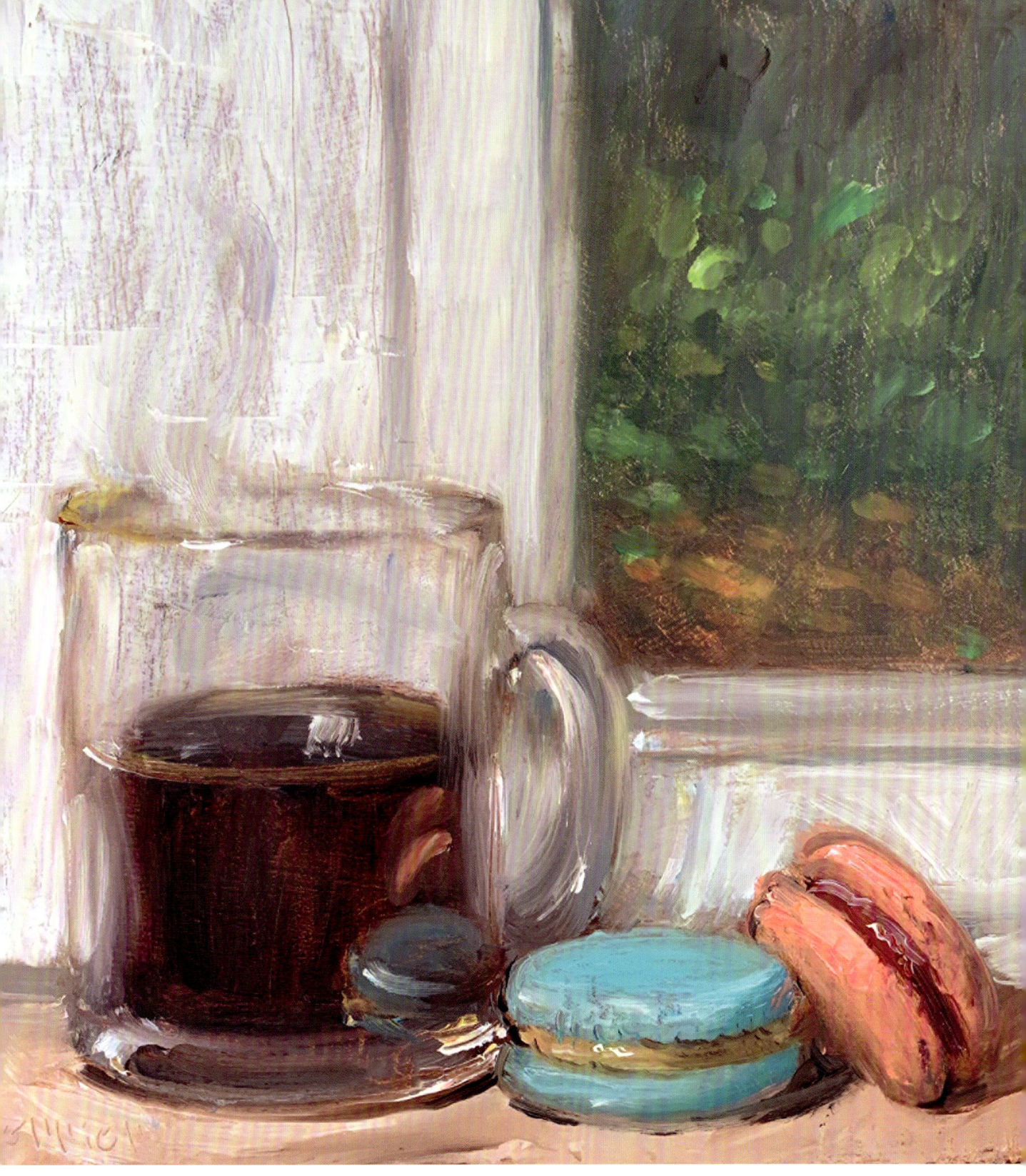

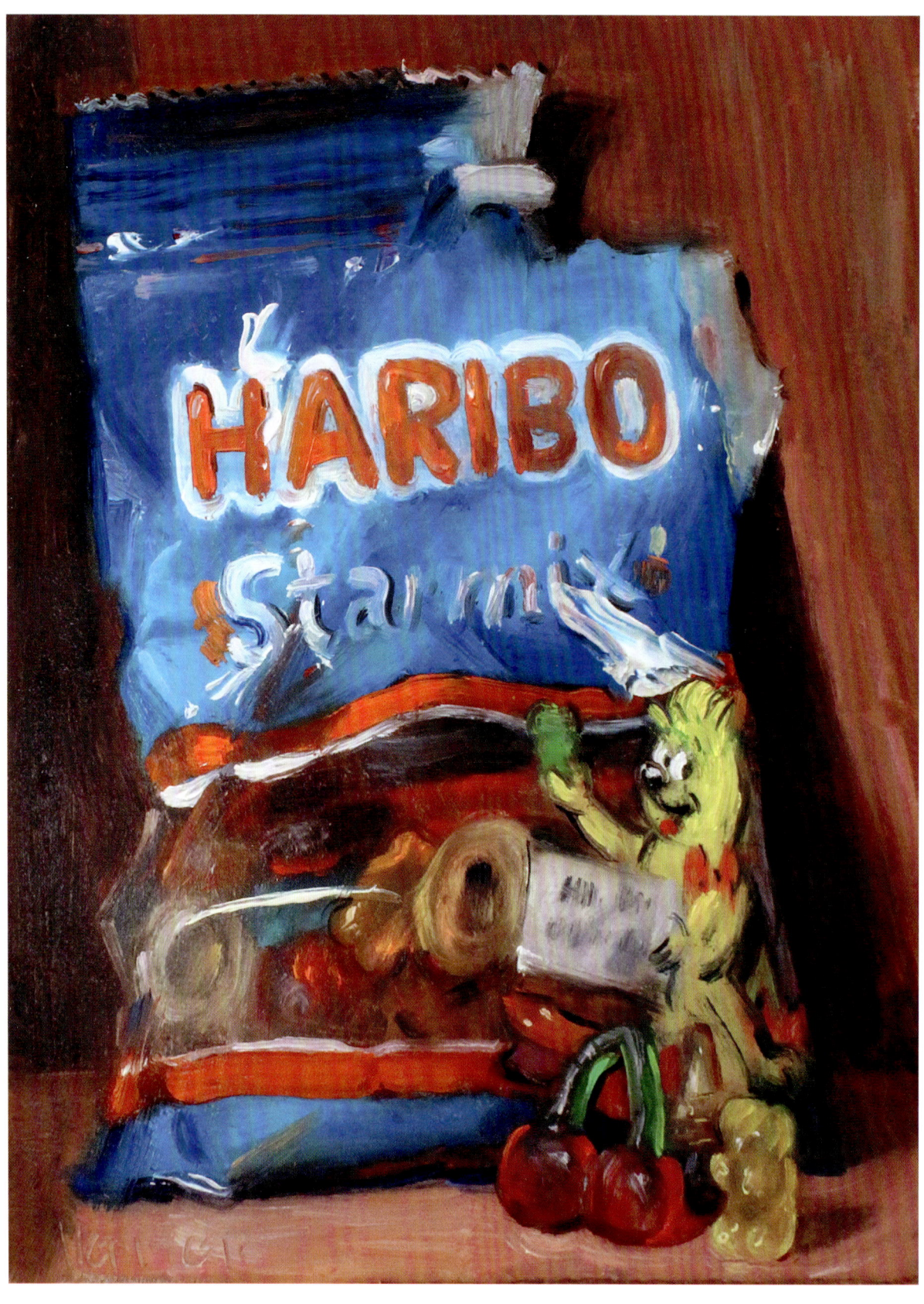

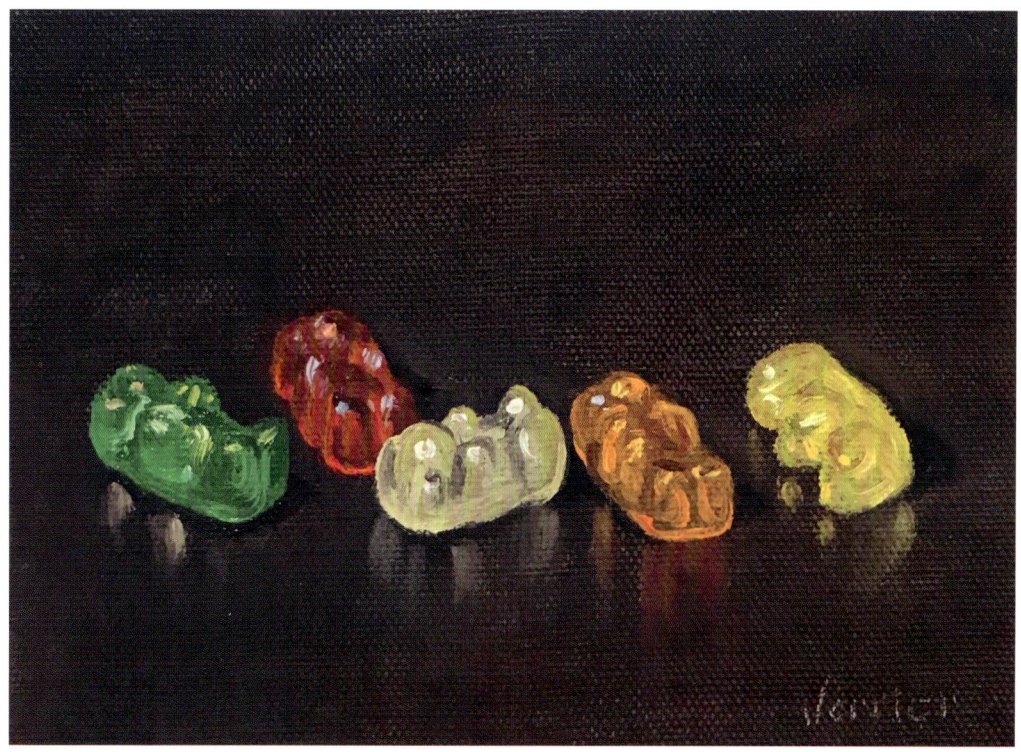

OPPOSITE PAGE:
Starmix
9 x 12 in.

5 Gummies
8 x 10 in.

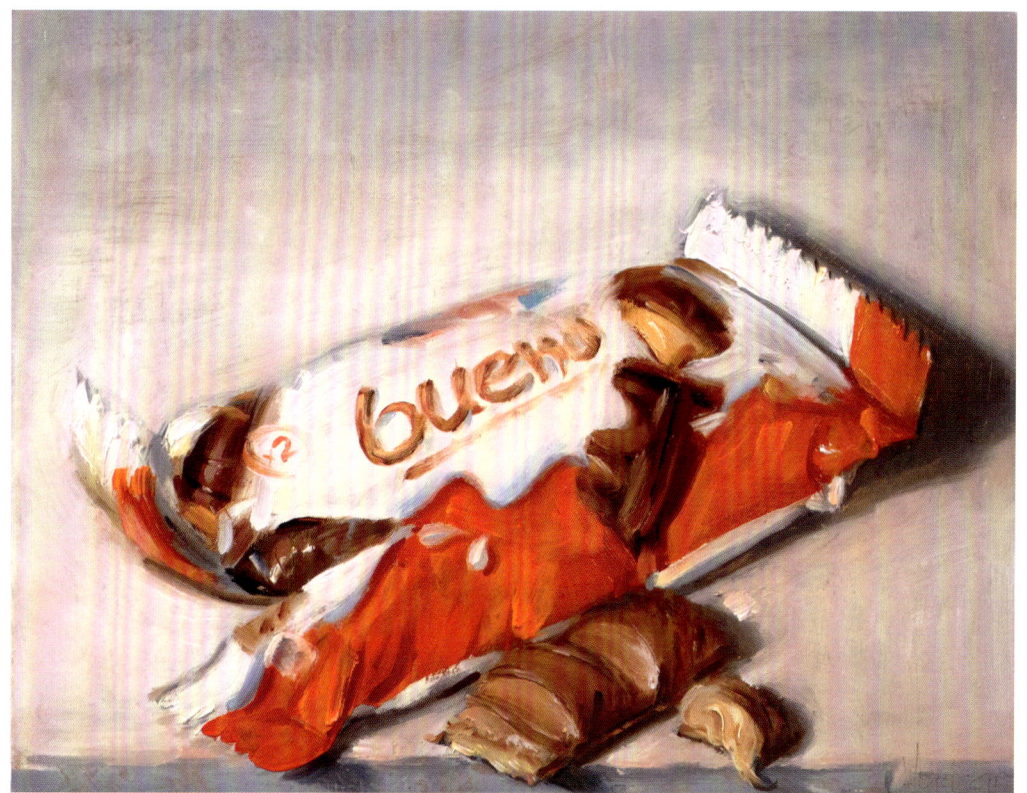

Kinder Bueno
8 x 10 in.

NATURAL DELIGHTS

Although I have been labeled a "junk-food painter," I am **actually** *a healthy eater who believes in moderation. I love portraying some fruit in a beautiful cup or bowl, especially the Birds of Britain pattern that I grew up with.*

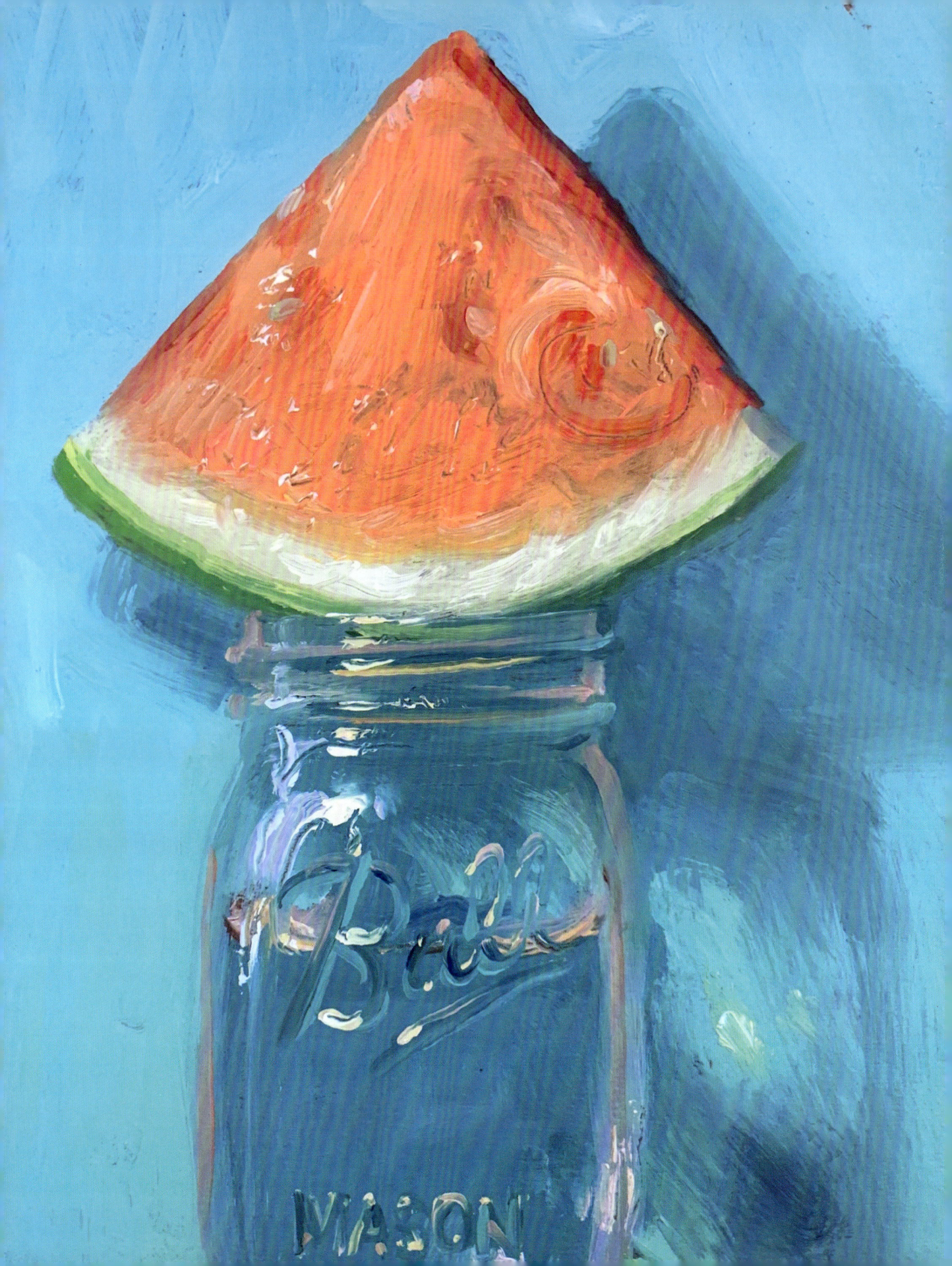

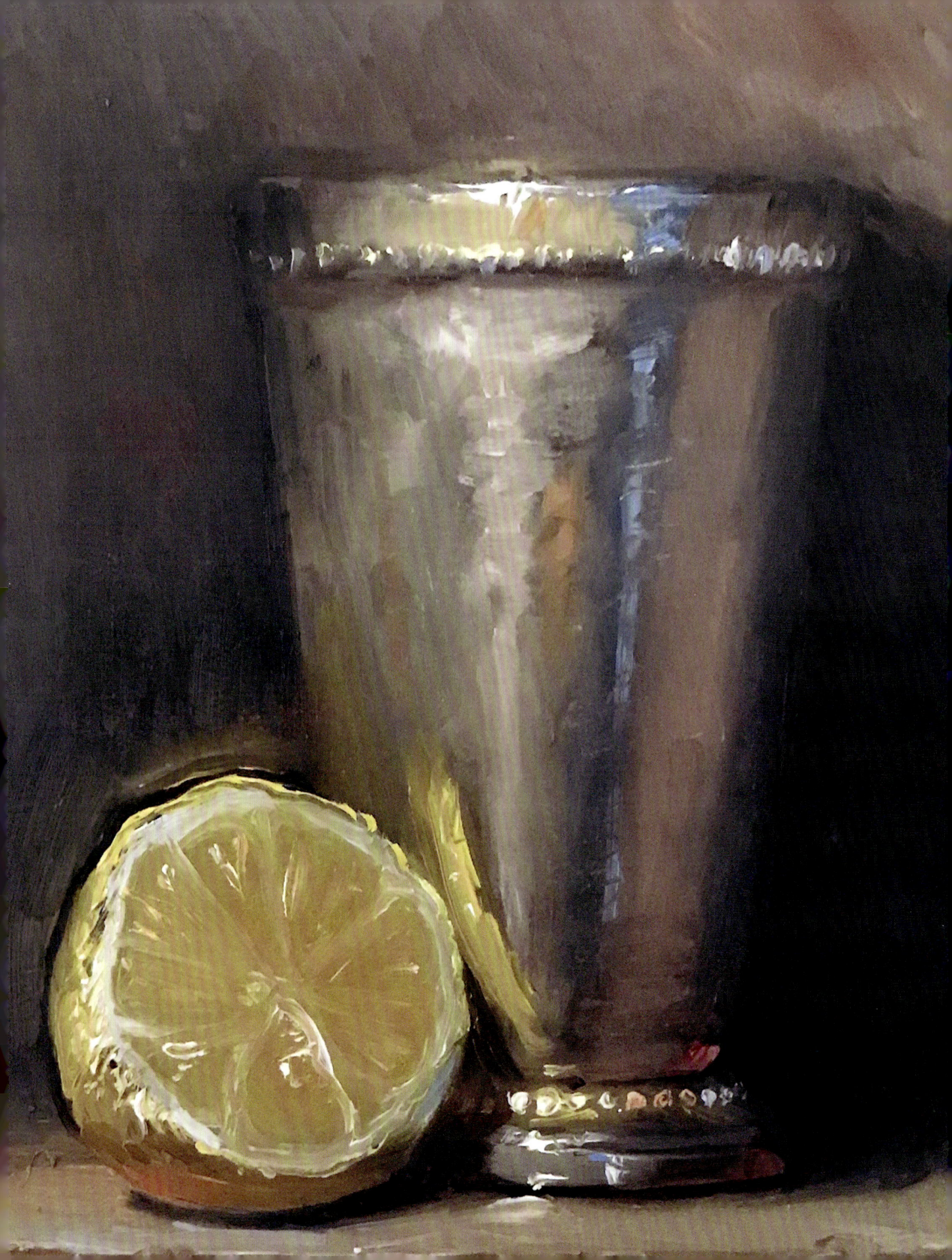

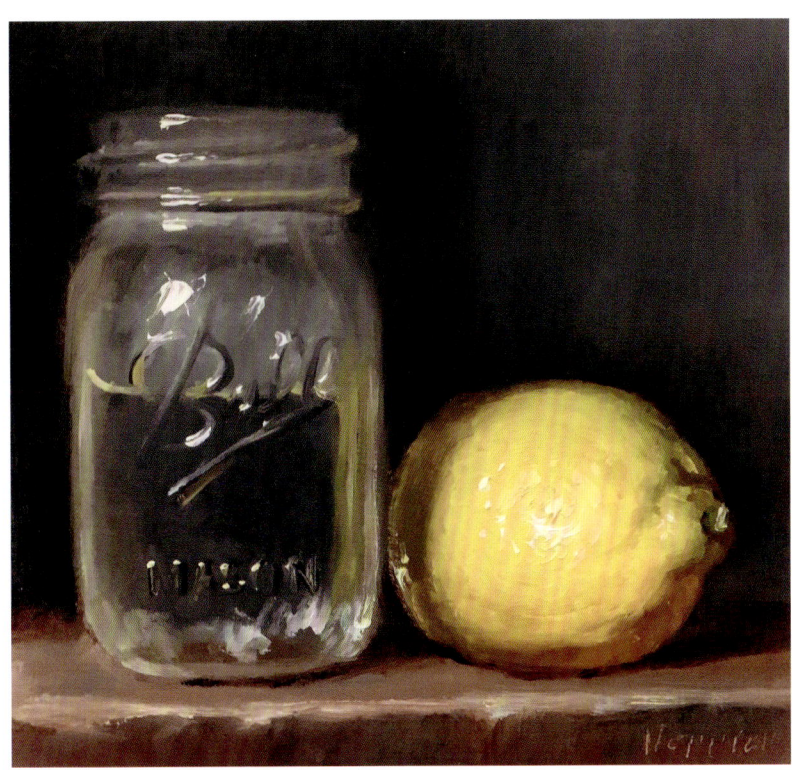

Lemon Water
8 x 9 in.

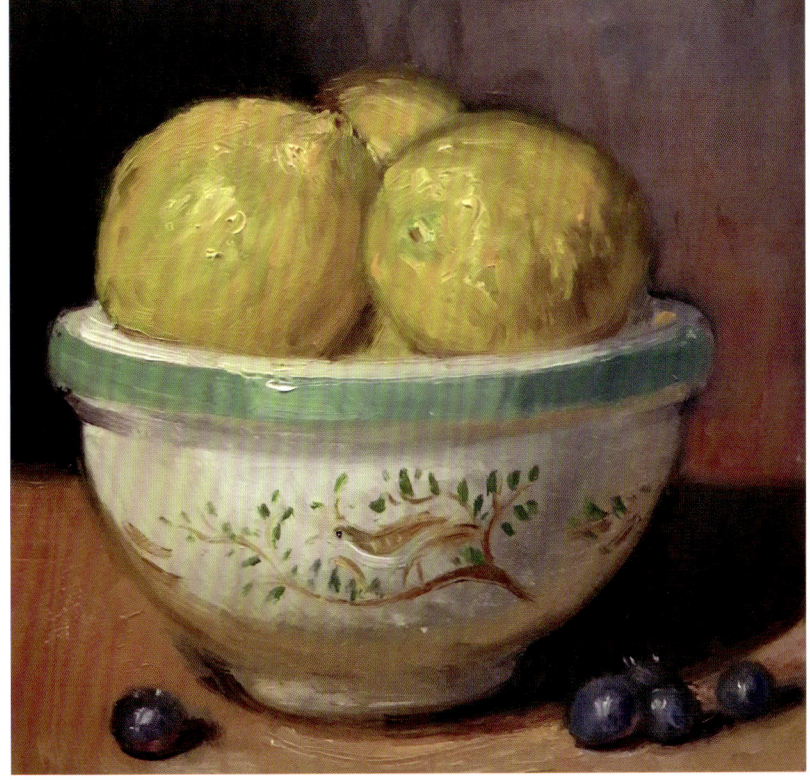

Lemons
8 x 9 in.

OPPOSITE PAGE:
Lemon & Silver
6 x 8 in.

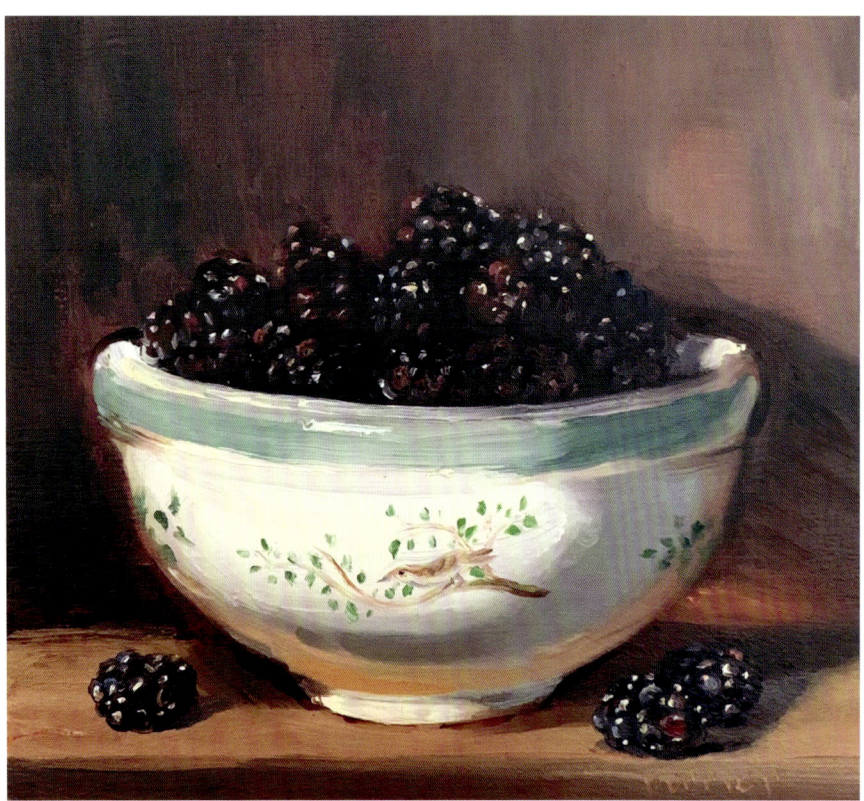

Blackberries
9 x 8 in.

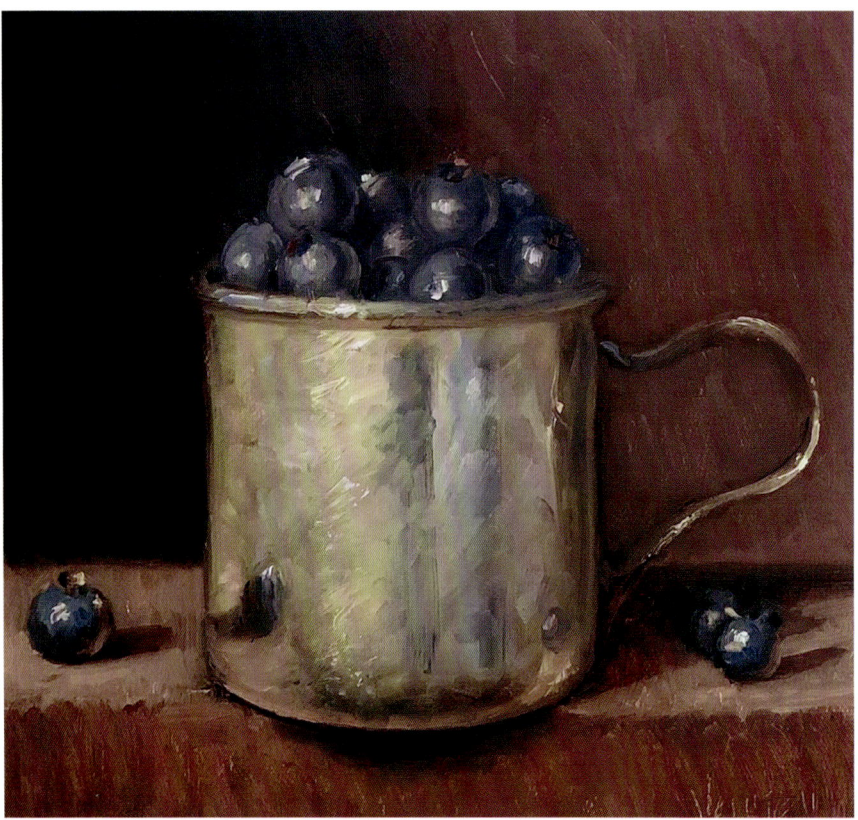

Blueberries & Silver
9 x 8 in.

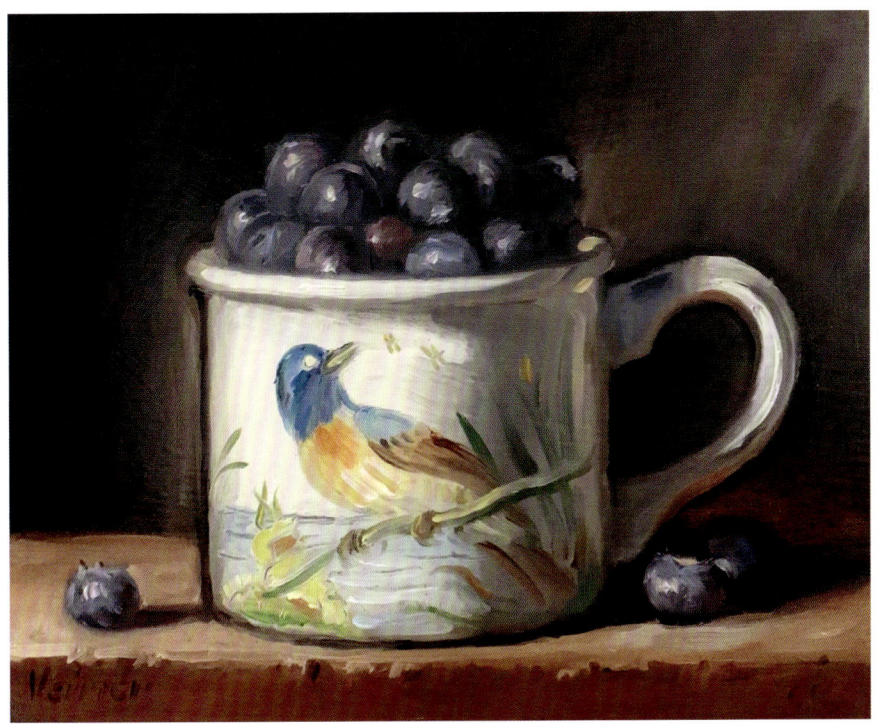

Blueberries in a Cup
8 x 9 in.

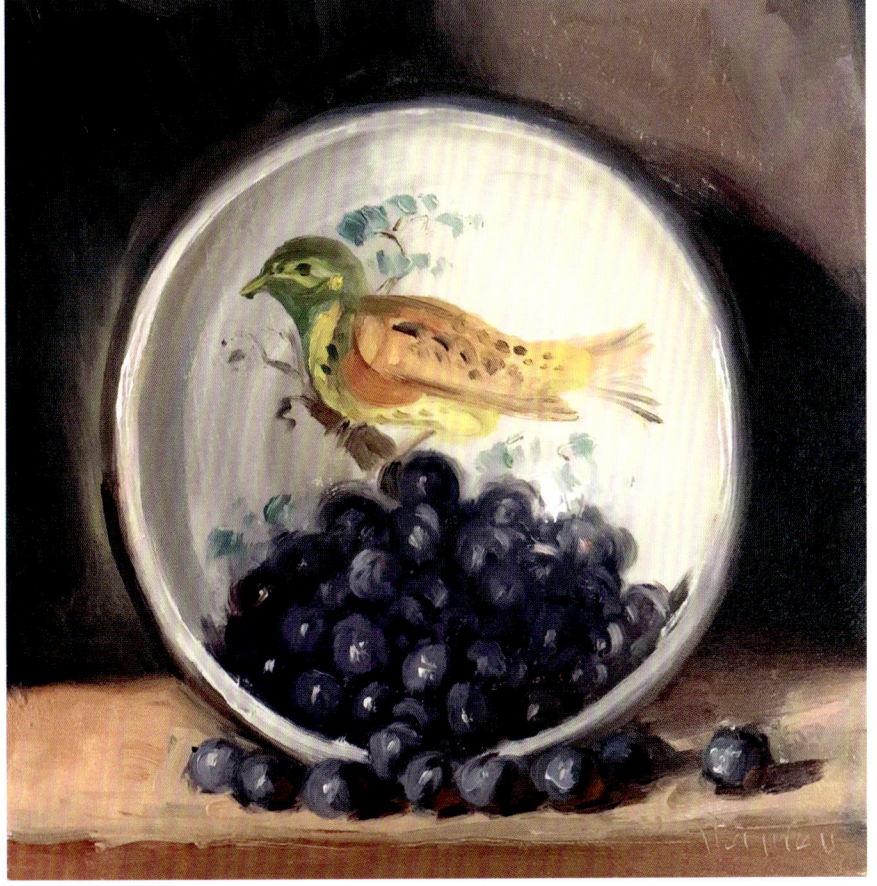

Blueberries Spilled
9 x 9 in.

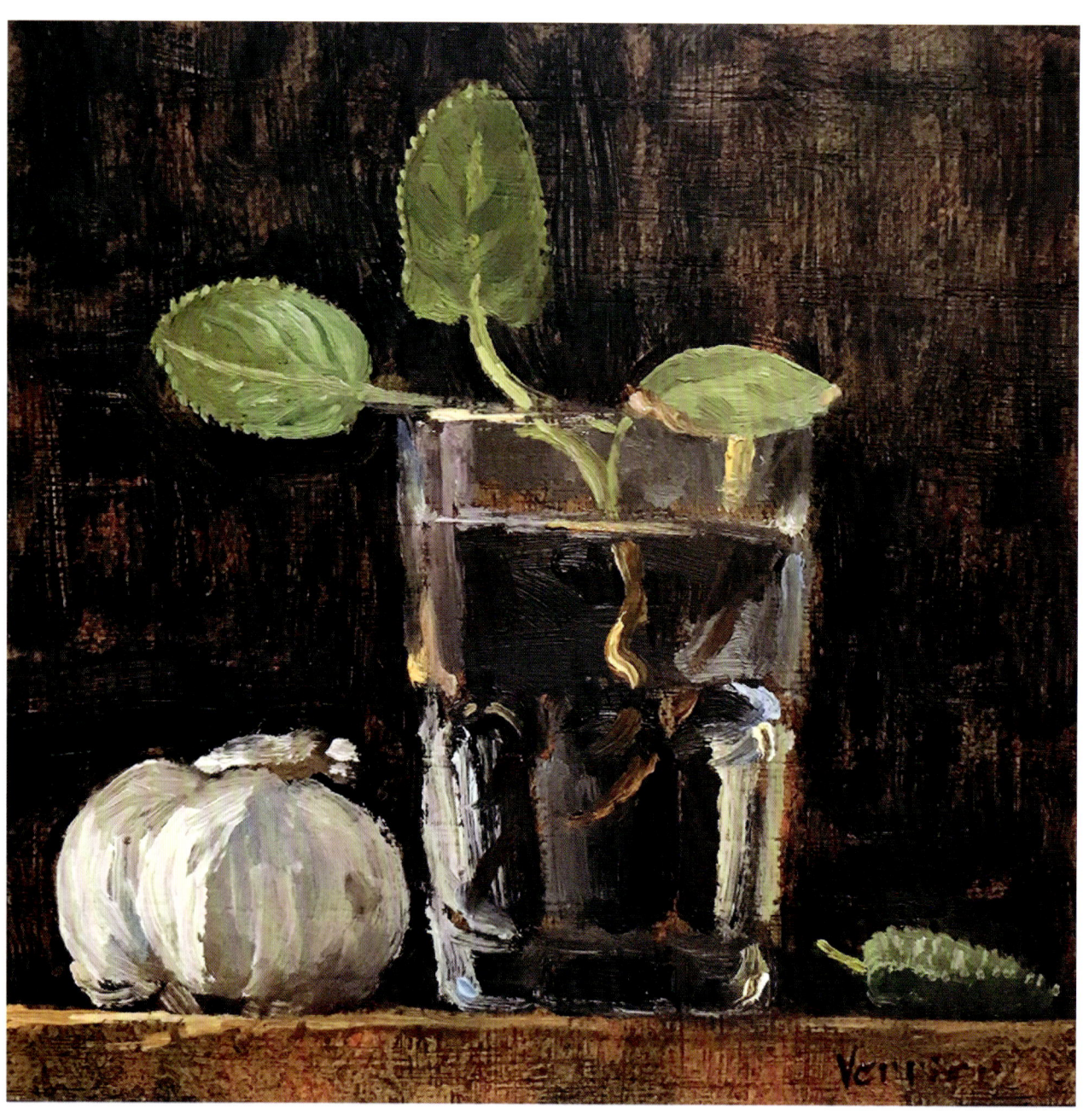

Garlic & Herbs
8 x 8 in.

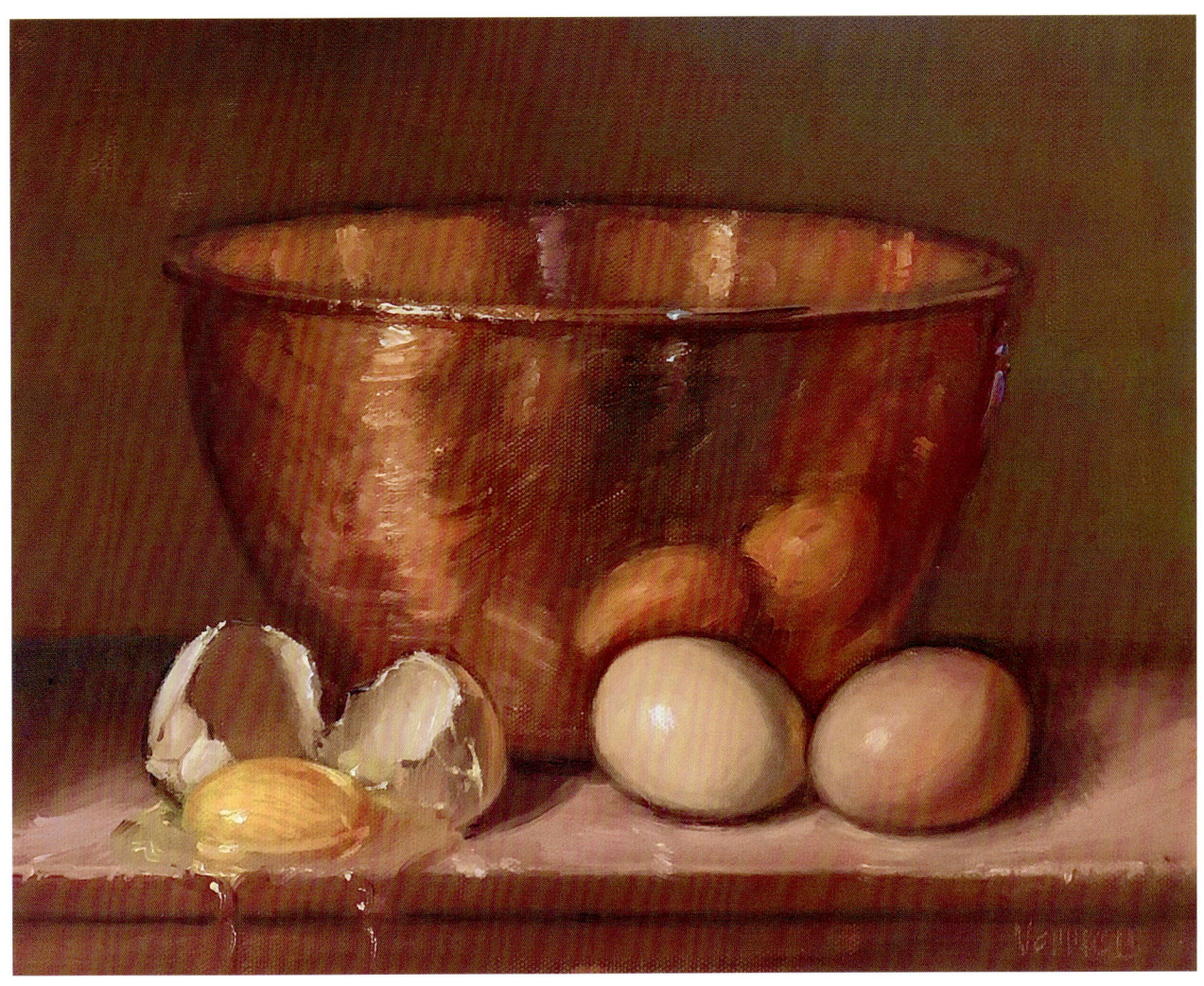

Eggs Copper

11 x 14 in.

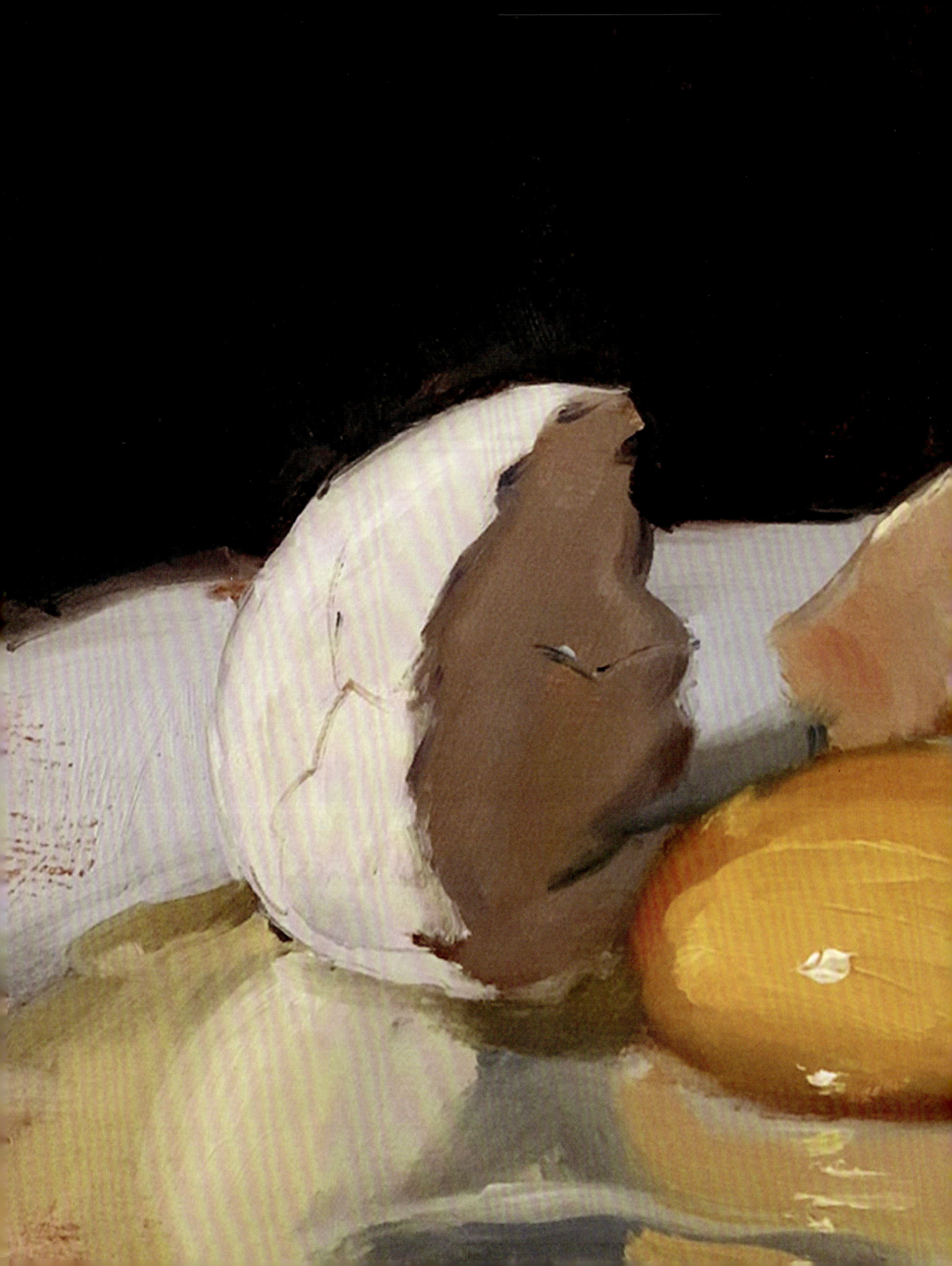

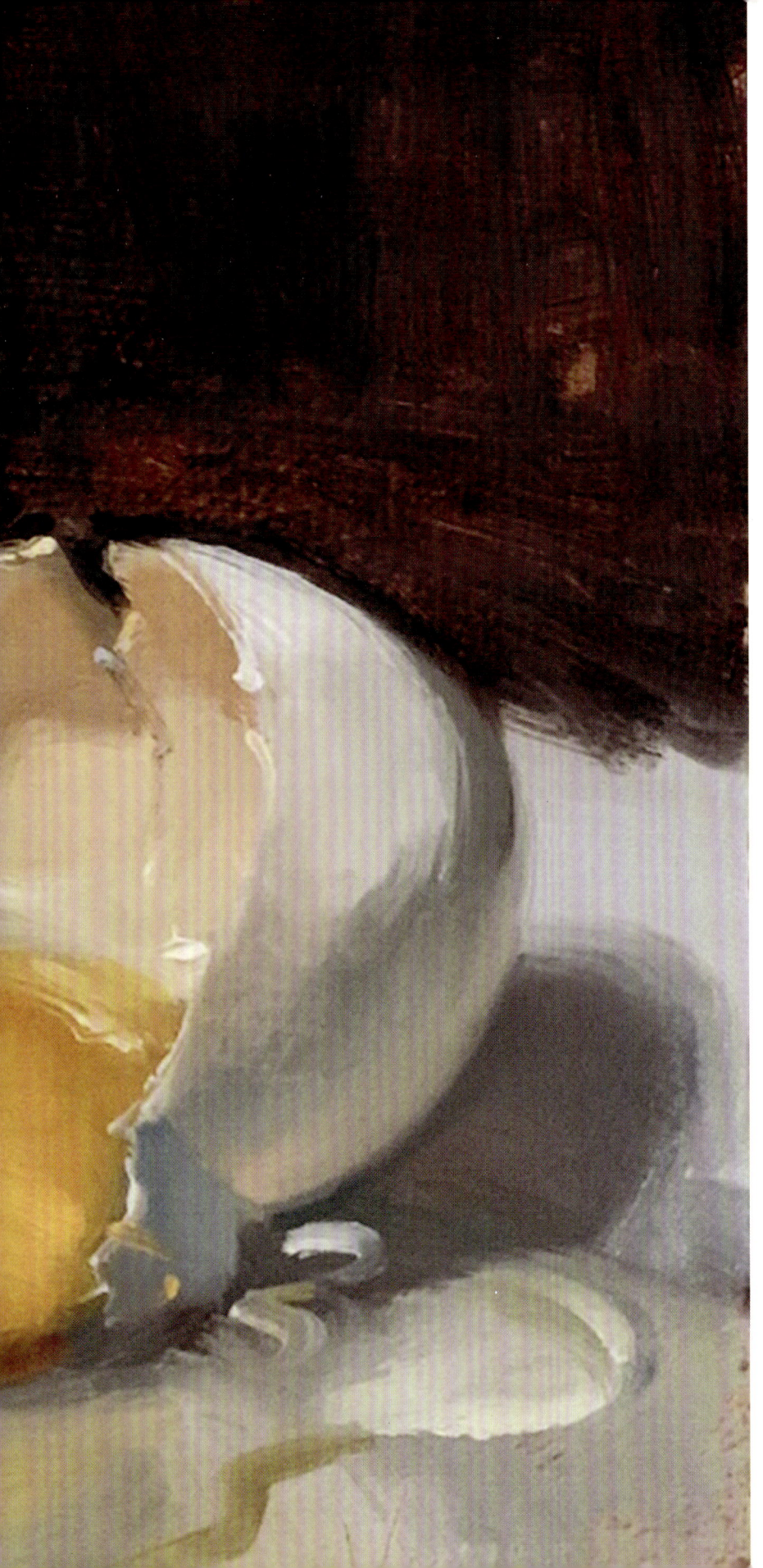

Broken Egg
8 x 9 in.

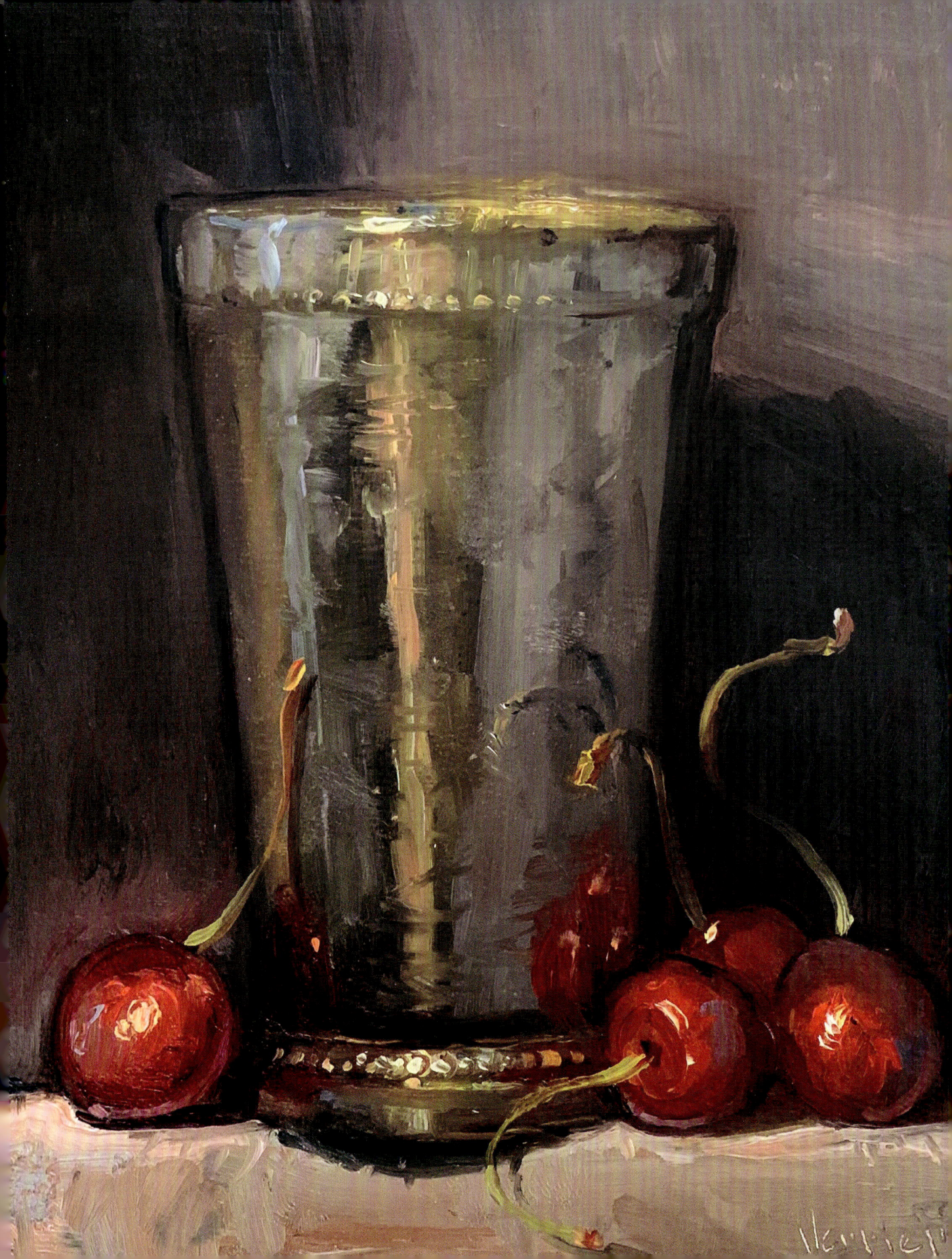

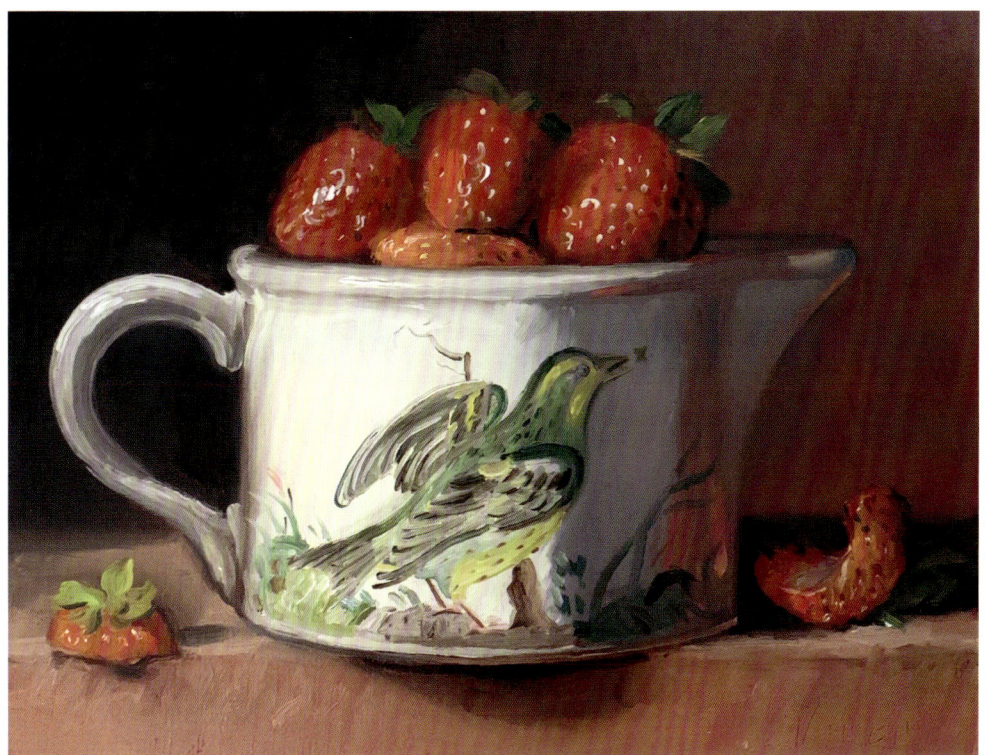

Strawberries
8 x 10 in.

Raspberries
9 x 8 inches

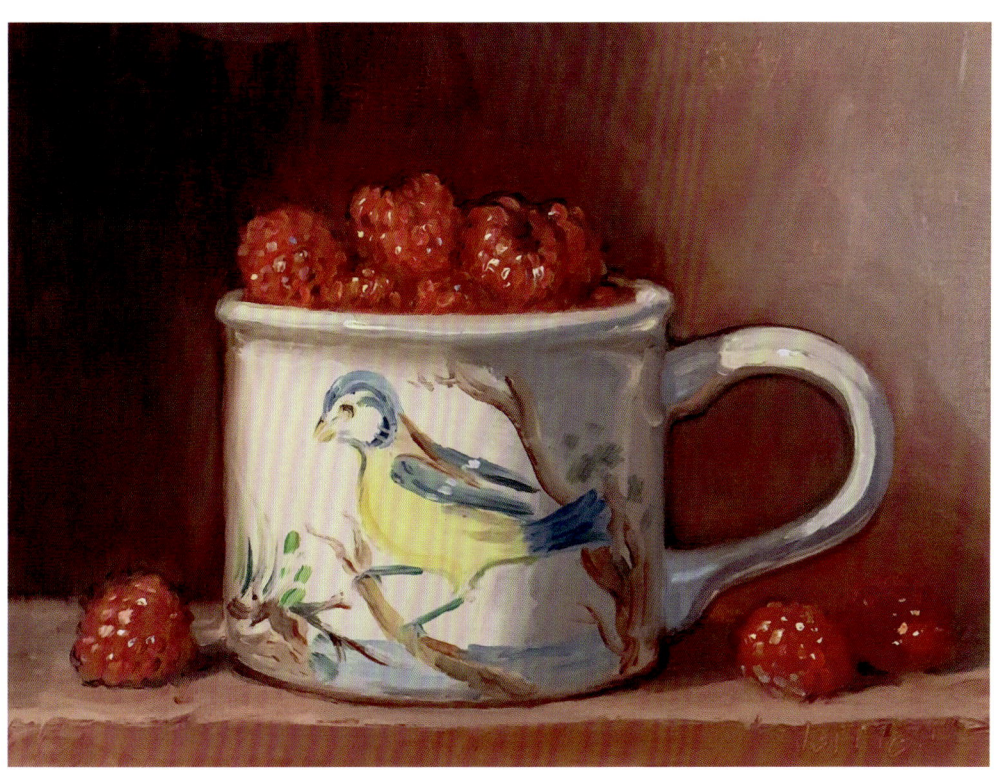

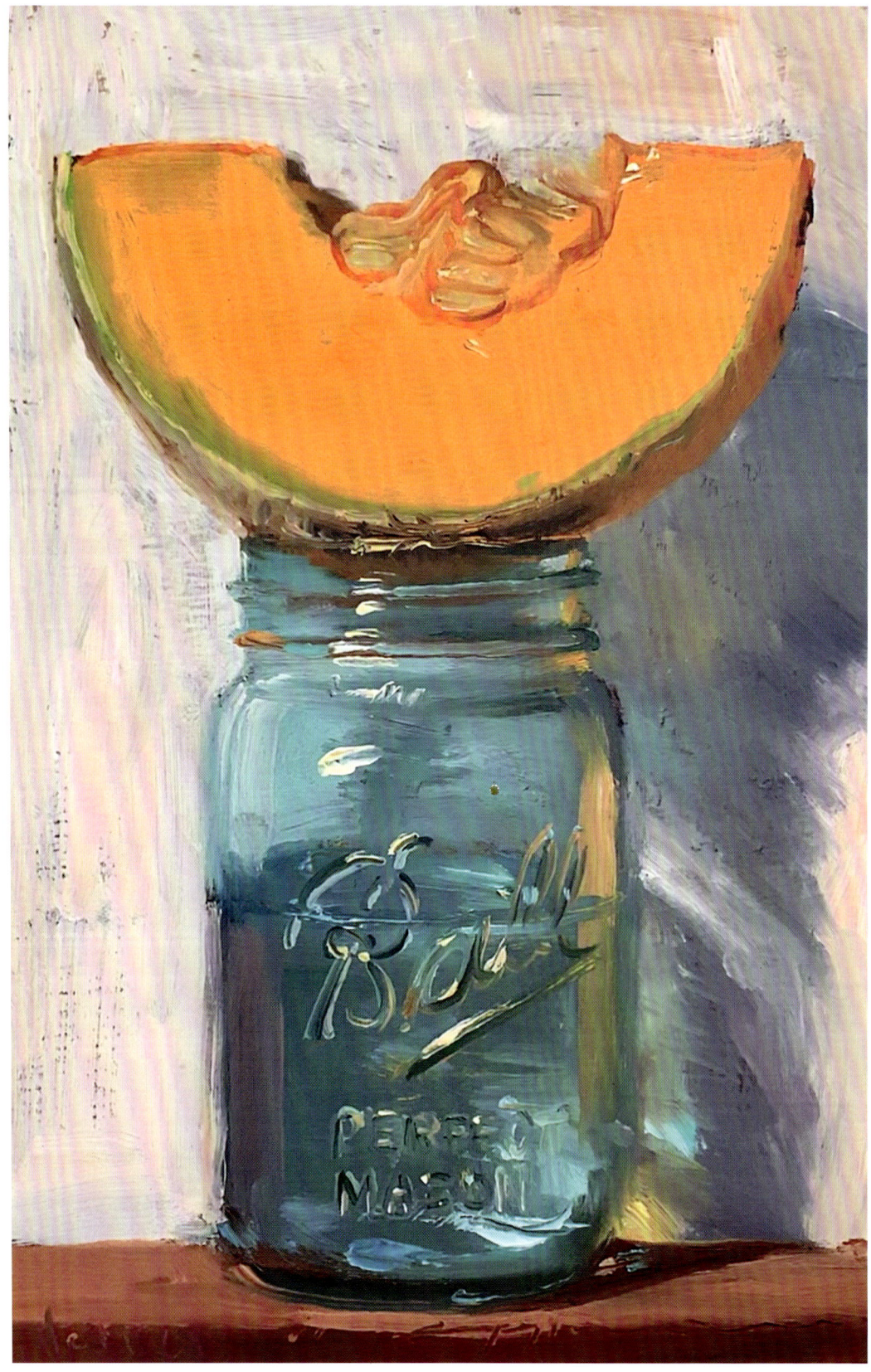

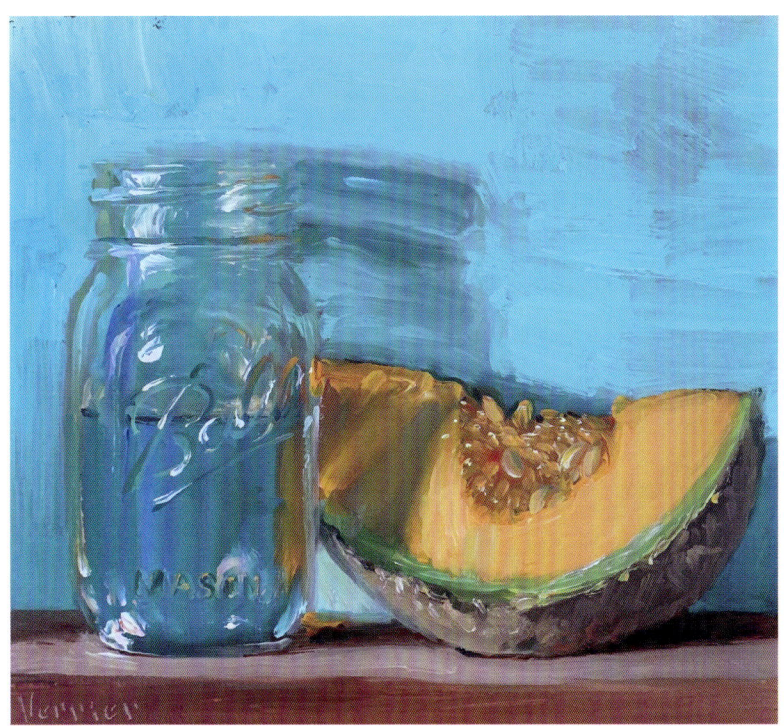

OPPOSITE PAGE:

Cantaloupe & Vintage Jar

7 x 10 in.

Canteloupe & Jar of Water

8 x 9 in.

Avocado & Spoon

9 x 8 in.

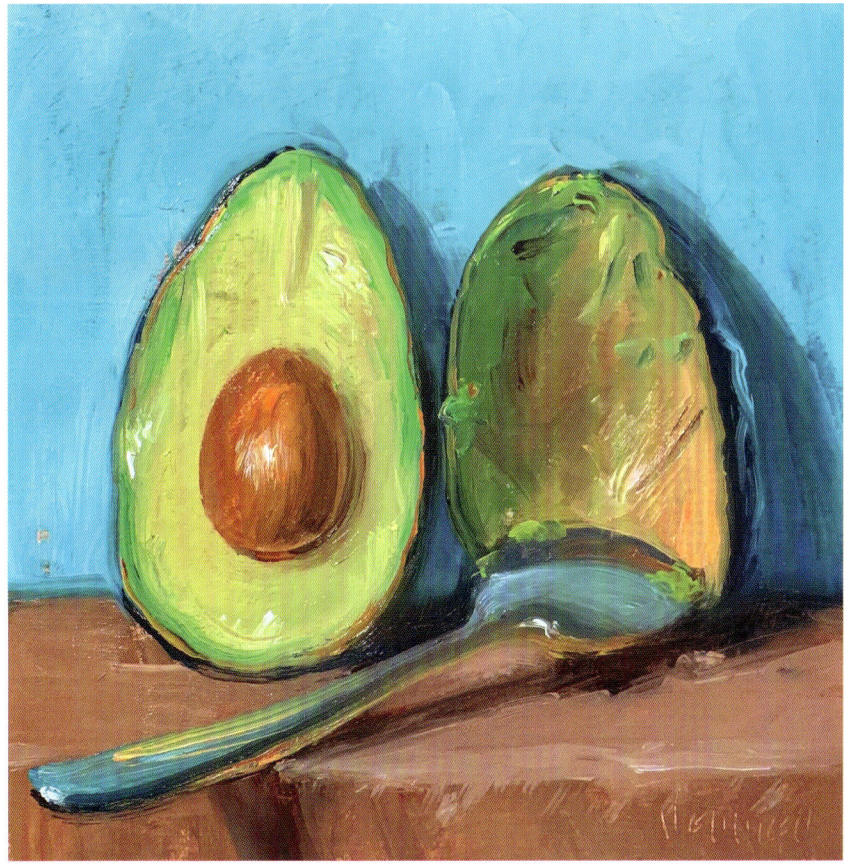

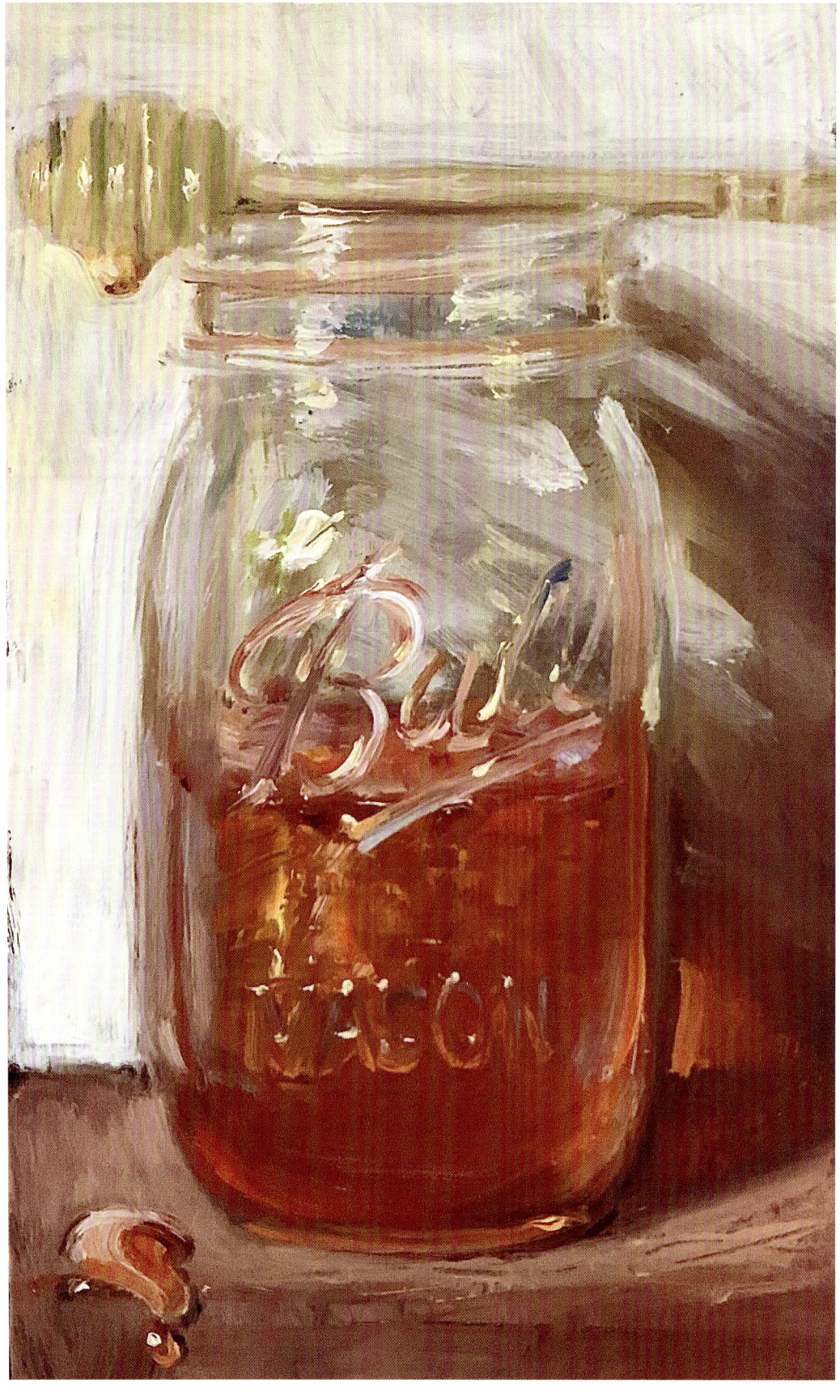

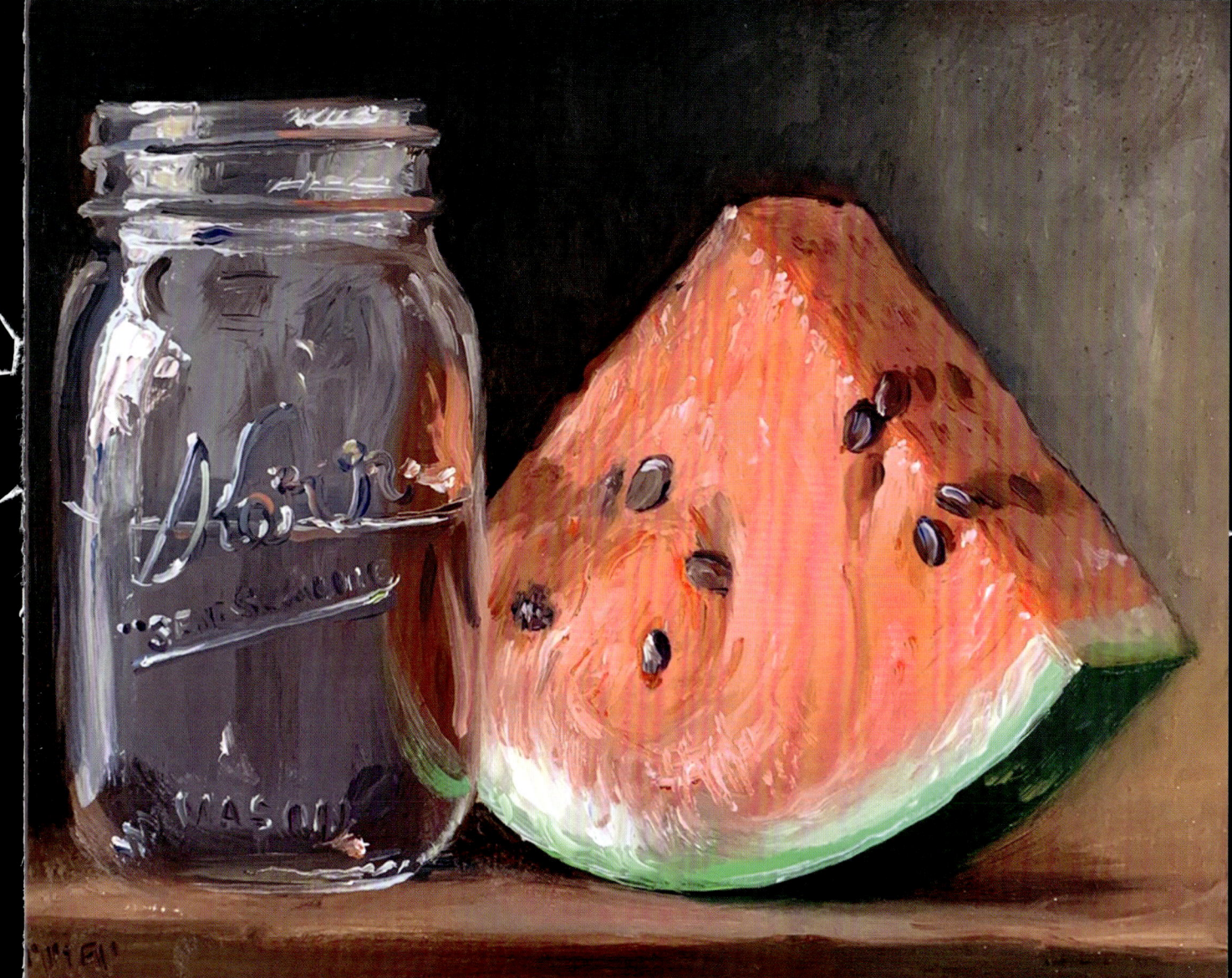

**Watermelon & Jar
of Water**

8 x 10 in.

Honey & Spool by Sarah Maisie

*This painting reminds me of so many trips to the farmers'
market with my family growing up. We'd always stop to get
honey because my entire house was plagued with sniffles
and itchy throats every allergy season. Popping Zyrtec and
Aleve can only get you so far, and we knew that getting
honey from the area would naturally help us combat the
pollen that would shower down on us (Thank you, bees!).
We'd consume it constantly throughout the year, in our
teas, breakfast oatmeal, homemade granola bars. I love
the shimmer and amber hue of the honey in the painting,
and how the white background makes the jar pop. I can
taste the wildflower honey on my tongue when I look at it,
and it's a testament how truly masterful Noah is.*

ACKNOWLEDGMENTS

I'd like to send love to Jesus, my wife Elizabeth; my kids Luke, Jude, July, and Lulu; my mom and dad; and my mentors Mark and Lilian. And thank you to all my fans! I would also like to thank posthumously my designer Maki, whose last project was laying out this beautiful book.

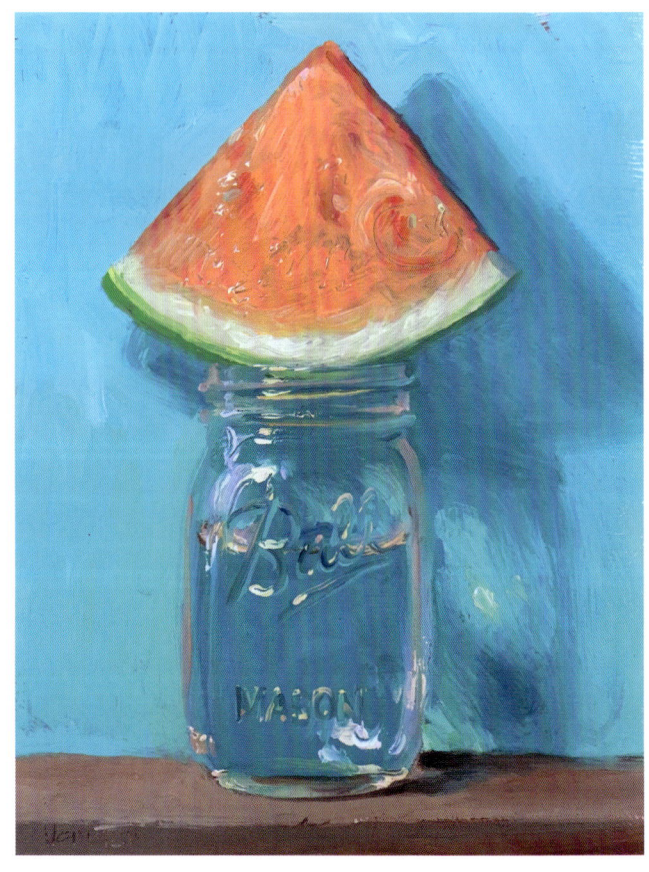

Watermelon Teal
Oil on canvas
18 x 24 in.